Nice Work

OTHER BOOKS BY CLAIRE HOY

Bill Davis (1985)
Friends in High Places (1987)
Margin of Error (1989)
By Way of Deception (1990)
Clyde Wells (1992)
The Truth about Breast Cancer (1995)

NICE WORK

The Continuing Scandal of Canada's Senate

CLAIRE HOY

M&S

Canadian Cataloguing in Publication Data

Hoy, Claire
Nice work : the continuing scandal of Canada's Senate

Includes bibliographical references and index.
ISBN 0-7710-4212-4

1. Canada. Parliament. Senate.   I. Title.
JL155.H69   1999   328.71'071   C99-931479-3

We acknowledge the financial support of the Government of Canada
through the Book Publishing Industry Development Program for
our publishing activities. Canadä

We further acknowledge the support of the Canada Council for the Arts and
the Ontario Arts Council for our publishing program.

Typeset in Sabon by M&S, Toronto

Printed and bound in Canada

McClelland & Stewart Inc.
The Canadian Publishers
481 University Avenue
Toronto, Ontario
M5G 2E9

1 2 3 4 5 6   04 03 02 01 00

To Sally
. . . with love

CONTENTS

PREFACE

Mention the word "Senate" and you're pretty well guaranteed to get a reaction, usually a negative one. Everybody, it seems, wants the place either reformed or abolished. Few want to leave it as it is. When I ran into Ontario premier Mike Harris at radio station CFRB this spring and told him I was writing a book on the Senate he said, without prompting, "Whenever anybody asks me about the Senate I ask when they're going to abolish it. That pretty well ends the conversation."

His is not an isolated view. But why is that? What is it about the Senate that bugs people so much? The Senate, after all, is a fixed part of our government, intended, as Sir John A. Macdonald put it, to function as a forum for "sober second thought." Most parliamentary democracies modelled on the British tradition do have a second house, apart from but linked to the legislative assembly. The Senate is ours. And, for the fathers of Confederation, its characteristics were crucial.

It was the deal-maker that broke a political impasse. Without the Senate, which assured equal representation for the regions regardless of population fluctuations, there might have been no Canada. As George Brown explained, "Our Lower Canada [Quebec] friends have agreed to give us representation by population in the Lower House, on the express condition that they shall have equality in the Upper House. On no other condition could we have advanced a step." And Sir John A. Macdonald, in the 1865 Confederation debates, said, "In order to protect local interests, and to prevent sectional jealousies, it was found requisite that the three great divisions into which British North America is separated should be represented in the Upper House on the principle of equality."

Yet few Canadians (except for the senators themselves) have ever been happy with the institution. They see it as a useless, expensive, undemocratic appendage of government. And, all too often, they view it, accurately, as a refuge and dumping ground for bagmen, party apologists, and failed politicians. Most Canadians agree that the place is overdue for change.

So why, if so many people want change, do we never get it? How is it that every prime minister promises reform, but it never happens? If we killed the Senate would public reaction reflect the sentiment expressed by the American writer Dorothy Parker after the death of President Calvin Coolidge when she quipped, "How do they know?" Would most Canadians know, or care, if the Senate died? In fact, the Canadian Senate is more significant than many people realize. It's not toothless. In fact, apart from the U.S. Senate, it's the most powerful upper house in the world. If more Canadians understood how often the Senate does exercise its power, there would be even more pressure to have something done about it. Without immense public pressure, not much is likely to change.

Still, concern over the Senate and its place in Confederation has had a profound impact on Canadian history. The most recent demonstration of that is the birth and remarkable growth of the Reform Party, the western-based populist movement that rode Senate reform as a vehicle to carry Preston Manning from nowhere just a little more than a decade ago to leadership of the second largest party in the Commons. Whether that's a good thing depends on your point of view, but there's no escaping the fact that Reform's view of the Senate as a potential equalizer against the power blocs of central Canada contributed significantly to the party's growth.

It was my long-time friend Roy MacGregor who got me into this. MacGregor, an accomplished author and senior columnist for the *National Post* – and arguably the sweetest writer we have in this country – grew tired of listening to me rant about the Senate and suggested I write about it instead. So I did.

My agent, Linda McKnight, took it from there, and I thank her along with McClelland & Stewart publisher Doug Gibson and senior editor Jonathan Webb for believing in the project too.

Nobody writes a book without a lot of help. At Canadian Press headquarters in Toronto, editor-in-chief Scott White and librarian Asma Khan gave me access to a world of information, especially the rare old microfiche files from the long-forgotten earlier years of the Senate, and I thank them both. At Southam's Toronto office, bureau chief Joan Walters and editorial assistant Moira Scott introduced me, a hopeless Luddite, to the wonders and mysteries of modern technological information recovery. In Ottawa, Carleton University student and press gallery associate Dan McHardie pored through old Hansards and dug up numerous essays on the Senate – including several of his own – to help fill in many of the blanks.

I also received kind and valuable assistance and advice from author Stevie Cameron in Toronto; in Ottawa from Michael Bate at *Frank* magazine; John Crupe in the Press Gallery; and, as always, staff at the truly magnificent Library of Parliament. Former Senate communications director Gord Lovelace was a lifesaver by loaning me his historical collection of nearly twenty years' worth of regular *Senate Bulletins*, the press clipping service which was a big part of the work he did during his tenure to keep the public and the media informed. And in Saskatoon, reporter Mark Wyatt of *Leader-Post* news generously offered his advice and assistance as did Don MacDonald of the Halifax *Chronicle-Herald*. Then there are a host of authors and journalists who, over the years, have chronicled the activities of the Senate, an invaluable resource in compiling the personal and political histories of the Red Chamber.

There are many others involved, especially people I interviewed both on and off the record. They know who they are, and I thank them all.

I

The Saskatchewan Roughrider

WHEN PRIME MINISTER Brian Mulroney went trawling for eight Tory loyalists in the summer of 1990 to stack the Senate in his zeal to push the hated GST past a rebellious, Liberal-laden Red Chamber, one of those he readily reeled into the partisan pond was Saskatchewan's recently retired deputy premier, Eric Berntson.

Like nearly every senator since Confederation, Berntson had demonstrated his worthiness for what has often been described as the "taskless thanks" by years of loyal service to both his political party and himself, precisely the sort of background that continues to guarantee that our 132-year-old Upper House retains its lowly reputation as a well-paid sinecure for a tawdry collection of bagmen, spent politicians, and assorted partisan hacks.

Berntson had served his party well. First elected to the Saskatchewan legislature in 1975, then re-elected in 1978, he won again in the 1982 sweep when Grant Devine's Tories took fifty-five seats, the largest majority in Saskatchewan history. Berntson was quickly named Devine's deputy premier and remained the province's most prominent and powerful minister for eight years, until he voluntarily stepped down from the cabinet in April 1990. Three months later, Berntson left the legislature altogether. On September 27, 1990, he became an instant member of the Senate's Hall of Shame by being named as one of the eight infamous GST senators.

Berntson was the most politically prominent of the GST senators. And as it turned out, not only had he served his party, he had served himself well too. On January 23, 1997, he was charged with fraud for his part in the largest political corruption scandal ever in Saskatchewan, and arguably the most far-reaching in Canadian history. Beginning in 1993, a total of twenty-one Tories, including eighteen former legislators, faced criminal charges in that scandal. On February 25, 1999, following a three-week trial in Regina, the fifty-seven-year-old senator became the fourteenth Saskatchewan Tory to be convicted in that scandal when he was found guilty of criminal fraud.

With that conviction, Berntson became the second current senator carrying a criminal conviction. He joined Quebec Tory senator Michel Cogger, another Mulroney appointee, who was convicted in 1998 of influence peddling for accepting $212,000 from a Quebec businessman who was seeking $45 million in federal and provincial help to build a silicon chip foundry near Montreal. Both senators are appealing their convictions. Berntson says if he loses his appeal, he will resign. He would likely face expulsion anyway, something that has never happened in the Senate, despite its long and often sordid history.

In choosing Berntson for the Senate in 1990 – nearly three years before the Saskatchewan political scandal broke – Mulroney picked the man who had served as Devine's Rasputin during that ill-fated Tory regime. Besides being deputy premier, Berntson at various times also doubled as House leader, minister of agriculture, minister of economic development and trade, provincial secretary and minister responsible for the Saskatchewan Water Corporation and SaskPower.

Regina-Lumsden-Lake Centre NDP MP John Solomon, now his party's federal whip, sat in the legislature with Berntson during most of the 1980s and says, "He ran things. He was the chief fixer. He handled the political strategy and determined in dramatic and significant terms the direction the government was going.

"Devine was happily encouraged to travel. He was gone eight to twelve weeks a year on various world junkets, so really it was left to Berntson much of the time to run the government," Solomon says. "And he and the Tories ran a scorched-earth policy across Saskatchewan. Watching them up close, it reminded me of the old saying about Nero fiddling while Rome burned. That's what they were doing to Saskatchewan."

In a lengthy feature called "All Devine's Men" in the September 1988 *Saturday Night* magazine, writer Andrew Nikiforuk put it this way: "If Devine was the happy face of government, Berntson was its hard muscle. As deputy premier, he made many of the day-to-day decisions, as well as playing a starring role in the GigaText fiasco. Not much happened in the Devine administration without Berntson's permission. Most former Tories still grow silent at the mention of the senator's name. 'He was a powerful guy,' says [former caucus chairman Lorne] McLaren."

Berntson, a farmer, masked much of his hard resolve behind a studied "aw shucks" exterior. Veteran Saskatchewan NDP legislator Ned Shillington said of Berntson that "the oldest con game in the world is you wander around in a set of big overalls with a straw stuck between your teeth, pretend you're a hick and all the while you're taking advantage of people who underestimate you. Eric in a way kind of did that."

The government in which Berntson was such a force had inherited a small budgetary surplus and an accumulated debt in Crown corporations of $3.5 billion. By the time they were booted out of office in October 1991 – in a provincial campaign Berntson directed – the debt had ballooned to nearly $15 billion. In a 1993 *Globe and Mail* article on Saskatchewan, journalist Stevie Cameron dramatically illustrated the scope of provincial pork-barrelling under the

Tories when she wrote that there were just four people working in public relations in Regina when they took office in 1982. By 1990, the number had swollen to 178 public relations operatives slurping at the government trough.

The government lost hundreds of millions of dollars by investing in ill-conceived projects. Many of these decisions resulted from a combination of partisan favouritism and plain poor judgement. One of those financial disasters was GigaText, a scheme that ironically brought Berntson and Senator Michel Cogger into contact with each other. Promoted by Quebec businessman Guy Montpetit, with a little help from his friend Cogger, the idea was to fund a new computer system that Montpetit claimed could translate provincial statutes from English into French. Despite clear warnings from federal officials that the translation system didn't work, and Ottawa's subsequent refusal to help fund it, Berntson helped arrange a $5-million grant to Montpetit to set up GigaText in Saskatchewan. It was a complete failure and the province ended up eating all of that money and more. While Berntson was guilty in this instance only of poor judgement, it was Cogger's relationship as a paid lobbyist with Montpetit that ultimately resulted in the Quebec senator being convicted of influence peddling.

The Saskatchewan Tory scam that resulted in the defeat of the government and the subsequent convictions of Berntson and thirteen other Tories grew directly out of a 1987 Conservative caucus meeting at a Cypress Hills resort. At this meeting, the caucus agreed to pool about twenty-five per cent of all communications funds – approximately $90,000 a year – supposedly to purchase province-wide advertising.

The pooling concept itself was not illegal, but caucus communications chairman John Scraba – who later plea-bargained for a two-year sentence plus $12,000 in restitution, and testified as a Crown witness against the others – was given the job of administering the fund by then labour minister and caucus chairman Lorne McLaren.

Scraba set up four companies: Communications Group Advertising; Airwaves Advertising; Images Consulting; and Systems Management Services Inc. As Nikiforuk explained in his *Saturday Night* article, "These unusual firms had no places of business, no employees, and no inventory. Whenever Airwaves or Images issued invoices for newsletters or radio ads, the work, if done at all, was actually produced by Tory caucus staff, and with equipment already paid for by the public. So the good people of Saskatchewan were now paying twice for communications allowance expenses." Between 1987 and 1991, these shell companies issued false invoices and claims worth $838,360, of which $229,000 may have been legitimate.

The scheme began to unravel in 1992, one year after voters had tossed out the Tories and given Roy Romanow's NDP a huge majority, when staff at the Canadian Imperial Bank of Commerce drilled open an unclaimed safety-deposit box and discovered $150,000 in $1,000 bills. The bank called the RCMP, which obtained a search warrant to drill open a second box, this one containing $90,000 for a total of $240,000. The bank, which was closing the branch, had tried unsuccessfully to notify the owner of the box by sending a registered letter to Fred Peters, the name under which it was listed. It turned out that Peters, a former colleague of Scraba's, had no knowledge of the scam, although he had to sweat through several visits from the RCMP before police figured out who really owned the boxes. Scraba, who said Peters's name just "popped into [his] head," had left the legislature after Devine's 1991 defeat. Police tracked him down in Verona, Ontario.

The discovery at the bank sparked a wide-ranging RCMP probe into the improper use of legislative expense accounts. In February 1993, the RCMP confirmed it was investigating several past and present members of the legislature, and in June, NDP Highways Minister Murray Koskie resigned from Premier Roy Romanow's cabinet after learning his expense accounts were under scrutiny. That prompted Romanow to introduce a tougher conflict-of-interest law and a code of ethics. Koskie, a twenty-year veteran of the legislature, was found guilty in February 1993 of defrauding the public of $4,000 by illegally pocketing money from a Regina advertising firm. His conviction came less than two weeks after the Saskatchewan Tories had booted MLA Gerald Muirhead out of the party after he too was convicted and fined $5,000 for falsifying an invoice for a saddle he bought in 1988 with money from his legislative expense account.

The continuing RCMP investigation led to charges against Scraba and former caucus chairman and labour minister Lorne McLaren in July 1994. In September 1995, McLaren was given three and one-half years in prison for defrauding taxpayers of over $1 million during the final term of the Conservative government. McLaren pleaded guilty to using false invoices to obtain $837,000 worth of legislators' communications expense allowances and admitted to stealing $114,200 by making loans to himself from the caucus and to diverting $125,000 in public money from caucus funds to the Tory party.

In April 1995, after the RCMP laid fraud charges against an additional eight former Tory MLAs and three sitting Tories, former premier Grant Devine, who has never been personally connected to the fraud, accused the NDP government of conducting a "witch-hunt," saying the charges were timed with an election looming to discredit the opposition, as if the Tories needed help in bringing discredit upon their party.

Among the eight charged at that time was former tourism minister John Gerich, an ex-RCMP officer. He had put in a claim for $3,600 worth of Christmas cards that had already been paid for from his communications allowance. But Scraba prepared a false invoice to one of the shell companies and delivered an envelope containing three $1,000 bills and six $100 bills to Gerich, which he then pocketed and which left no paper trail. At Gerich's subsequent trial in 1997, he was sentenced to two years less a day and ordered to pay $12,264 in restitution. In sentencing him, Justice W.R. Matheson said, "Political corruption is endemic to Latin American countries, Asia . . . and perhaps Eastern Europe jurisdictions. But [it has] never seriously been suggested that corruption permeates Canadian politics, at least until a fraud of this scale was revealed."

While everybody knew in 1995 that the RCMP investigation was continuing and more criminal charges were likely, Berntson had not been implicated at this point. But the RCMP began to take an interest in his affairs in February 1995 after RCMP Sgt. John Leitch stumbled on some intriguing evidence. Leitch, a veteran commercial crime investigator, was poring over warehoused documents searching for evidence against former justice and finance minister Robert Andrew – who was subsequently fined $5,500 and ordered to pay $4,500 in restitution for his part in the fraud. During this search, Leitch found a $5,000 cheque written on the account of Dome Advertising Ltd. and addressed to Berriedale Management Inc., a company that Leitch knew belonged to Berntson.

Dome, which went out of business in the early 1990s, was run by Phil Kershaw, a one-time president of the Saskatchewan Roughriders and chairman of the Canadian Football League. It was one of two advertising agencies of record for the Devine government, sharing the gravy train with Robertson Pole. The two firms cornered ninety per cent of the government advertising market. During the disastrous 1991 election, directors for both companies worked together as directors of Blue Wave, putting together the Tory election advertising campaign. A provincial commission found later that Dome was paid thousands of dollars by the government for no apparent reason. It had also funnelled $500,000 to Strategy West over two years, an unrelated agency operated by Cy Macdonald, a former Liberal cabinet minister and close friend of Devine. There was no record of a contract with him in public accounts.

Leitch, his interest piqued by the discovery of the first cheque to Berntson's company, soon discovered another, this one for $8,450. Leitch subsequently found evidence of a third transaction between Dome and Berriedale and ultimately ended up with a three-foot stack of bank records and computer printouts that formed the basis for fraud charges against both Andrew and Berntson. On

January 23, 1997, Berntson, Andrew, and four other Tories were added to the list of individuals charged as a result of the RCMP investigation. Berntson was charged with breach of trust and two counts of fraud. The next day, he resigned from the federal Conservative caucus and stepped down as the Conservative's deputy leader in the Senate. That brought to nineteen the number of Tories charged in the scandal at that point. Of the thirteen previously charged, seven had been convicted, three acquitted, and three were still before the courts.

While Berntson was not publicly connected to the Tory caucus scam until charges against him were announced in 1997, considerable public interest in his activities during the Devine years was sparked by a February 6, 1993, article in the *Globe and Mail* written by prominent investigative journalist Stevie Cameron. This article focused on Berntson's personal and political connections with his good friend Robert Stromberg, head of the prominent law firm Robertson Stromberg, which grew from a small Saskatoon business to become one of the biggest law firms in Saskatchewan during the years the Tories were in power.

Robertson Stromberg was handed most of the legal work for the 1988 merger of two large Crown corporations – the provincially owned Saskatchewan Mining Development Corporation and Eldorado Nuclear Ltd. of Ottawa – to form a new privatized company called Cameco, the world's largest uranium company. The same firm also handled the work required to privatize the Potash Corporation in 1989. Berntson was not only a vocal supporter of the uranium industry and of privatization, he was also the minister for economic development in charge of the Saskatchewan Mining Development Corporation during the period of the merger in 1988 and 1989. As soon as he left the government, Berntson was employed as a consultant to Cameco through Robertson Stromberg "to accommodate the needs" of Cameco in connection with the company's privatization in 1991.

The *Globe* article cited "reliable sources" reporting that Berntson was paid $100, 000 in consulting fees for his efforts, but Berntson, asked about it, told Cameron, "I won't answer that question one way or another." No wonder. After the story was published, Cameco quickly issued a press release to say it had paid Berntson $355,000 as a consultant during 1990 and 1991.

All of this caught the interest of the Law Society of Saskatchewan, particularly after a letter written to them by Emmet Reidy two weeks after the *Globe* piece alleged that "the Robertson Stromberg law firm performed a great deal of legal work during the 1980s that could only have come with the blessing of the Devine Government, of whom Senator Berntson was a very influential member." Reidy asked the law society to "investigate the activities of Robertson Stromberg and Senator Berntson. . . ."

Five weeks later, the law society wrote Reidy to say it had no jurisdiction to investigate Berntson, a non-lawyer, and that allegations of kickbacks had been denied by the firm. It added, however, that in view of the perception resulting from the *Globe* article, the matter was being referred to the discipline committee chair. But in a small province like Saskatchewan, it proved difficult to set up a committee of people who did not have a personal conflict of some sort with either Berntson or Stromberg. At the time of Reidy's complaint, for example, Leslie Prosser of Saskatoon was president of the law society and also a partner in Robertson Stromberg. R. Peter MacKinnon was appointed by the law society as chairman of a three-member investigation committee in June 1993, but he stepped down as chairman in September, then left the committee altogether in October, after complaints that his wife was a cabinet minister in the NDP government that had replaced Berntson's Tories and therefore he could be seen as having a political axe to grind against Berntson. Committee member Matthew Miazga also stepped down after an interim report found no evidence of kickbacks by Robertson Stromberg but did discover money had been paid by Cameco through the law firm to Berntson's Berriedale Management Inc. Miazga's wife was a member of Cameco's board of directors.

The law society tried again in January 1994, setting up another investigation committee to study the payment of money by Cameco through the law firm to Berntson's company and in June recommended laying a formal complaint against Robert Stromberg for "conduct unbecoming a lawyer." It accused Stromberg of having entered into a "scheme" with Berntson that "was disguised and misrepresented . . . in order to avoid public knowledge of [Senator] E.A. Berntson's involvement" and of a breach of Section 121 of the Criminal Code, commonly known as "influence peddling." It also accused Stromberg of assisting Berntson in breaching the Code "and attempting to conceal the breach. . . ." The committee also recommended a second complaint of conduct unbecoming a lawyer against twenty-one current and former members of the law firm, saying "they did fail to report . . . the actions of Stromberg to the Law Society."

After considerable legal wrangling, Mr. Justice G.W. Baynton of the Saskatchewan Queen's Bench tossed out the law society complaints, primarily because they had not stuck strictly to matters of unprofessional conduct but had made accusations of criminal conduct. "Unless the committee found that the lawyer had entered into the alleged scheme and that he improperly aided a possible breach of S. 121, it could not find for unprofessional conduct," he wrote. "The unprofessional conduct aspects of the alleged acts were insignificant compared to their criminal aspects respecting named individuals, including non-lawyers. . . . The contact between the police and the Law Society made the disciplinary proceeding a form of preliminary inquiry. It could be used to help the police investigation and bypass many individual rights under the Criminal Code. . . . Further, the public would consider a finding of the lawyer's unprofessional conduct an inherent finding that the politician or client had done something illegal."

Judge Baynton's comments about the "police investigation" are not to be confused with the much wider probe the RCMP was conducting into the Saskatchewan Tory caucus scandal, but referred to a specific investigation launched almost simultaneously with the law society probe by RCMP Staff Sgt. L.D. Jacobs into the activities of Berntson and Stromberg. In a June 23, 1995, letter from Jacobs, the NCO in charge of Saskatoon's commercial crime section, to the law society, the Mountie wrote, "I believe that it may be in our interest to work together, where possible, to ensure that our mutual efforts are successful. . . . I expect that the investigation conducted by the Law Society would have produced evidence beneficial to our criminal investigation. It would be helpful if, after consideration, the Law Society chose to review with the RCMP what information and evidence relating to influence peddling exists."

Jacobs also asked the law society to look into an intriguing 1990 real estate deal. Even though Berntson's personal bank account was $50,000 overdrawn at the time, he and his second wife, Joan, acquired clear title to an upscale home at 102 Saskatchewan Crescent West in the tony university area of Saskatoon. The home was owned by Amok Ltd., a uranium firm, which had bought it in 1981 for $260,000. The Berntsons paid $160,000 in 1990. A year later, they obtained a mortgage for $200,000 on the house from the Royal Bank of Canada. They sold it in 1993.

Jacobs wrote that the transaction "may be of interest to your investigation committee. . . . We believe the statement of adjustments will show that $5,000, which was part of the selling agent and broker commission, was forgiven in favour of the purchasers, Mr. and Mrs. Berntson. This resulted from Robert Stromberg (acting for Mr. Berntson) asking the agent and broker to help the purchaser. Mr. Berntson was the Deputy Premier at the time." The RCMP continued to investigate the matter, but no charges were ever laid, and in early 1999 an RCMP official told me that the investigation had been dropped and they had no further comment.

Berntson's only other brush with the law during this period came in February 1992 when he was fined $500 and suspended from driving for three months on a charge of impaired driving after he pleaded guilty in the provincial court in Hanley, near Saskatoon. He had been stopped by the RCMP on a highway south of Saskatoon on January 7.

In addition to his Senate duties and his work for Cameco, Berntson was keeping himself busy elsewhere as well. He was elected to the board of directors of Platinum Capital Management Inc., and when he spoke to Cameron for her 1993 *Globe and Mail* article he said he was spending most of his time working on private deals with other investors in the Caribbean and South America. "It's nothing to do with my public life," he said, refusing to discuss the deals or his partners. "I keep those confidential."

He was also chairman at that time of Toronto-based Transprairie Energy Ltd., a natural gas wholesaler owned by Toronto business-man Mark Silver. The company president was Regina lawyer Gary Drummond. The three businessmen were also directors of Eurotech Building Technologies Inc., formerly called Zaba Lee Developments Ltd. Vancouver Stock Exchange records showed that Berntson received 100,000 shares of Eurotech in 1991 and was listed as a director. But by March of that year the company was hit with a cease-trading order and a temporary suspension after fighting with VSE regulators over its failure to file timely financial disclosures. The new management team, which included Berntson and Silver, had invested $1.4 million in a product called Flexibrick.

In an information circular distributed by International Thunderbird Gaming Corp. of Vancouver in advance of its annual meeting on June 22, 1995, the company announced that it had paid Berntson $15,000 in director's fees but, oddly, he was not shown on the list of company directors. The firm, which had some interest in gambling licences in Saskatchewan, owns the Landmark Inn on Albert Street in Regina.

Berntson also garnered considerable publicity across the country in 1996 when former Saskatchewan Conservative party whip Michael Hopfner called him to be a witness at his trial. When a subpoena was issued to compel Senator Berntson to testify, it could not be served because he was hiding behind his parliamentary privilege. Three weeks later, following massive media and political criticism of his actions, Berntson wrote an open letter denying that he was trying to evade testifying by using his Senate privileges, even though he had been doing exactly that, and he did subsequently take the stand in Hopfner's trial. Hopfner was found guilty of collecting more than $57,000 through false expense claims, sentenced to eighteen months in jail, and ordered to repay the taxpayers' money. The former Lloydminster MLA was acquitted of a more serious charge of helping to organize the million-dollar fraud ring that operated in the Tory caucus from 1986 to 1991.

Berntson's action provoked a debate on the question of privilege in the House of Commons on November 25, 1998, when Regina New Democrat MP John Solomon, who had sat in the Saskatchewan legislature during much of Berntson's term there, introduced a private members' motion seeking to "eliminate the privilege of members of the House of Commons and Senators to evade an obligation to testify before a court or civil proceeding."

Solomon told the Commons that "many people in Saskatchewan two years ago told me they thought Senator Berntson was exercising his privileges not out of a sense of importance of his work in the Senate, but to avoid giving testimony at one trial that might later lead to his own criminal charges. Although I do not want to comment on a matter that is currently before the courts, I can say that it was not so impossible to see how they might come to that conclusion."

Despite his best efforts, however, Solomon found little support for his motion in the Commons. "I do not believe MPs or Senators should have an unfettered privilege to refuse to testify in court as witnesses," he said. Perhaps not, but since politicians rarely agree to give up any privileges they enjoy, Solomon's efforts to send the matter to the Procedures and House Affairs Committee for further study failed.

The Saskatchewan Tory scandal discredited the people involved in it and destroyed the provincial Conservative Party. But perhaps its most tragic ramification was the February 1995 suicide of former cabinet minister Jack Wolfe after the RCMP made a routine call to him as part of their investigation, which was named "Operation Fiddle." The police simply wanted to know how Wolfe had acquired a computer, but the thirty-nine-year-old veterinarian, who suffered from bouts of depression, telephoned his lawyer, Clyne Harradence, to say that the police "found some evidence that I've been lying" at a preliminary hearing for one of the Tory caucus workers. Harradence told him not to worry – and police would say later that Wolfe had done nothing wrong. But later that same day Wolfe put a shotgun to his head and pulled the trigger. He left behind his wife, Gail, who was pregnant with their fourth child at the time, and a short, bittersweet suicide note saying, "I love you all too much to have you bear the pain of having my name and reputation destroyed because of [the] partisan political interests of others."

Besides costing Wolfe his life, ruining the careers of so many public officials, and further undermining public confidence in the political system, the litany of crimes also wiped out ninety years of Saskatchewan political history on November 9, 1997, when delegates at a Regina meeting voted 130–22 to make the Saskatchewan Conservative Party "inactive" for the next two provincial elections, leaving it up to ten trustees to decide when – or if – the party should end its self-imposed hiatus at that time. As things stand, it's not likely. That's because a new party has already sprung up to replace the Conservatives. Earlier in 1997, four Conservative MLAs joined with four Liberal MLAs to form the Saskatchewan Party, grabbing Official Opposition status in the legislature from the remaining six Liberal MLAs.

Berntson's trial got under way in Regina in January 1999, two years after charges were laid against him. Berntson, who was easily the most powerful and prominent of the twenty-one Tories who had been charged since 1993, was facing one charge of fraud over $5,000 and one count of breach of trust. The charges contained five separate allegations of wrongdoing:

- That he used false invoices provided by Dome Advertising to obtain $18,450 from his MLA communications allowance;
- That he used false invoices from 582806 Saskatchewan Ltd. (Airwaves Advertising) – one of the four numbered companies operated by Scraba on behalf of the Tory caucus – to obtain a further $7,870 from his communications allowance;
- That he made false claims on his secretarial services expense allowance to obtain $31,046;
- That he made false claims on his constituency office allowance to obtain $10,689;
- And that he played an instrumental role in the diversion of $125,000 from the PC caucus bank account to Progressive Conservative Party coffers after the 1986 election.

Much of Berntson's defence against these charges was that he was simply a poor bookkeeper. He described himself in court as a "shoebox accountant" and his wife, Joan, testified that she still takes a shoebox to collect his Senate expense receipts in his Ottawa office. She apparently does a good job, since the 1997–98 public accounts show that Berntson is one of the leading spenders in the Senate, costing taxpayers more than $260,000 to keep him in the style he's become accustomed to. He charged $97,855 for travel expenses plus $92,596 in research assistance, staff, and other expenses; claimed his entire $10,100 tax-free allowance; and collected his senatorial pay of $64,500.

During the fourteen-day trial, Court of Queen's Bench Justice Frank Gerein heard the testimony of twenty-two Crown witnesses. When the trial ended early in February, Judge Gerein announced he would return with his verdict in three weeks. On February 25, 1999, Gerein tossed out the breach of trust charge and two of the other charges, but he did find Berntson guilty of criminal fraud for funnelling $42,000 from his constituency expenses into Berriedale Management Inc., a company he owned, instead of giving it to his secretary as the legislature had intended.

During the trial, Berntson's former secretary, Audrey Young, who worked for him from 1987 to 1990, testified that she never saw a dime of the more than $10,000 Berntson received in 1988 to offset secretarial expenses. Young said she was paid directly by the legislature and had no idea where Berntson obtained receipts indicating he paid her an additional $860 to $1,000 a month for working in his Carlyle constituency office in 1988. She acknowledged that her signature appeared at the bottom of the receipts, but testified someone else filled in the rest of the information because the handwriting was different from her own.

Judge Gerein called it an "illicit scheme" and wrote that Berriedale was Berntson's "alter ego. . . . It was used for the purpose of obtaining monies from the constituency office and services allowance and the constituency secretarial allowance. This was done through the presentment of false invoices." The judge added that Berntson "was a very busy man. . . . He was the sole shareholder and operating mind of Berriedale Management Inc. He knew the company rendered no services and employed no person who did." He added that "I consider the testimony of the accused [Berntson] to be rather questionable. I have no doubt that the accused had knowledge and played a role in what transpired."

Judge Gerein also dismissed Berntson's claim that the money was used to pay both his former and present wives for secretarial duties in their home. "According to him [Berntson] they [his wives] were not paid directly, but the women and children enjoyed the benefit of the money paid for secretarial services because it went towards the cost of their shelter, food, clothing, utilities, and general living expenses," wrote Gerein. "In my opinion, that is not a lawful justification. It is at best a retroactive rationalization of illegal conduct."

The judge also wrote that he was "satisfied that there was no agreement, arrangement, or even understanding between the accused and either of his wives that they would be compensated for their labours on his behalf. Thus, there was never any fee payable for services of any sort, including secretarial services. It follows that the accused was not entitled to access the particular allowances in order to obtain a fee for service." Finally, Judge Gerein wrote that "money flowed from the public purse into his [Berntson's] pocket absent any legitimate entitlement. Had the true situation not been concealed by deceit and dishonesty the money would never have been paid."

Berntson, who spent much of the trial sitting in the court with his arms crossed in front of him, and flatly refusing any public comment, showed no emotion as the verdict was announced. Outside the court, however, the usually bombastic, tough-talking senator was sombre but still unrepentant. "As far as I'm concerned I did nothing wrong," he said.

On March 15, Berntson's characteristic bravado was considerably diminished when he made an emotional appeal for leniency at his sentencing hearing before Judge Gerein. "I ask you to balance my positive contributions to society against that for which you have found me guilty," he said, his voice cracking. "My service has been with the belief that honesty, integrity, and hard work would make a difference." No doubt it would, but as Crown attorney Sharon Pratchler told the court, public officials have an obligation to set a good example.

"A very clear and unequivocal message needs to be sent by the court. If those who make the law will not uphold it, who will?" she said, asking the judge to impose a jail sentence.

Berntson's lawyer, Mike Megaw, asked for a conditional sentence, which would mean no jail time, emphasizing the senator's years of public service and volunteer work with street kids and literacy projects. Megaw said the trial had drained Berntson's financial resources and destroyed his political career. At fifty-seven he has no job prospects and "doesn't know what he will do . . . to support himself and his family."

The next day, Judge Gerein sentenced Berntson to one year in a provincial jail and ordered him to repay the $41,735 he defrauded from taxpayers. "It should be made known to others in like circumstances that dishonesty in public office will result in harsh consequence. . . ." said the judge. "Society expected you to act with probity; you failed to do so. The public finds that offensive in the extreme. The sentence must reflect that denunciation."

Berntson gave his tearful wife a quick kiss before he was led out of the courtroom in handcuffs. He immediately filed an appeal of his conviction and was released a few hours later after a bail hearing. He said if he loses his appeal, he'll resign from the Senate.

His political opponents, however, weren't prepared to wait that long. Saskatchewan NDP MP Chris Axworthy said Berntson should do the honourable thing and resign immediately. "Each day that the public witnesses the spectacle of a senator hiding in his office behind the questionable cloak of an appeal, the public's trust and respect of each of us withers."

Reform MP Deborah Grey, her party's deputy leader, said the convictions of both Berntson and Cogger prove that something must be done about the Senate. "The Senate is so outdated," she said, "that the prime minister can't even fire these two."

As for the senators themselves, they have made it clear they won't do anything about Cogger or Berntson until their appeals have been exhausted.

In the meantime, both men continue to sit in the Senate and draw their senatorial salaries and enjoy the generous perks of power.

2

In the Beginning

O N SEPTEMBER 6, 1856, George Wilson Allan, a wealthy and popular Toronto businessman, was sailing across the Atlantic Ocean, a journey that in those days took about three weeks. Unknown to him, a coalition of both Liberal and Conservative activists was rallying in a downtown Toronto hall to make a decision that would directly affect his future life.

When he arrived home on September 11 and stepped off his Grand Trunk Railway car onto the platform of the old wooden station built not far from the site of the current Union Station, Allan was presented with a petition signed by nearly two thousand electors – all men, of course – informing him that he had been nominated as the Conservative candidate for the Legislative Council, the original name for the Senate, for the united Upper and Lower Canadas.

While bands played and people sang and waved banners, Allan, who had been mayor of Toronto the year before, accepted the nomination. In an age when communication was by no means instant, participatory democracy did not necessarily require participation.

The first experiment with an upper house in British colonial history dates to the 1791 Constitutional Act, which divided the colony of Canada into Upper and Lower Canada. Both parts were given an elected assembly along with a legislative council, or Senate, whose members were appointed for life by the governor.

As things turned out, the real power rested with both the executive council (a forerunner of our modern cabinet) and the legislative council. The unelected councils quickly became powerful, autocratic oligarchies composed of wealthy government, business, and religious figures who paid little heed to the wishes of the elected legislatures and even less to the public at large.

These councils became known as the Chateau Clique in Lower Canada and the Family Compact in Upper Canada. They wielded enormous power even after the 1841 Act of Union created the United Province of Canada and brought responsible government to British North America for the first time. The elected Assembly was given eighty-four seats, forty-two from each of the provinces, including a cabinet of ministers responsible to the Lower House. The arrangement created considerable resentment in francophone Lower Canada, which, at the time, had a population of about 720,000 compared to just 400,000 in English-speaking Upper Canada. (Mind you, within a decade Upper Canada's population surpassed that of Quebec.)

The unelected council continued to dominate government after the Act of Union took effect. Pressure for reform, however, grew steadily. Matters came to a head when the legislative council and its Tory allies in the Assembly lost a bitter fight over the Rebellion Losses Bill in 1849. The governor-general, Lord Elgin, sided with Reformers when he signed the bill that Tories said compensated those who rebelled against the Crown in 1837. On his way home to

Monklands, his official Montreal residence, Elgin's carriage was pursued by a Tory-organized mob that pelted him with eggs, rocks, and garbage. That same night a mob of about fifteen hundred English-speaking Montrealers broke into the House of Assembly, where the politicians were in session, took an axe to the Throne, stole the mace, and sacked the chamber itself. A fire broke out after someone smashed gas mains, and after some confusion the politicians ran from the building, while the mob outside hooted and howled with delight. The building burned to the ground. As a result of this and continuing attacks by Tory-inspired hooligans against legislators, Lord Elgin and his government moved to Toronto. In 1859, after years of political infighting, the sod was officially turned on the new Parliament buildings in Ottawa, Queen Victoria's personal choice as the capital of Canada.

About this time, various groups began to lobby hard for an elected senate. In 1855, a year after Sir Allan MacNab formed a coalition government, a bill was introduced and approved in the House of Commons "to change the constitution of the Legislative Council by rendering the same elective." Sir John A. Macdonald, leader of the Tory party, supported the bill, but George Brown, publisher of the *Globe* and leader of the Reform movement, did not. The Conservative politicians wanted an elite counterweight to the assembly and cabinet. The Clear Grits, who usually didn't agree with the Conservatives on anything, favoured the move because they believed all public institutions should be elective.

Despite the strong vote of support for an elective senate, however, the unelected, life-tenured legislative councillors flatly rejected the bill. The same bill was re-introduced a year later and carried in the Assembly by a vote of eighty-one to twelve. After much debate and a number of amendments, it was finally accepted by the Council and given royal assent on June 24, 1856.

The original bill had called for the immediate retirement of all current unelected councillors, but that was voted down by the Council and it was agreed they could keep their seats under the life tenure of their appointments. The act did, however, provide for the election for an eight-year term of forty-eight members, each representing an electoral division, half of them in Upper Canada and half in Lower Canada. To provide for a gradual changeover to a fully elective Council, the act decreed that six members from each province should be elected at two-year intervals, the first twelve in 1856 and the last twelve in 1862. No time was lost. Writs were issued for the election of the first twelve councillors on September 1, 1856 – about the time that George Wilson Allan began his long voyage home.

Toronto at this time was combined with the Township of York to form the electoral division of York. Because it fell into the second round of voting, the election there would not take place until 1858. George Brown tried to persuade some of his followers to run for the job, but no one wanted it. Both he and they were, however, horrified, when former alderman Charles Eward Romain announced that he would be an independent candidate and produced the necessary signatures to validate his intentions. Romain, a colourful, somewhat rowdy sports figure of questionable ethics, was decidedly persona non grata with the city's upper crust and, indeed, with most people who knew him. The *Montreal Pilot*, for example, wrote, "Things have come to a pretty pass when such a person as Mr. Charles Romain proposes to contest the chief electoral division in Upper Canada as a candidate for the Legislative Council."

Romain's candidacy had the effect of uniting both Tories and Grits and led directly to their selection of Allan as their candidate. The great irony of his selection was that the argument for an elected Council was that it would make the councillors more responsive to the people and break the hold that the monied Establishment had on the government. But nobody could have been more Establishment than Allan. His father, William Allan, had been a charter member of the Family Compact, and the president and founder of the Bank of Upper Canada, which was the Compact's official bank.

George Allan, a prosperous merchant, was chancellor of Trinity University and at various times president of two of the early voluntary educational organizations, the Mechanics' Institute and the Canadian Institute. An avid gardener, Allan is perhaps best remembered for his donation in 1860 of an oval of five acres of land near Sherbourne and Carlton streets, which quickly became the home of the Toronto Horticultural Society, the first horticultural society in the province. Additional land was leased from the municipality in 1864, and in 1888 it was turned over to the city. It was named Allan Gardens in 1901 and remains today as an oasis of greenery in the grey heart of the city.

Under the system of voting in the pre-Confederation days, the formal election of candidates was often an exciting and downright riotous procedure. In late September an estimated three thousand people gathered around the hustings in Yorkville, then a flourishing suburb of Toronto. Both Allan and Romain delivered election speeches and then the presiding officer, Sheriff Jarvis, called for a show of hands. He quickly declared that Allan had won, prompting Romain's friends to demand a formal poll, which was set for October 5 and 6.

The first day's voting went so strongly in favour of what the *Colonist* newspaper called "Allan and Respectability," that Romain acknowledged defeat. His followers wouldn't quit, however, and by the end of the second day of voting, the ballots cast were 2,869 for Allan and 1,456 for Romain, a resounding majority of 1,413 for Allan.

The country's only experience with an elected senate did not change much, because most of the successful candidates came from the same class as their appointed predecessors. Anyway, it wasn't given much time to work. Within a few years the idea of a confederation of all the British North American colonies began to take hold as the preferred route to political and economic salvation.

The rocky road to Confederation was mapped out in three conferences by the collective Fathers of Confederation: Charlottetown in
September 1864, where Maritime union was the major issue but a
delegation of Canadian politicians sold the idea of confederation;
Quebec City in October 1864, where a series of seventy-two resolutions on a wider union were approved; and London, England, in
December 1866, resulting in the British North America Act.

In June of 1864, Reform leader George Brown, chairman of the
parliamentary committee studying the constitutional question,
strongly advocated the federative union of the British North
American colonies. About the same time, Governor-General Lord
Monck asked Macdonald and Brown to set aside their bitter political differences and form a coalition. On June 22, the governing
Tories and opposition Reform announced they had indeed joined to
fight for a united British North America. In July the lieutenant-
governors of the three Maritime provinces, in response to a letter
from Monck, told Canada's governor-general that Canadian delegates would be welcome at the September Charlottetown Conference
on Maritime union.

And so it was that in late August 1864, Macdonald, Brown,
French-Canadian leader George-Étienne Cartier, and five other
federal ministers boarded the luxury steamer the *Queen Victoria*.
They arrived in Charlottetown three days later. The conference
began September 1 and by the time the twenty-three delegates
wrapped it up five days later, the Canadians had managed to over-
come much of the original hostility against confederation that ani-
mated the Maritime leaders. Indeed, the Maritime delegates decided
that the union of their provinces was hopeless but unanimously
agreed that, given the right terms, a broader confederation of British
North America was highly desirable. They agreed to attend another
conference in Quebec City.

In October 1864, the delegates from Canada, New Brunswick,
Nova Scotia, Newfoundland, and Prince Edward Island locked
themselves into the spacious crimson second-floor reading room of

the Quebec Legislative Council and spent eighteen exhausting days privately hammering out seventy-two resolutions aimed at uniting British North America.

Few would have predicted going into the Quebec Conference that the make-or-break issue for a deal was the composition of a new Canadian Senate. But that's exactly what happened.

On Thursday, October 13, 1864, the fourth day of the Quebec Conference, Macdonald introduced a resolution drafted by the Canadian cabinet on just what would happen to the Senate. The proposal ignited a full week of rancorous debate over both the composition of the Senate and whether members would be appointed or elected. When it all ended, Macdonald conceded that "in order to protect local interests, and to prevent sectional jealousies, it was found requisite that the three great divisions into which British North America is separated should be represented in the Upper House on the principle of equality." And Brown explained, "Our Lower Canada [Quebec] friends have agreed to give us representation by population in the Lower House, on the express condition that they shall have equality in the Upper House. On no other condition could we have advanced a step."

It's important to recall the population disparity between the various players at the time of the Confederation debate since fears from the smaller groups of being smothered by the larger ones were at the heart of the disagreements. By 1861, Upper Canada's population, having tripled over the previous twenty years, had reached 1,396,091. Lower Canada had 1,111,586 people. Nova Scotia, the largest of the Maritime colonies, boasted a population of 330,857, while New Brunswick had 252,047, and Prince Edward Island, 80,857. Newfoundland and Labrador's population at that time was approximately 140,000. None of the others was growing at even close to the same rate that Upper Canada was, so the population disparities were bound to broaden as time went on. The combined population of the four Atlantic colonies was less than one-third that of the existing Canadian provinces.

Population, of course, wasn't the only consideration. At the time of Confederation, religion played a major role in the lives of most people and there was considerable antipathy between Roman Catholics and Protestants. About eighty-five per cent of the people of Lower Canada were Roman Catholic in 1861. In Upper Canada the ratio was reversed, with almost eighty-three per cent adhering to Protestant faiths. Join the two provinces together and the split was relatively even. But because Protestants had significantly higher numbers in all four Atlantic colonies – from a high of seventy-four per cent in Nova Scotia to a low of fifty-six per cent in Prince Edward Island – a union of all the colonies meant that Roman Catholics became a distinct minority, another reason why opposition to Confederation was stronger in the Atlantic region and why support in Lower Canada was less pronounced than it was in Upper Canada.

Macdonald, a veteran negotiator and wily politician, understood these things better than most. That's why the Canadian Senate proposal at the Quebec Conference offered "sectional" equality. There would be three sections, Ontario, Quebec, and the Maritimes, each with the same number of seats in the Upper House. Macdonald presented the plan as a concession to the Maritimers, pointing out that it would give them "equality" in the Senate even though their collective population was much smaller than either of the two Canadas.

Maritimers, however, had a different view. New Brunswick premier Leonard Tilley, Nova Scotia's chief delegate, Charles Tupper, and New Brunswick attorney-general Charles Fisher all tried to convince the Canadians to expand the Senate representation from their provinces. The Canadians wouldn't budge. In fact Brown, who had absolutely insisted that representation in the Commons must be based on population, suggested that if the Maritimes could have extra seats, then so should Upper Canada, since it had so many more people. That idea, of course, infuriated the delegates from Quebec.

Things were so bad that P.E.I. cabinet minister Edward Whelan – whose strong union support would cost him his seat in 1867 – wrote shortly before the first grand ball on the Friday night that "matters do not certainly look very promising."

Nor did they improve after the Sunday break when Prince Edward Island introduced an even more serious challenge to the process.

Andrew Archibald Macdonald, a prominent P.E.I. merchant and ship owner, argued that if rep-by-pop had to prevail in the Commons then "the upper house should be more representative of the small provinces, as it was to be the guardian of their rights and privileges." He argued that each province, not just each section, ought to have equal representation in the federal upper house, the same as they did in the U.S. Senate. (This, indeed, is the same argument now made by Reform leader Preston Manning and his supporters when they call for a "Triple E" – Elected, Effective, Equal – Senate.)

After Andrew Macdonald's Monday morning bombshell, the Canadian delegation held a private caucus and decided to change its tactics, reviving a motion that Nova Scotia's Sir Charles Tupper had made at the start of the debate, that the three Maritime provinces would start on an equal footing with Ontario and Quebec in the Senate, but there would be additional seats for the Atlantic region if Newfoundland joined Confederation. It worked, and Tupper's resurrected motion was quickly passed.

The Canadians had budged, but only slightly, since the other part of the plan was that Newfoundland's Senate seats would be balanced by future seats for the northwest when it joined Confederation. Prince Edward Island still wasn't happy and suggested that if the Canadians "made no allowance" it might prefer to remain out of Confederation.

In his instructive book, *1867: How the Fathers Made a Deal*, author Christopher Moore writes, "The other Maritime delegations had turned a deaf ear to Andrew Macdonald's plausible contention that the Senate could not be the guardian of provincial interests unless all provinces were equally represented. No Maritime delegate gave an unequivocal explanation of why they accepted a mere handful of extra seats in the Senate as a substitute for provincial equality there. But a hint at an answer emerged from the next big issue of the conference: how senators were to be selected."

Should they be elected or appointed? If appointed, who should appoint them – the federal or provincial governments? And what about members of the existing upper houses? Should they have priority in their appointments and should opposition as well as government parties be represented? That debate took up another two full days. Brown did not want an elected Senate because he did not want a Conservative upper house that felt it was entitled to challenge the Commons. He argued that election was certain to give senators that sense of entitlement. Finally, Nova Scotia Reformer Jonathan McCully, a teacher, lawyer, and editor, and one of the most enthusiastic advocates of Confederation, moved that senators be appointed for life by the federal government – although the initial Senate would be a bipartisan one, appointed from all the parties in proportion to their existing strength in the Upper House of each province. It was approved unanimously.

"The decision for 'sectional' or regional rather than provincial equality had already established that the Senate was unlikely to become an effective guardian of provinces' interests," wrote Moore. "The decision to let the federal cabinet appoint the senators killed any possibility of that.

"The Confederation-makers, despite all the days they spent wrangling over details of the Senate, agreed on one thing about it: it must be weak. The Senate they designed was attacked from the start as unrepresentative, unable to defend provincial interests, a retirement home for party hacks, but no one has ever successfully shown the Senate to be strong, or to pose a credible challenge to the authority of the House of Commons. That was the essential requirement of the men who designed it."

By the end of the debate, it was clear that the delegates from Prince Edward Island were having great difficulty accepting that agenda. The delegates from Nova Scotia and New Brunswick, on the other hand, had no such problems, although they would run into considerable problems trying to sell the principles when they returned to their own jurisdictions.

The unelected principle was ridiculed at the time in the Canadian Legislative Assembly when Christopher Dunkin, a Quebec MLA, called the appointed Senate "just the worst body that could be contrived. Ridiculously the worst." He joked that the best defence of it was that its appointees would be old men "upon whom death would provide a strange kind of constitutional check when nothing else did."

Macdonald justified the Senate as a mechanism for "sober second thought" to keep a check on the "democratic excesses" of the elected Lower Chamber. Keep in mind that the prevailing view of men in positions of religious, political, and economic power at the time was that the masses, who were generally poorly educated, weren't to be trusted with the serious business of running the country. Macdonald, addressing the concerns of the smaller provinces, went on to say that "we must protect the rights of minorities, and the rich are always fewer than the poor."

The truth of the new Senate, despite all the noble and newsworthy rhetoric about protecting the minorities and acting as a check on democratic excesses, is that the new Senate was a deal designed by and for the rich and privileged. Its main purpose was to protect that privilege from the great unwashed, a goal that, in truth, is about the only thing the Senate has managed to do well in its 132-year history. After all, in order to qualify for this appointment you had to be at least thirty years old, a resident in the province you represented and – here's the kicker – you had to own property worth at least $4,000. That was a significant sum at the time, equal approximately to the annual salary of a Superior Court judge. It certainly wasn't designed to accommodate your average carpenter or clerk.

When the Quebec Conference wrapped up, the real selling job began, as the delegates streamed out of the ornate Legislative Council chambers in Quebec City and drifted back to their home turf.

Within two weeks some formidable opposition came from Antoine-Aimé Dorion, leader of the Parti Rouge, who called the Quebec deal a "sham. . . . This is not the confederation we were proposed, but simply a legislative union disguised under the name of confederation." Dorion, who became Quebec's chief anti-confederate leading up to 1867, feared a strong central government would leave provincial legislatures only minor powers.

He saw the resolution to appoint the initial senators from the existing Legislative Councils for what it was, "a transparent bribe to curb the opposition in the upper houses." He predicted – wrongly, as it turns out – that since most British North American governments were Conservative, "For all time to come . . . you will find the Legislative Council controlled by the influence of the present government."

Quebec's chief negotiator at the conferences was Sir George-Étienne Cartier, a pivotal figure in the events, and also a bona fide, blue-blood, Establishment figure. He was a man who travelled easily among senior Church officials, who was seen as a spokesman for Conservative French-Canadian opinion, and who was approved by the tycoons of English Montreal's "Square Mile." He dominated politics in Canada East.

Supporters of the Quebec pact replied to Dorion that Article 14 of the Quebec Resolutions answered his fears of a Senate dominated by Conservative power-brokers. It reads, "That in such nomination due regard shall be had to the claims of the members of the Legislative Council in opposition in each province, so that all political parties may as nearly as possible be fairly represented." In other words, the prime minister of the day was called upon to appoint senators from all the parties. It sounds good in theory, but in practice that article has never come close to being acted on. Look at the current Senate, for example. Apart from a smattering of independents, all the senators are either Liberal or Conservative, even though the Conservatives stand in fifth place in the House of Commons. The two largest opposition parties in the Commons – the Reform Party and the Bloc Québécois – do not have a single senator between them.

The bitter split over the deal was evident in March 1865, when after an intense, five-week debate, Parliament voted to accept the terms agreed upon at Quebec City. The members from Canada West (Ontario) overwhelmingly endorsed the deal, voting 54–8, but in Canada East (Quebec) the vote was 37–25 in favour. Twenty-one of the forty-eight French-Canadian members were opposed, yet another manifestation of the French-English split that has plagued Canada since the beginning.

That same month, voters in New Brunswick, worried the union would mean higher taxes and a loss of local control, tossed out pro-confederate premier Leonard Tilley – who even lost his own riding – along with two other delegates who represented the province at the Quebec Conference, a clear win for anti-confederate leader Albert Smith, who easily won his seat.

In Nova Scotia, prominent anti-confederate Joseph Howe continued to stir up opposition to Confederation by publishing his *Botheration Letters*. In Prince Edward Island, pro-confederate Edward Whelan conceded that the island was "dead set against union in all shapes and forms."

In the midst of the growing controversy, however, the pro-confederate forces received significant help from an unexpected source: the United States. With tensions mounting between England and the North because of the Civil War (British sympathies lay with the South), pressure was developing within the northern states to annex Canada. Massachusetts passed a resolution calling for the annexation; the *Chicago Tribune* wrote that Canada "would be snatched up by this Republic as quickly as a hawk would gobble up a quail"; in July 1866, a bill clearing the way for the annexation of Canada was introduced and debated in Congress.

To many Maritimers, the prospect of joining Upper and Lower Canada, and remaining loyal to the Crown, was more attractive than the spectre of being gobbled up by the Americans. When in April 1866, the Nova Scotia Assembly received news that an army of Irish Americans (Fenians) in Eastport, Maine, was planning an attack, it wrapped up a fifteen-hour debate by voting 31–19 in favour of Premier Charles Tupper's resolution to arrange "a scheme of union."

One anti-confederate politician who switched sides during the debate said he hoped he'd "never live to see the Stars and Stripes floating on Citadel Hill."

The Fenians actually did cross the border from Maine into New Brunswick but were easily beaten back by British soldiers and local militia. But the raid was enough to convince New Brunswickers to elect a pro-confederate government, one week after Albert Smith's administration resigned. Lieutenant-governor Arthur Hamilton Gordon called on Peter Mitchell to form the government, but the party's real leader was the venerable Leonard Tilley.

Still, the issue wasn't settled. A delegation of sixteen led by Macdonald and Cartier set off for London, England, in December 1866 and spent three weeks fashioning a deal with British officials. It was similar to the 1864 Quebec Resolutions, but achieving agreement wasn't easy. Once again, the issue of the Upper House dominated the agenda. New Brunswicker Jonathan McCully, a member of his province's Legislative Council and a delegate at the London talks, said, "I feel that we are now touching the very life of the whole scheme." Making matters more difficult, Nova Scotia's fiery anti-confederate Joseph Howe was in London at the same time hoping to sabotage negotiations. Among other things, he sent Lord Carnarvon a copy of a stinging George Brown article from the *Globe* headlined "Drunkenness in High Places," describing a drunken Macdonald clinging to his desk in Parliament to keep from falling on the floor. The article prompted personal visits to Carnarvon from Macdonald, Cartier, and Sir Alexander Galt. Whether Carnarvon was reassured is open to question. After a visit to Carnarvon's Highclere Castle, Macdonald fell asleep while reading his newspaper in his hotel and his candle set his bedding afire. Despite serious burns, however, Macdonald showed up to chair the next day's meeting.

At the end of the day, although both Prince Edward Island and Newfoundland bowed out of the deal, the Confederation forces won. On March 29, 1867, three weeks to the day after Britain's Parliament passed third reading of the British North America Act setting up the new Dominion of Canada, a delegation from British North America watched Queen Victoria give royal assent to the bill. On June 21, Governor-General Lord Monck returned from England to announce, in the Queen's name, that July 1 would be the day the BNA Act would be proclaimed, creating the new confederation of Canada.

BOMBS AND BEAUHARNOIS

ALMOST FROM THE beginning, there was considerable dissatisfaction with the operation of the Senate. Calls for reform were
frequent – and as frequently ignored. In 1874, Lord Dufferin, the
country's third governor-general, called it "an absurdly effete body –
nothing but a political infirmary and a bribery fund." Other critics
focused on its unrepresentative nature. During a Commons debate
in May 1886 on Senate reform, Liberal leader Wilfrid Laurier said
he did not favour abolishing the Senate, but that people "must see
the difference between having a Senate which is not responsible to
anybody whatever and a Senate which is responsible to the people."
He called it "a perfectly irresponsible body which can defy the power
of the House, set itself against all legislation, and which cannot be
brought to change its opinion."

In response, Prime Minister Macdonald said, "Our constitution
is a good one as it is and it is satisfactory for all purposes; the country
is going on well; the laws passed by this House are good laws and

are not objected to by the other House; the country is developing very rapidly."

The Liberals didn't agree. They opposed abolition but argued for change. In a 1906 speech in the Commons Laurier outlined his party's position: "But if we are to have reform I would not be averse to adopting the system of our neighbours and having each province represented by an equal number of members whether that province be large or small." Two years later, Laurier, now speaking as prime minister, elaborated on his views to the *Times* of London, saying that the Senate, with eighty-seven members, was too large, and if each of the nine provinces were given six senators "they would have a body sufficiently large and not cumbersome. . . ." He also argued that the life tenure is "wrong" and "led to the result that members of the Senate were regarded as pensioners of State. . . ."

The phrase was well-chosen. For more than a few senators, the upper chamber has been a very comfortable retirement home that they have occupied well into their twilight years. Canada is the only country in the world that has had a centenarian member of its Parliament. Better still – we've had two. New Brunswick Conservative senator David Wark moved comfortably from his colony's Legislative Council to the Senate in 1867 and stayed there until he died at age 102 in August 1905. Then there was Quebec Liberal senator George C. Dessaules. He sat in the Upper Chamber from March 1907 to April 1930 when he died, also aged 102. Parliamentary historian Arthur Beauchesne once described Dessaules as "a quiet and retiring man who rarely took part in debate." That doesn't quite do justice to his career. Dessaules made exactly two short speeches: one when he first entered the Senate, to deny that his appointment was part of a corrupt bargain; the second twenty-three years later when his colleagues presented him with a portrait marking his hundredth birthday. Other than that, he never uttered a peep.

In 1911, Laurier told the House that he favoured a twelve- or fifteen-year term for senators, some of them appointed by the provincial legislatures. "I have heard it said: 'Why does not the government itself select senators from the different political parties?' Well, I have only to say that the government is composed of men who are very human. . . ."

Indeed, after sixteen years of Liberal rule under Laurier – who appointed eighty-one senators, all of them Liberal – the days of the Macdonald-appointed Tory majority were long gone, leaving the Liberals with a majority of forty-five in the ninety-six-seat upper chamber. Macdonald had named seventy-two senators to form the Upper House. Later he named ninety-two to fill vacancies, all of them Tories. In the decade after Laurier, under Conservative and Unionist rule, the situation was exactly reversed, with the Conservatives holding a majority of forty-five in the Senate. Robert Borden managed to pick sixty-one senators, all Tories, during his term, and Arthur Meighen squeezed in another fifteen Tories. During the next nine years under King's Liberals, the Liberals closed the gap, but the Conservatives still had a slight edge, forty-seven to forty-three, with one Progressive. Conservative prime minister R.B. Bennett reversed the trend again between 1930 and 1935 by making eighty-three Senate appointments, all Tory, before getting booted out of office. Then it was King's turn to load it up with Liberals and by 1940, with King already making seventy Liberal appointments, the Liberals had a clear majority in the Senate, their first one since 1911. For most of the next fifty-nine years, except during part of the Mulroney years, the Liberals have held on to that majority in the Senate.

This pattern of appointment by party affiliation was bound, eventually, to lead to conflict. The first serious clash between the pampered Senate pensioners and the elected House of Commons came in 1913 when the senators refused to approve Sir Robert Borden's Naval Aid Bill. Borden wanted the federal government to spend $35 million to have three battleships built in British shipyards and manned by British sailors. It was a policy that had attracted considerable public opposition but it had also been a major plank in Borden's successful election platform two years before. The Senate blocked the bill, and after a series of threats and counter-threats, Borden felt he was losing public support and backed down.

In 1911, Britain's House of Lords rejected the government's budget. The Liberal prime minister responded by obtaining an order from the King empowering him to appoint as many peers of the realm as he needed to override the decision. The threat was enough to force the Lords to pass the budget. The same order also took away their power of absolute veto. The reaction from Canadian senators to the events in Britain was to issue a defiant declaration stating that "the House of Commons of Canada . . . [can't] drag the Senate beneath it as the Commons did the House of Lords in England."

And just to show they meant business, the Tory-dominated Senate in 1926 voted forty-five to twenty-one to veto the main plank of Liberal Mackenzie King's platform, the old-age pension. During a Commons debate that June, Comox-Alberni Liberal A.W. O'Neill ridiculed the Senate for having sat "an average of less than five days each month. . . . The average point of view of the man in the street towards the Senate is one of mild derision, rising in some cases to rather hostile dimensions, and I am afraid that when the people in general find that a body which costs them three-quarters of a million a year has rejected not the details of this measure, but – and this is the vital point in respect of which the common man will be most embittered – the very principle of the measure itself. . . they will be most upset with the whole notion of a Senate. The details of the bill could have been adjusted, but the vital principle of the whole thing has been rejected."

The senators claimed that King did not have an electoral mandate to enact the legislation and insisted that they had a public responsibility to veto it. The public, it seems, did not agree. In the election that followed, the Liberals were returned to power with a large majority.

The election result, however, did not stop the Tory senators from vetoing King's efforts to rescind the notorious Section 98 of the

Criminal Code. This bill had been introduced by the Borden Unionist government and enforced by Solicitor-General Arthur Meighen to brutally quash the Winnipeg General Strike of 1919. The law expanded the definition of "seditious intent" so broadly that almost anybody, certainly any labour leader, could be jailed under it for up to twenty years. Four times between 1926 and 1930, King and the Commons approved a motion to kill the section, but each time the Senate exercised its veto powers, again using the bizarre explanation that King – who had been quite public in his opposition to the measure for years – did not have a mandate to repeal the section.

The current shape of the Senate was actually settled in March 1915 when Conservative prime minister Sir Robert Borden introduced a motion to increase the number of seats in the Senate from seventy-two to ninety-six to account for the new western provinces. The motion increased the "sectional" divisions from the original three to four, the fourth comprising Manitoba, Saskatchewan, Alberta, and British Columbia, each of them represented by six senators, compared to twenty-four each for Ontario and Quebec, ten each for New Brunswick and Nova Scotia, and four for Prince Edward Island. The motion was unopposed. Since then, of course, Alberta and British Columbia in particular have blossomed into the country's third and fourth largest provinces, creating an imbalance that continues to cause considerable political friction west of Ontario and contributing significantly to the spectacular growth of the Reform Party.

Borden's bill, which the Senate had already agreed to support, also amended Section 26 – which Brian Mulroney would use sixty-five years later to load the Senate in the GST fight – increasing the number of senators who could be added from three or six to four or eight. It also limited the size of the Senate to 104, at least until Newfoundland joined (which it did in 1949). Newfoundland's allotment was increased from four to six senators, raising the maximum size of the Senate to 110.

And finally, the bill provided that "a province shall always be entitled to a number of members in the House of Commons not less than the number of senators representing such province," a provision that was tossed in as a sop to the Maritime provinces, Prince Edward Island in particular, that were worried about ending up with little representation in the Commons if adjustments continued to be made on the basis of population shifts. The motion was approved by the Commons without opposition.

Throughout the 1920s, barely a year passed without a debate in the Commons either to abolish the Senate or reform it. In his reply to the Speech from the Throne in March of 1922, Conservative MP Thomas Church, the colourful, long-time Toronto mayor, called for a referendum in the next election to amend the BNA Act "with a view to abolishing the Senate altogether, because I feel that its usefulness has gone."

In March of 1923 the Commons again had a major debate, this one sparked by a motion from Joliette MP Jean J. Denis to elect senators for six-year terms in special senatorial divisions. Under his scheme, half of the senators would be elected every third year. Once again, lots of talk but no action.

In July of 1924, Labour Minister James Murdock and Conservative leader Arthur Meighen fell into a debate about how best to inform the senators that the Commons was unhappy with their decision, for the second consecutive year, to amend the Industrial Disputes Investigation Act. Murdock said the amendment "introduces a new feature in the said bill and would complicate rather than simplify procedure." Meighen said he had no objection to the motion "but I think the reason given is inadequate; it should be made more specific."

That prompted Justice Minister Ernest Lapointe to show what the Liberal government thought of the Tory senators. Even after the Speaker intervened on Meighen's side, citing parliamentary rules saying "specific reasons must be enumerated in a message of this character to the upper House," Lapointe said, "I do not know why we could be so generous as to give all details to the Senate when we do not concur with that body. They are not overwhelmingly generous in their conduct towards us. They merely say they do not concur, without giving one single reason. That is the way the Senate is proceeding. . . ." In fact, twice during the life of that parliament, the Senate had thrown out bills for the construction of much-needed branch railway lines in western Canada because it wasn't in the interest of their friends – and some of their colleagues – in private ownership.

In March of 1925, the Commons easily approved a motion from Prime Minister King, who had delivered several fiery speeches railing against the Senate during the election campaign, that "the Senate as at present appointed and constituted is not of the greatest advantage to Canada." To correct the situation, King proposed to call a dominion-provincial conference to "consider the advisability of amending the British North America Act in respect of the constitution and powers of the Senate."

In June, Opposition leader Meighen, who would later become a senator himself, asked King when the conference would be called: "We are now approaching the end of the session, and we are reminded of the anniversary of the same threat a year ago." King said, "The government has not as yet had time to consider the agenda," to which Meighen presciently quipped, "For my part, I now bid good-bye to all prospects." In 1926, responding to the same question from Meighen, King offered a new twist for his lengthy prevarication, saying, "The conference should be preceded by a general election at which the reform of the Senate is a principal issue, in order that its deliberations may be influenced by the known will of the people."

One prominent MP who put the Senate into proper perspective was Quebec Conservative Henri Bourassa, who argued that the "traffic in Senate seats" to raise money for the party in power was a normal part of doing business. "I well remember one day when Sir

Wilfrid Laurier told me his propaganda fund was empty, but that before long perhaps two or three seats could be disposed of in the Senate, and therefore the [cash] flow might come again. Of course, all these things are known. We might just as well make no bones about them, and not be hypocritical. I believe no reform can be accomplished by cant and hypocrisy. . . . I think from time to time efforts could be made to prevent the evils from becoming too great. You have a certain piece of machinery. It gets dirty. You clean it, although you know it will be dirty again five years hence."

Back in 1873, the government of Sir John A. Macdonald had been brought down temporarily by a bribery scandal involving a Chicago entrepreneur who had plans of his own for the Canadian Pacific Railway. The scheme was denounced at the time by millionaire businessman David MacPherson, who called it "one of the most unpatriotic conspiracies ever entered in this Dominion. An audacious, unpatriotic and gigantic swindle."

He was really ticked. And no wonder. MacPherson, it happens, had headed a rival syndicate hoping to win the CPR contract. He was also a senator, a mix of public and private duties that was commonplace in the politics of the day. Indeed, his colleague in the upper chamber, Senator Frank Smith, was not only a wholesale grocer and railway executive, but also a minister without portfolio in Macdonald's government and active in the project when it finally did get on the rails in 1881.

Since the beginning, Canada's senators have freely mixed public and private business with little apparent concern about anything beyond their own bottom lines. In the late nineteenth century, most elected bodies had the same problem, but over the years, chiefly in response to public outrage at ongoing scandals, the House of Commons and provincial legislatures have introduced tougher conflict-of-interest laws. The Senate, however, continues the old tradition of mingling private and public duty. Granted, it too has introduced some rules, but they're so weak that no senator has ever received more than a gentle tap on the wrist for breaking them.

There have been many attempts at reform over the years. In 1927, CCF leader J.S. Woodsworth, angered by the veto of the old-age pension bill a year earlier, launched a devastating attack on the Senate, calling it "the champion and safeguard of . . . the big interests." Citing a story in the *Canada Forward*, a labour newspaper, Woodsworth read: "In the Senate fifty members of that body control and direct the economic life of Canada. That is to say that fifty senators are directors of 334 commercial and financial institutions."

Woodsworth added there were twenty-seven lawyers in the Senate, twelve of them Tories and fifteen Liberals. Twelve of them were directors in eighty-eight different corporations. There were eleven journalists, editors, and publishers, six of whom were directors in thirty-four commercial and financial institutions. There were eleven manufacturers and capitalists who were directors in 131 commercial and financial institutions. In addition, eight doctor-senators were directors in twenty-two corporations.

Woodsworth went on to list the directorships of six senators, one of whom, Senator N. Curry, was listed in the *Canadian Parliamentary Guide* of 1926 as "president of twelve companies and director of thirty." Another, Senator L.C. Webster, was a director or senior officer of forty-one corporations, most of them among the biggest in the country.

Any list of the major captains of industry of the day would have to include Montreal senator Wilfrid Laurier McDougald, whose nephew Bud McDougald went on to become one of the major players in the giant Argus Corporation, the company that gave Conrad Black his start.

McDougald, just recently appointed to the Senate by King, was listed by Woodsworth as a director of the following corporations: Hollinger Gold Mine Co. Ltd., Ogdensburg Coal and Towing Co. Ltd., Sterling Bond Co., Canada Steamship Lines Ltd., Tidewater Shipbuilders Ltd., Davie Shipbuilding and Repairing Co. Ltd., Great

Lakes Transportation Co., Midland Shipbuilding Co., George Hall Coal Co., Richelieu and Ontario Navigation Co., Inland Lines Ltd., Niagara Navigation Co., Thousand Island Steamboat Co., Merchants Montreal Line, Century Coal and Coke Co. Ltd., The Coal Co. Ltd., St. Lawrence Realty Co., Superior Sales Co. Ltd., and Labrador Pulp and Paper Co.

McDougald's elevation to the Senate may, at least in part, explain King's reluctance to match his anti-Senate election rhetoric with concrete actions.

McDougald had a vision. He wanted to divert the St. Lawrence River and build a dam to generate electricity. It would have three times the power capacity of any dam in the world. At the time, apart from requiring a federal licence, the industry was completely unregulated. Any entrepreneur lucky enough to get a licence was virtually assured of making massive profits. Well, lucky isn't the right word. McDougald understood that obtaining a licence had little to do with luck. It happened that he was a close friend of R.A.C. Henry, the powerful deputy minister of railways and canals, a good man to know if you wanted to get into the business of using water power to generate electricity. Together, the two men formed Sterling Industrial Corp. and successfully purchased the Beauharnois power site on the St. Lawrence River.

Next, they sold Sterling Industrial Corp. to the Beauharnois Power Syndicate, each pocketing a cool $500,000 profit. But they were far from finished. Using their positions to their own advantage, they set out to convince the government that the Beauharnois Power Syndicate should be given the right to build canals and dams on the site. Senator McDougald became chairman of the Beauharnois board, while Henry, still a deputy minister, became general manager of the Beauharnois Power Corporation. Both men were given insider's opportunities to buy Beauharnois stock at rock-bottom prices. As the stock skyrocketed on the open market, they each made hundreds of thousands of dollars in additional profits.

McDougald wasn't the only senator on the Beauharnois board.

Joining him were senators Andrew Haydon and Donat Raymond, both Liberal bagmen, and Liberal senator Philippe Jacques Paradis, a director of many other companies as well.

To make sure they had their ducks in a row, McDougald treated King to a Beauharnois-financed Caribbean cruise. The company also donated $750,000 to King's 1925 and 1926 election campaigns. In return, King appointed McDougald chairman of the Montreal Harbour Commission and a member of the National Advisory Committee on the St. Lawrence Seaway, both blatant conflicts of interest that allowed McDougald further leverage to steer the hydro-electric business toward his own company.

As if that weren't enough, McDougald chaired the Special Senate Committee on the St. Lawrence Waterway. There was some political pressure at the time to hand control of such hydro-power mega-projects over to public corporations, but McDougald's committee was having none of that. The committee voted to award exclusive development rights to private interests, such deserving corporations, for example, as the Beauharnois Power Syndicate. The National Advisory Committee, helped along by McDougald, came to the same conclusion.

To buttress his case that private development was preferable to public expenditure, McDougald turned to an "expert" witness – none other than deputy minister R.A.C. Henry – who solemnly swore before both committees that it was better for consumers to have these resources developed by private corporations. And just in case Henry may have been caught off guard when he gave his testimony, McDougald, after meeting with his colleagues on the committee, slipped Henry a list of the questions the other senators would ask.

Finally, in 1931, with Conservative R.B. Bennett in power and Senator Arthur Meighen leading the charge in the Senate, the political dam broke. A Commons committee decided to investigate the profits of the Beauharnois Power Syndicate. The Beauharnois affair remains one of the biggest scandals in Canadian political history. It turned out that in addition to funding King's election campaigns directly, Beauharnois Power Project president Robert O. Sweezey had raised $864,000 for a no-questions-asked Liberal Party slush fund. Hundreds of thousands more went to the Quebec Liberal Party as well.

Prominent Ontario Tory senator John Aird, Jr., whose father John Aird, Sr., ran the Canadian Imperial Bank of Commerce, made off with $125,000 in profits after convincing Beauharnois officials that he represented the Ontario Tories and could guarantee a government purchase of Beauharnois power. It was a lie: Aird simply pocketed the money. Years later, his nephew, John Black Aird, served as Ontario's lieutenant-governor and then as a senator in the Red Chamber.

Meighen was so outraged he even tried to have Raymond, Haydon, and McDougald expelled from the Senate. The Senate was asked to determine if the three senators were "gentlemen" worthy of retaining their seats. They may indeed have been crooks, but apparently they were "gentlemen" since the Senate failed to expel them, perhaps because the Liberals still enjoyed a slight majority in the chamber.

In an oddly schizophrenic speech during debate of the Beauharnois report, Senator J.J. Hughes began by demanding that all senators sever all their business and professional contacts when appointed. He would exempt farming, however, "because there is no danger of anybody making any money at farming." Hughes also demanded that senators divorce themselves completely from political activity. He added that all parliamentary inquiries and royal commissions could then be conducted by the Senate, which would become a semi-judicial body.

As for his three wayward colleagues, Hughes believed they had harmed Canada "but it is the system under which they lived, and not primarily the men who were to blame. The exploitation of natural resources by captains of industry is recognized by the system and legalized under it." Hughes said if the senators "were punished for doing what hundreds of other men had done, it would be adding political partisanship to injustice."

All three of the tainted senators disappeared from public view. None of them left with empty pockets. Haydon, for example, had struck a rather unusual deal on behalf of his law firm to handle the legal work for Beauharnois. The firm received $50,000 when Ottawa approved the application, while Haydon himself was awarded $600,000, an outright bribe. By the time the scandal blew up, however, Haydon was so ill he was confined to his bed – and would die soon afterwards – so nobody had the heart to pursue the matter.

Raymond, who had sat with McDougald on the Senate committee that approved the Beauharnois bid while at the same time sitting on the company's board, was offered Beauharnois shares at $37.50, when their market value was $100. For a mere $30,000 investment then, Raymond made a profit of $529,600. Raymond, who would become Liberal Party treasurer, also accepted $200,000 from Sweezey to pass along to Senator Haydon en route to the Liberal Party campaign fund. Raymond was criticized by the investigative committee in 1932 for failing to mention this $200,000 in his sworn testimony. He quietly fled back to his corporate boardrooms.

In his book, *Survival of the Fattest*, author Larry Zolf described King's affection for McDougald as "almost carnal. McDougald was the largest walking conflict of interest in Canadian history. He was also the stingiest. When McDougald turned over his chits for King's meals, towels, suntan lotion, steamship tickets, dirty laundry, cabin and entertainment to the Beauharnois company for a tax write-off, he was more than indiscreet, he was cheap and stupid. When headlines proclaimed 'Mr. King's Holiday Bills Paid By Beauharnois,' King's written-off dirty laundry was aired in public. McDougald sat idly by as King's career looked as though it was approaching an inglorious end."

McDougald, who had made at least $2 million from this caper, flatly refused to participate in the House Beauharnois inquiry on the grounds of senatorial privilege. He claimed he was immune to questions from the plebs in the Lower House. This was a bit much even for his fellow senators, who voted down McDougald's request for immunity from testifying. No matter, he still refused to testify and was ultimately cited for contempt, becoming the first (and only) senator ever to be locked up in the Peace Tower. Finally, with great reluctance, he resigned his seat, taking his money with him, of course.

As for King, he never did accept any responsibility for the scandal, even though he was a party to it. But in politics, memories are short, and four years after the affair ended, King was once again back in power.

Judson King, an advocate of publicly owned power and intimate of U.S. president Roosevelt, described the Beauharnois scandal as "the most astounding attempt to corrupt the Dominion Government in Canadian history."

It remains unmatched.

WOMEN ARE PEOPLE TOO

O N HER FIRST day as Canada's first police magistrate in 1916, Judge Emily Murphy, presiding over Edmonton's newly created Women's Court, so enraged a defence lawyer whose client she had declared guilty that he told her point-blank that since women were not legally "persons" under the British North America Act, she had no right sitting in judgement of anybody.

And so began Murphy's valiant thirteen-year journey, which ended October 18, 1929, when the Justice Committee of the Privy Council of England ruled that women were indeed "persons" and were eligible for appointment to the Canadian Senate.

Emily Murphy was an odd radical. An Ontario transplant, she came from solid Tory stock. Her grandfather, Ogle Robert Gowan, was a Tory MP for twenty-seven years and a founder of the Orange Lodge of Canada. Murphy graduated from Bishop Strachan, the ultra-exclusive private girls' school in central Toronto. She married a fundamentalist minister turned capitalist.

On April 13, 1883, a year after he returned to power in the Commons, Prime Minister John A. Macdonald personally introduced a bill that included a clause giving the vote to widows and unmarried women with sufficient property qualifications. The bill died on the order paper. It was re-introduced in 1884 and again in 1885, but again it got nowhere.

By 1900, most of the provinces did permit women to vote for school trustees and municipal officials, although here again, these voting rights were often restricted to widows and unmarried women. In 1912, even though women were practising law in Ontario and New Brunswick, the British Columbia Court of Appeal unanimously refused Mabel French's appeal to be admitted to the provincial bar by interpreting the word "person" in the Bar Act to include men only, prompting federal attorney-general William J. Bowser to rush through a new Bar Act allowing women to practise law, both as barristers and solicitors.

On January 28, 1916, Manitoba became the first province to give women the right to vote and run for provincial office. Within six years, every province but Quebec – which held out until 1940 – had followed suit.

The breakthrough on the federal level came on May 16, 1917, when Prime Minister Robert Borden startled the Commons by saying that during the war women "have showed themselves worthy to take a part in the government of this country and they have thereby made abundantly clear what I believe was clear before, their right to a voice in the government of the country in which they live." He said the question should be decided before the House prorogued for the next election, slated for that October.

Borden's new-found sympathy for women's suffrage was surprising, but it wasn't long before his motives became clear. In September, he introduced the Military Voters Act, giving the vote during the war years to all British subjects, male and female, regardless of their age (twenty-one was the legal voting age then) who were active in any branch of the Canadian armed services.

Section 33A of the act read: "Every female person shall be capable of voting and qualified to vote at a Dominion election in any province or in the Yukon Territory, who, being a British subject and qualified as to age, race and residence, as required in the case of a male person . . . [who] is the wife, widow, mother, sister or daughter of any person, male or female, living or dead, who is serving or has served without Canada in any of the military forces, or within or without Canada in any of the naval forces, of Canada or of Great Britain in the present war. . . ."

Critics accused Borden of making the move in order to get electoral support for his contentious compulsory conscription bill. In an effort to ensure his re-election, Borden fashioned a coalition with a group of pro-conscription Liberals, taking office on October 12, 1917, as the Union government. Conscription was bitterly fought in Quebec, where much of the population saw it as England's war, and in parts of the west, where many people had left overseas countries where compulsory military service laws were at least part of their motivation for immigrating to Canada.

Because Borden was seriously ill, however, the unenviable job of steering the bill through the Commons was handed to Secretary of State Arthur Meighen. (On July 10, 1920, Meighen became prime minister after Borden retired because of his health.) Meighen argued that it would be "unfair and unreasonable" to extend the franchise to all women because so many of them had become naturalized simply by marrying British citizens. Even though many women's organizations did not approve of the government's tactics, it did give many Canadian women a federal vote for the first time, making it easier to extend the principle after the war.

That is what happened in 1920 when the Union government approved the Dominion Elections Act giving voting rights in federal elections to both men and women who were British citizens, twenty-one years or older and who were residents of Canada for a year and residents of the electoral district for two months before the elections. A year later, when all women electors could vote for the first time, Meighen was defeated by Liberal William Lyon Mackenzie

King, even though Meighen had become the first prime minister to promise to appoint women to the Senate. In that election, four women ran as candidates but just one, Agnes Macphail of Ontario, an independent, got elected, the beginning of her historic nineteen-year political career.

Agnes Macphail is generally honoured as Canada's first female parliamentarian, but she was not the first woman elected to a high office. That honour is shared by two Alberta women, Louise M. McKinney and Roberta MacAdams, who were elected in the June 1917 provincial elections there. Their more famous colleague, Nellie McClung, who would later join Murphy's crusade in the "persons" case, was elected to the legislature in 1921.

Alberta Liberal premier A.L. Sifton was a strong advocate of a greater public role for women. When he named Emily Murphy to the bench in 1916, she became the first female police magistrate not only in Canada, but in the British Empire. A year after that, Mr. Justice Scott of the Supreme Court of Alberta, in a case based on the "persons" issue there, ruled that "reason and good sense" say there is "no legal disqualification" for holding public office "arising from any distinction of sex."

In 1919, with Murphy as chairperson, delegates from all eight provinces attending the Federated Women's Institutes of Canada convention unanimously endorsed a resolution requesting Borden to appoint a woman to the Senate. Two years later, the Montreal Women's Club got more specific, asking Meighen to appoint Emily Murphy as soon as a vacancy occurred. Meighen replied that the law officers of the Crown had advised him that it wasn't possible under the terms of the BNA Act.

After King defeated Meighen, Murphy sent a letter to the new prime minister saying she would like to become a Senator. King was non-committal, although he did say he was prepared, if necessary, to amend the constitution. In June 1923, Senator Archibald McCoig waded into the dispute with a motion to amend the BNA Act to permit women to sit in the Senate. But when it came time to move the motion, McCoig didn't show up in the Red Chamber.

The entire issue revolved around one word – "persons" – in Section 24 of the BNA Act. The act reads:

"The Governor-General shall from time to time in the Queen's name, by instrument under the Great Seal of Canada, summon qualified persons to the Senate; and subject to the provisions of this Act, every person so summoned shall become a member of the Senate, and a Senator."

Murphy's brother, Mr. Justice William Nassau, advised her that under Section 60 of the Supreme Court Act any five interested persons could petition the government for an order-in-council directing the Supreme Court of Canada to rule on a constitutional point involving an interpretation of the BNA Act. Not only that, if the case was considered important, the government would even pay the legal expenses. Armed with that information, Murphy asked justice department officials if the issue of women being allowed in the Senate fit the criteria. After being told it did, she set out to choose four women to champion the case with her.

She began with Irene Parlby, the first woman ever to sit in a provincial cabinet. Louise McKinney, who was one of two women sharing the honour of being Canada's first elected female legislators, was also a natural, as was Henrietta Muir Edwards, founder of the Working Girls Association of Montreal, editor of *Working Woman of Canada* and for thirty-five years convenor of laws of the National Council of Women. Finally, Murphy turned to Nellie McClung, the country's most famous author, social activist, and suffragette.

In mid-October 1927, the Supreme Court was asked to decide "Does the word Persons in Section 24 of the British North America Act, 1867, include female persons?"

The case got under way in March 1928, with federal solicitor-general Lucien Cannon arguing the government's side and Toronto lawyer Newton Wesley Rowell representing the five women. Rowell, a former Ontario Liberal leader and fanatical prohibitionist, was also hired by Alberta to represent the province in supporting the five women, while Quebec dispatched special counsel Charles Lanctôt to oppose them.

On April 24, Chief Justice Frank Anglin announced that the court favoured the historical view that the court accepts the BNA Act as it was intended in 1867, when women had no political privileges. "The question is answered in the negative," he said.

Rowell telegraphed Murphy with the bad news and although disappointed, she fired letters off to her four colleagues advocating an appeal to the House of Lord's justice committee, saying, "Of the ultimate results, I have not the slightest doubt, nothing can prevent our winning."

With the federal justice department paying the costs and Alberta sending its own attorney-general, J.F. Lymburn, to help Rowell, the scene shifted in July 1929 to a chamber in London's 1 Downing Street before five of Britain's law lords at the Justice Committee of the Privy Council of England. The hearing took four days. The decision three months.

On October 18, 1929, Lord Chancellor Sankey delivered the verdict. "Their Lordships have come to the conclusion that the word persons includes members of the male and female sex, and that therefore the question propounded by the governor-general must be answered in the affirmative; and that women are eligible to be summoned and become members of the Senate of Canada."

Murphy had won, but she would never get personally to enjoy the spoils of victory. She died in 1933 without ever getting to sit in the Senate.

On February 15, 1930, King passed over Murphy and instead appointed an old family friend, Cairine Wilson, as Canada's first female senator. A wealthy, bilingual Ottawa matron from Rockcliffe, Wilson, unlike Murphy, was devoted to the Liberal Party. Her father, Robert Mackay, was a Liberal senator. Her husband, Norman Wilson, had served as a Liberal MP. She had been a leader in establishing the National Federation of Liberal Women of Canada and of the Twentieth Century Liberal Association of Canada, an organization for young people.

The appointment of Wilson certainly did not undermine the clubby, big-business character of the Senate. Four years after her appointment, her daughter Jane Marie married Charles Burns, a Bay Street baron who would become president of Burns Fry Ltd., one of Canada's largest investment firms. Two years later, Wilson loaned her entrepreneurial son-in-law $50,000 to buy a seat on the Toronto Stock Exchange.

While the gender ban had finally been lifted, there wasn't exactly a flood of women filling up the cushy Senate seats. In 1931, the death of an Alberta senator raised hopes that Murphy would finally be appointed, but Conservative prime minister R.B. Bennett appointed another man instead, saying that because the dearly departed had been a Roman Catholic, he was morally obligated to appoint another Catholic. Perhaps. But one assumes there were at least a few female Roman Catholics in Alberta at the time. Bennett did appoint Iva Campbell Fallis, a former vice-president of the Dominion Conservative Association of Canada, in 1935. There were no other women appointed to the Senate in the 1930s and none in the 1940s either. Four women were appointed during the 1950s and just three in the 1960s. The balance began to even out after that.

On May 3, 1955, Wilson again made history, becoming the first woman ever to occupy the Speaker's chair, albeit only temporarily, after regular Speaker W. Wishart Robertson was sick and couldn't answer the bell. On December 12, 1972, Senator Muriel Fergusson, a New Brunswick Liberal, became the first woman to be the permanent Senate Speaker. The Commons wouldn't appoint its first woman Speaker until April 1980 when Pierre Trudeau appointed Jeanne Sauvé. The Senate also beat the Commons in introducing female pages, when Elaine Robillard, twenty, and Claire Lafleche, nineteen, two university students, showed up in the Senate on September 15, 1971.

In November 1997, Senator Colin Kenny, one of the biggest spenders when it comes to enhancing Senate facilities and perquisites and certainly the best publicity hound in the Senate, introduced a bill to turn a 1.1-acre site near the Parliament Buildings into a national historic park commemorating the "Famous Five" from the "persons" case. In a subsequent article in the *Ottawa Citizen*, Kenny wrote that Murphy "was a woman of such obvious merit that various groups recommended that she be appointed Canada's first female Senator." His sentiments were certainly echoed by the non-profit Famous Five Foundation, which raised money to put a statue of the Famous Five in the park. In December, after the motion was given all-party consent in the Commons, the Senate formally requested that the government allow the statue to be erected on Parliament Hill, previously the exclusive preserve for statues of monarchs, former prime ministers, and Fathers of Confederation.

Mind you, in order to deify Murphy and her colleagues, it was necessary to overlook some of the views they espoused during their lifetimes. After all, no need to sully the ceremony and dampen the delight of those wanting to celebrate their accomplishments. Murphy, for example, was an outright racist, well known for her virulent anti-Chinese writings, and three of the five women advocated population control through the forced sterilization of mentally disabled people.

Today, 30 of the 103 senators are women, and most of them, like most of their male counterparts, are there as a reward for services rendered to the party that appointed them.

Easily the most controversial woman senator is Toronto's Anne Cools. She is Canada's first black senator, currently its longest-serving female senator, a two-time losing federal Liberal candidate, and the only senator who has ever served a jail sentence. One thing that can be said about Cools, however, is that she works hard at being a senator. It's a split decision whether the results of her labours are helpful.

Appointed by Pierre Trudeau on January 13, 1984, the Barbados-born Cools was born into one of the island's most illustrious political families. Her cousin was the country's first female cabinet minister; another was a senator. One uncle was a cabinet minister, another a member of parliament. Her grandfather was a prominent municipal politician.

After a married sister moved to Canada, her family followed. Cools was thirteen. By the time she was nineteen, Cools was in what she has described herself as her radical period, triggered she says when she visited war graves and viewed paintings about war while travelling alone in Europe.

She was at McGill University in 1969 when a thirteen-day occupation of a Sir George Williams University building culminated in the $1.5-million destruction of the university's computer equipment.

The troubles began when six West Indian students accused twenty-eight-year-old assistant biology professor Perry Anderson of racism. Four different investigations found no validity in the charges against Anderson, but by that time the damage had been done. The racism charge was the central issue in the student sit-in, which began peacefully but erupted when some of the protesters – Cools insists she wasn't among them – moved into the university's ninth-floor computer centre and set fires and began smashing equipment.

Cools has been quick to serve legal notice to any publication suggesting that she played a role in damaging the computer – and several published apologies have been won. She insists she wasn't even in the room at the time. In a February 1984 feature interview with the *Toronto Star*, Cools – who was twenty-five at the time – portrayed herself as a heroine in the riot. She told reporter Jackie Smith, "Everybody could have been killed. That thing came close to being a holocaust. . . . I'm one of the reasons people are alive today."

In Montreal on April 30, 1971, Mr. Justice Kenneth Mackay of Quebec Superior Court sentenced Cools to six months (she served four) and fined her $1,500 or an additional six months for her part in the affair. Two other protesters were sentenced with her: Roosevelt Douglas, twenty-nine, of Dominica, was given two years less a day and a $5,000 fine; Brenda Dickonson-Dash, twenty-five, of Montreal, was fined $2,000 or six months in jail.

In passing sentence, Mackay described both Douglas and Cools as "leaders" in the occupation, at which point Douglas shouted, "Long live Black power!" Mackay said that "compassion, not confrontation should be used to fight racism." The trio had been convicted April 22 by a court of Queen's Bench jury after deliberating for just two hours. Cools was convicted of wilful obstruction.

She was appointed a part-time member of the National Parole Board by the Liberals in 1980. She subsequently applied to the parole board for a pardon. She points out she was not on the board that awarded the pardon in 1981.

Cools turned to social work and became a well-known advocate of women's shelters, helping set up the much-heralded Women in Transition. In 1978, she lost a bitter Liberal nomination fight against then University of Toronto president John Evans for a by-election in the Toronto riding of Rosedale. The next year she ran against incumbent Tory David Crombie, Toronto's immensely popular one-time tiny perfect mayor. She lost. Again in 1980, she faced off against Crombie, who missed most of the campaign because of a heart attack, but still defeated her by 1,891 votes. Crombie told his supporters on election night, "This is the first time in Canadian history that a campaign was won without a candidate." Cools refused to walk around the corner to Crombie's committee room to concede defeat.

The one-time darling of the radical women's movement is now reviled as an anti-Christ by much of the feminist sisterhood, mainly because of her work on divorce and child custody issues in which Cools argues – quite sensibly – that men have been getting a raw deal from the system. Cools has taken it upon herself to counter many of the strategic lies that have been spread against men by the feminist movement for years, lies that have become the common wisdom and are rarely questioned by anyone. In a March 1995 speech in the Senate, for example, she cited twenty-three separate researchers whose work has found that women are as likely as men to physically abuse their children. Veteran *Calgary Herald* political columnist Peter Stockland, after a 1996 interview with Cools, wrote that her point is "not to demonize women but to challenge feminist shibboleths of females as a) natural loving nurturers and b) perpetual victims." Cools also claimed that women have "hijacked" the issue of domestic violence and are "helping women turn into hating men."

Her work with Liberal MP Roger Gallaway – currently famous for a campaign to abolish the Senate – on the Special Joint Committee on Custody and Access prompted Hedy Fry, the secretary of state for the status of women, to allow the Women's Justice Network to use her Web site to launch a vicious attack against the committee. The network called on women's groups to "discredit" the process and "nullify any recommendations" and complained that women appearing before the committee "were strongly subjected to a pro-male bias." Gallaway and Cools had simply argued that shared parenting should be the legal cornerstone of the Divorce Act, thereby affording fathers more rights in these cases.

At the height of the storm, Cools said that opposition to the committee was being driven by "a minority of gender-based feminist ideologues who are having difficulty accepting the fact that history has passed them by."

Fry told the *National Post* that "it is better to err on the side of safety" and let children live with their mothers in cases in which women accuse their spouses of abuse, hardly a male-friendly position. The policy perpetuates the myth that fathers are not as fit as mothers to care for their children, something Cools, to her credit, has taken considerable flak for standing up against.

If Cools is the most controversial woman senator, Vancouver's Pat Carney is the most disagreeable. Some people say her chronic arthritis and bad back make her grumpy. Whatever it is, Carney's personality could be described as containing all the warmth of a piece of sandpaper being rubbed over a cake of ice.

Mulroney appointed Carney to the Senate in August 1990 after several years in various senior cabinet posts in the Conservative government. Her attendance record is not terrific, but she is a passionate defender of British Columbia. She successfully blocked a federal plan to close a series of historic B.C. coastal lighthouses, fought coast-guard cutbacks, and scorched the Liberal government for what she saw as its mishandling of the west coast salmon fisheries.

She got a bit carried away, however, in October 1997 when she moaned that British Columbians have been "betrayed and ignored" by the federal government. She added that as a result the province shouldn't rule out separation as an option if it can't negotiate a new deal for itself in Confederation. Carney, a former newspaper columnist and reporter, then attacked the "hysterical central Canadian pig media" because she didn't like their critical reporting of her comments. "In the eyes of the central Canadian media," she added, "Senator Pat is just another fat lady who sings in French to [Quebec premier] Lucien Bouchard's tune."

Prime Minister Jean Chrétien wasn't impressed with her separatist rhetoric either. He told a Vancouver audience, "Overblown rhetoric gets headlines but it does nothing to help solve problems." And federal fisheries minister David Anderson, a British Columbian, said that people who threaten B.C. secession are "losers" and blackmailers. Public opinion polls in the province indicated widespread dissatisfaction with Ottawa, but precious little support for B.C. separation.

In 1991, Senator Lowell Murray, then the government leader in the Senate, unceremoniously bumped Carney from the constitutional committee. Murray said Carney is "unreliable," that she can't be counted on to show up for meetings and her poor attendance record is "bad for morale" in the upper chamber's Tory caucus. "My job is to have three Conservative senators at that committee at all times," said Murray. "I cannot depend on Senator Carney to be there."

Carney, who blames everybody but herself for her problems, complained that she was being punished for voting against the government's compromise abortion bill a week earlier. The bill, sponsored by then justice minister Kim Campbell, died in the Senate on a rare tie vote. But nobody was buying Carney's excuses. The late columnist Marjorie Nichols, a long-time colleague and close friend of Carney, wrote that the senator "may not be quite the martyr that her supporters proclaim." Nichols said Carney told her that she had informed Murray she would not return to Ottawa for the abortion vote and then, without a word of warning, jetted back to Ottawa to vote against the bill. "After the vote," wrote Nichols, "Carney continued her furtive game, hiding in a Senate anteroom to avoid . . . Campbell until departing to catch her flight back to Vancouver. I leave it you to decide whether Carney's actions were those of a woman of great conviction and courage who is being unfairly punished."

Recently, Carney got embroiled in a bitter battle with CBC television's hit comedy show, *This Hour Has 22 Minutes*. Carney was unhappy that the Citadel Hotel, an Ottawa establishment popular with out-of-town senators and MPs, wouldn't serve low-fat bagels with its free continental breakfast. Carney sent a letter, on Senate letterhead, to some four hundred MPs and senators, suggesting the Citadel breakfast should be labelled "Warning, This Food Is Dangerous to Your Health." She said later that her letter was a "lighthearted" attempt to "encourage parliamentarians to promote heart-healthy food in their workplace – airplanes, hotels and parliamentary functions." Perhaps because Carney is not noted for her "lighthearted" style, her letter was not generally perceived that way. But it made terrific fodder for comedian Rick Mercer's weekly televised tirades on the CBC comedy show.

Carney wasn't amused. Gerald Lunz, creative producer of the show, told reporters that Carney "phoned one of our staff researchers . . . screaming and yelling like a crazy person because she heard that *22 Minutes* was going to do a story."

It is not known whether Carney ever considered another option: buying her own low-fat bagels with her high-protein Senate salary.

During the dying days of Pierre Trudeau's reign in 1984, when he compiled a gross list of patronage pay-offs – which would help condemn John Turner to a prime ministerial footnote – one of the recipients of the philosopher king's largesse was his long-time legislative assistant, Alberta native Joyce Fairbairn.

Fairbairn, a former journalist, attended the same high school as both Joe Clark and Jim Coutts and has shown herself over the years to be an effective advocate of many causes, including literacy and Senate reform.

Fairbairn, who was replaced after the last election as government leader in the Senate by Cape Bretoner Al Graham, still effectively runs the Liberal Senate caucus. The affable Graham, a genuinely nice guy, is too busy travelling the world on freebies and rubbing shoulders with the high and mighty. Anyway, he's not as politically astute as Fairbairn, but with the loss of Liberal seats in the Maritimes, somebody from the region had to be put in a position of authority. With the departure of former senator Allan MacEachen, Fairbairn is easily the most adroit legislative tactician in the place. She spent fifteen years working for Trudeau. As the only woman in his powerful PMO with daily access to the boss, it was her job to brief him each day before he went into Question Period in the House of Commons, a job that taught her a thing or two about politics. She also stood out as the most human and helpful member of a staff that was not noted for either trait.

When Trudeau appointed her on June 29, 1984, she and her husband, Michael Gillan, who was director of communications in Trudeau's PMO, formed what Zolf called "the longest-running executive assistant act in Ottawa." Her appointment as one of Alberta's representatives in the Upper House does, however, underscore a serious flaw in the current process. The Senate was always intended to represent the regions, but it's difficult to see how Fairbairn, who has lived more of her life in Ottawa than she did in Lethbridge, can really be seen as a representative of Alberta, particularly as a Liberal, since that province isn't exactly prime electoral territory for Liberals, although Fairbairn has always made a point of making regular trips back to her home town and travelling to rural southwestern Alberta to keep in touch with local concerns.

"I would not have taken the job if I didn't believe that there is first of all a regional representation component that is fundamental to what I do," she told Ottawa editor Joan Cohen in an extensive 1990 interview with the *Winnipeg Free Press.* "You not only reflect your region here in Ottawa, but to do so you have to go back to your area regularly and listen and communicate and travel and take part in local activities."

Still, Fairbairn has said many times that she wishes the voters and not her former boss had put her in the Senate. She told Cohen that the Senate performs valuable services, "but no one knows this work is being done. People seem only to see the Senate when it is engaged in some kind of struggle on an issue of principle.

"One reason, certainly, is because the Senate isn't elected. There is no connecting link directly to the people. There is no accountability to the people. Although you have all the power you need, without that connecting link you do not have credibility."

If more Senators reflected Fairbairn's work ethic and parliamentary skills, credibility would be less of a problem than it is.

While studies have shown that the female senators tend to spend more time working at their Senate jobs than their male counterparts, there's no reason to think they are any more or less effective. They do, however, tend to have fewer outside distractions, such as corporate directorships, to keep them away from the Upper House.

But nearly all of the women, both the useful and the useless, share one thing in common with male senators: they got their jobs as payment for political services rendered.

Nobody reflects that better than Tory senator Marjory LeBreton, appointed June 18, 1993, by Brian Mulroney just before the former prime minister rushed out of town under cover of darkness to avoid the pent-up wrath of the Canadian people.

During most of the Mulroney years, LeBreton was the chief engineer in charge of the Tory patronage machinery. Though Mulroney was elected in 1984 at least partially on his promise to clean up the sleazy Liberal patronage record, the only real change in patronage was that it was dispensed largely to Tories instead of Liberals. And LeBreton was a key player in that partisan pursuit.

This doesn't make her a bad senator or a bad person. In fact, she's a good person and an effective senator, but there can be no doubt how she earned her job.

There are more than 2,600 order-in-council appointments to boards, agencies, and commissions to be filled by the government in power. When the Tories took power in 1984, Mulroney decreed that thirty per cent of those appointments had to go to women. He actually surpassed that target thanks in large part to LeBreton's assistance.

One of the more intriguing senatorial appointments was Jean Chrétien's September 23, 1997, announcement that Nova Scotia native Sister Peggy Butts would become the first nun to sit in the upper chamber. Sister Peggy, as she calls herself, was the second youngest child and the only girl in a family of five children whose brothers played hockey both with and against another noted Cape Bretoner, Senator Al Graham, the government leader in the Senate.

Taking her vows with Montreal's Congregation de Notre Dame, located directly across from the old Montreal Forum, Sister Peggy didn't get to go to the hockey games, but she was involved in some fancy stickhandling in massaging the rules to make her eligible for a Senate seat.

As a nun who had taken a vow of poverty forty years ago, Sister Peggy did not meet the qualification of owning at least $4,000 worth of "real and personal property." After being asked by the PMO if she would take the job, she contacted Notre Dame headquarters. After several weeks of wrestling with the dilemma, the canon lawyers and theologians devised a plan: they transferred a small piece of scrub land, worth about $4,000, in the Antigonish area into Sister Peggy's name. The scheme is certainly legal, but given the nature and the business of the appointee, it does raise ethical and moral questions about its propriety. To her credit, she is donating her entire salary to charity.

(While Sister Peggy's case is unusual, the late Jean Marchand did not own property in the Quebec district that he was chosen to represent in the Senate either. So off he went to the Nicolet region on the south shore of the St. Lawrence River to find some farm land. When he was told that one parcel was selling for $3,000, he offered $4,000. The farmer, realizing he was onto a good thing, countered by offering him two non-adjacent plots for $7,000. After Marchand's death, Pierre de Bane was named to the Senate to represent the same district in 1984. He bought the land and is still using it to meet the Senate property qualifications.)

Another oddity about Sister Peggy's appointment, however, is that it will last only twenty-two months. Already past her seventy-third birthday, she'll have to retire when she hits seventy-five. This has led to considerable speculation that she was simply keeping the seat warm for former Liberal cabinet minister David Dingwall, Chrétien's loyal Maritime lieutenant. Dingwall became so unpopular in Nova Scotia that he is credited with – or blamed for – the loss of so many traditional Maritime Liberal seats in the last election.

Most of the pundits responded to the Sister-senator's appointment by praising her work for the poor and dispossessed. *Ottawa Citizen* columnist Jane Taber's column, for example, was headlined: "As scholar, feminist, senator, Sister Peggy works for greater good." It helps, however, if you're Liberal. NDP leader Alexa McDonough, also a Nova Scotian, described the appointment as "patronage politics as usual. . . . Sister Peggy Butts has been one of the most faithful Liberal partisans in Cape Breton and, I'm prepared to say, all of Nova Scotia." Told that Sister Peggy claimed she had no Liberal affiliation, McDonough, the former Nova Scotia NDP leader, paused and said, "I think you'd better report me speechless."

While much is made of the advantages of increasing the number of women in the Senate, the fact is that most of them, like their male counterparts, are chosen primarily on the questionable basis of partisan politics rather than on some meritorious or noble quality.

Former Manitoba Liberal leader Sharon Carstairs, about as

partisan a practitioner as you can find, was rewarded for her undying devotion to Chrétien on September 15, 1994. Carstairs, whose father was also a senator, is best remembered for her emotional breakdown during the final days of the Meech Lake Accord, something she has called the "absolute worst week of my life." She's also not shy about spending the public coin since her now-defunct Special Committee on Euthanasia in 1996 spent $206,587 writing a report that was shelved, along with so many of the other reports that the Senate constantly brags about as its biggest contribution to Canadian life.

One-time Prince Edward Island premier Catherine Callbeck, who did not particularly distinguish herself in that job, which came after an undistinguished career as a Liberal MP from the island, made it to patronage heaven two years after Carstairs did. Ten years earlier, then senior New Brunswick Tory cabinet minister Brenda Robertson was tapped by Mulroney to enjoy a well-paid life of semi-retirement in the nation's capital. Robertson's reaction when Mulroney called her in late December 1984 was, "It certainly is a good Christmas present." Hard to argue with that. Robertson, who was New Brunswick social reform minister when she left, was a major cog in the political machine of the late Richard Hatfield, an administration so admired by the people it served that it became one of only two governments in Canadian history to finish an election campaign without a single seat.

Mulroney also chose Manitoban Mira Spivak in 1986, and while Spivak was not an active politician, it's hardly a coincidence that her husband, Sidney, was the former Manitoba Conservative leader. Mulroney also appointed two other women on the same day Spivak was given the nod: Ethel Cochrane of Newfoundland and Eileen Rossiter of Prince Edward Island. Cochrane's most appealing qualification to become Newfoundland's first woman senator was that her husband had served as executive assistant to Newfoundland's colourful Tory heavyweight John Crosbie in the 1970s. As for Rossiter, her brother-in-law was a veteran provincial cabinet minister on the island.

Chrétien's November 1997 appointment of Albertan Thelma

Chalifoux made her the first Metis person and the first aboriginal woman appointed to the Senate. An educator and activist, Chalifoux was appointed less for her special skills and more as part of Chrétien's highly political campaign against the express wishes of Alberta's government and population to have its Senate appointees elected. Edmonton Reform MP Rahim Jaffer called Chalifoux's appointment an affront to the people of Alberta. "We are sick of the prime minister appointing senators to an unelected, unaccountable, undemocratic haven of patronage. How much longer will the prime minister disrespect the expressed wishes of Albertans?" Deputy Prime Minister Herb Gray, ignoring the fact that Reform has consistently attacked the appointment process, accused Jaffer of attacking Chalifoux because she's Metis, an unusual cheap shot from a politician who normally shows more class. Chalifoux responded by pleading helplessness. "If it was elected, I never would have had a chance," she said. "I'm a woman, I'm Metis and I don't have the finances." Neither did Pearl Calahasen, a three-term Tory MLA for Lesser Slave Lake. Even Chalifoux agreed, when asked by an Edmonton reporter, that Calahasen is proof that native women can set up election fundraising machines and win. Mind you, being handed the winning lottery ticket by the prime minister is a lot easier than working for the position. Chalifoux offended some and pleased others with her opening gambit as a senator when she introduced a bill to rewrite history and exonerate the mad Metis murderer Louis Riel. Chalifoux's bill argues that the Metis were simply defending their homes and that Riel was "wrongfully tried, convicted and executed for high treason by the government of Canada." It didn't take Chalifoux long, however, to get into the real spirit of the Senate. In February 1998, about two months after her appointment, claiming she was working twelve-hour days, Chalifoux referred to her "measly" salary and said she agreed with a task force that recommended that senators, who work sixty-nine days a year, should earn $83,000 and get a $6,000 housing allowance.

While we're on the subject of Senate firsts, Prime Minister Jean Chrétien named Toronto Liberal Vivienne Poy to the Senate on September 17, 1998, becoming the first Canadian of Chinese descent in the Senate and undoubtedly the first fashion designer as well.

"My line had a lot of flair, always classic but pretty," Poy said in an *Ottawa Citizen* interview after her appointment. "I love colors. I did a lot of things in black because there was a demand for it. But I'm a color person. I never wear black because color affects not only your own mood, but other people's mood. And I always dress to make other people happy."

On her Senate duties, Poy, who also sits on the board of an Asian bank, says she'll bring her "sense of caring in the community . . . health care, better conditions for children, better conditions for women. This is my usual community involvement. And we need art. Without it we have no soul."

Chrétien's April 9, 1997, appointment of prominent Quebecker Lucie Pepin was his twentieth Senate appointee since assuming office, eleven of them women. Pepin was the head nurse at the first outpatient birth-control clinic in Canada and in the 1970s was national coordinator of the Canadian Committee for Fertility Research. She also served as president of the Canadian Advisory Council on the Status of Women from 1981 to 1984, but what likely brought her most to Chrétien's attention were her bona fide Liberal Party credentials. She won the federal riding of Outremont for the Liberals in 1984 but lost in 1988. In accepting the pre-eminent patronage post from Chrétien, however, she had to give up another one: her job with the appeal division of the National Parole Board. Who says public service doesn't require self-sacrifice?

On August 26, 1996, shortly after Conrad Black's company took over the *Montreal Gazette*, the paper's editor-in-chief Joan Fraser became a bit of a celebrity in some circles with her decision to resign. Fraser, whose editorial position was uncomfortably cozy with Quebec separatists, was lauded by that element of society that views

Black as the personification of evil. In fact, under Fraser's editorship, the *Gazette* had been steadily losing both its political clout and its customers in that divided province.

Not to worry, salvation was at hand! In September 1998, Chrétien came calling with a Senate seat.

On July 14, 1993, a *Gazette* editorial published while Fraser was the editorial boss, said: "The fact is that the Senate is both more and less than the pig-trough that has become a staple of Canadian humour." It went on to say that senators "rarely do any harm and quite often do some good. Far better to let them carry on, than launch a whole new constitutional shouting match."

In an interview with her former paper after her Senate appointment, Fraser said it is "very useful to have a second chamber." She doesn't agree that senators should be elected because it would usurp the powers of the elected House of Commons. Asked how she felt about leaving her job as director at the Centre for Research and Information on Canada – a division of the Council for Canadian Unity – Fraser said: "This is one of the greatest honours and privileges that your country can give you. It's very humbling."

It's also very rewarding, what with the "pig-trough" and all.

5

KING AND COYNE

SOME THINGS DON'T change.

On June 5, 1939, in the midst of a bitter Commons-Senate dispute over Mackenzie King's Central Mortgage Bank bill, Conservative senator Arthur Meighen, a former prime minister, noted with disgust that there were only twenty-five senators present in the chamber.

"We are taking kangaroo leaps into national socialism and all that involves," he complained, yet hardly anybody was there to worry about it.

The government was anxious to close its fourth session of the eighteenth Parliament, but the Conservatives, with a majority in the Senate, were balking, prompting Fort William MP Rev. Dan McIvor to ask a question that is still often asked today: "Who is governing this country? Fifteen members of the other chamber, or the elected representatives of the people?"

As it turned out, the bill was sent back and forth between the two houses several times before Meighen finally relented. The process prompted CCF leader M.J. Coldwell to say, "If the government had reformed the Senate, they could deal with this."

King, of course, like prime ministers before and after him, continued to deal with Senate "reform" the normal way – by appointing party loyalists at every opportunity. One of those loyalists was John J. Duftus, the sitting Liberal MP for Peterborough West.

Duftus, who had been treasurer of the local Liberal association for twenty-five years before seeking election, had been duly nominated as the Liberal candidate, had rented his campaign headquarters, and was actually out knocking on doors just before lunch on February 15, when he was approached by an emissary from Ottawa who told him that King wanted somebody else to run in the riding and that he, Duftus, was now a senator.

"Mr. King's message was a decided shock to me this morning," said Duftus. He wasn't so shocked, however, that he turned down his ticket to patronage heaven.

The appointment of Duftus and W.J. Hushion, a Montreal Liberal, had come five days after King had named six other Liberals to the Senate. One of them, Salter Adrian Hayden of Toronto, a senior member of McCarthy & McCarthy, a Toronto law firm, former president of the Young Liberal Club, would most effectively represent Bay Street in the Senate for the next forty-three years.

Hayden, a senior director of the Bank of Nova Scotia and board member on eighteen other corporations, chaired the powerful Banking, Trade and Commerce Committee for nearly thirty years. Under his leadership, the committee rejected all financial legislation that he viewed as "impractical, unfair or disruptive," which is to say, anything that might interfere with the unfettered pursuit of profit by himself and his corporate buddies. Hayden was certainly not alone in that pursuit. He was, however, as author Larry Zolf called him, "the Capitalist Capo," running a committee composed of an elite group of twenty lawyers, bankers, and businessmen whose first loyalty was always to the shareholders. Hayden retired at age eighty-three because of ill health, just three years after he instituted what is now called the "Hayden formula," which enables the Senate to study a bill immediately after it is tabled in the Commons instead of waiting until it makes its way through successive readings. This allows the senators to get their hands on the bill sooner and keep it there longer, all the better to make certain that the plebs in the Lower House are not trying to do anything to inconvenience the corporate moguls and their Senate surrogates.

In November 1943, King appointed two prominent newspaper executives to the Senate, Kingston *Whig-Standard* publisher W. Rupert Davies, whose son Robertson became one of Canada's finest novelists, and Pamphile R. DuTremblay, president of Montreal's *La Presse*. Although they were both in the same business, that's where the comparison ended. Davies, who emigrated from Wales at age fifteen, earned his apprenticeship as a printer at the Brantford *Expositor*, worked for a while as a journeyman then leased the *Herald*, a local weekly printed at Thamesville, Ontario. DuTremblay, on the other hand, was born into wealth and power, studied law at Laval and McGill, married Angelina Berthiaume, the boss's daughter, sat as Liberal MP for Laurier-Outremont from 1917–21, and illustrated his inordinate interest in money by giving new meaning to double-dipping while serving as a paid member in two Senates at once: Quebec's Legislative Council from 1924 until he died in 1955, and the Senate of Canada from 1943 until his death. (Quebec's Legislative Council, the only remaining provincial upper house in the country, was finally abolished in 1972, part of a government bill that also changed the name of Quebec's Legislative Assembly to the National Assembly.)

In April 1943, by which time the Liberals had re-established their rightful control over the Senate, King was asked in the Commons why DuTremblay was not asked to resign his seat in Quebec's provincial senate before his appointment to Ottawa. King dismissed the question out of hand, saying there was no legal obstacle to belonging to both upper houses and he had absolutely no problem with it.

In November 1945 DuTremblay was arraigned in Montreal's Court of King's Bench, charged with stealing $9,076.66, the property of his late father-in-law, Trefflé Berthiaume, the founder of *La Presse*. The charge followed several years of civil action over the affairs of *La Presse* and was brought against him by Eugene Berthiaume, his brother-in-law and chairman of the board of *La Presse*, who accused the senator of falsifying the books. A month later the charge was dismissed, but the family feud eventually sparked a Montreal newspaper war in 1961 when Senator DuTremblay's wealthy widow, Angelina, used part of her personal fortune of $25 million to launch *Le Nouveau Journal*. This short-lived daily newspaper was aimed at undermining *La Presse*, which, at the time, was run by her three nephews and a niece. The feud over control of the family empire spilled into the political arena, provoking Quebec's premier, Jean Lesage, into passing a bill making it illegal for *La Presse* to be sold for at least fifteen years.

King's most controversial appointment came in 1944 in the midst of the Second World War and the great Conscription crisis, when he appointed four Quebec Liberals, one of them the provincial public works minister T.D. Bouchard of St. Hyacinthe. In his maiden Senate speech on June 22, 1944, Bouchard proposed a dominion-provincial conference to draft a Canadian history text that would be acceptable to all provinces. He accused the Roman Catholic Church of supporting a secret cabal called the Jacques Cartier Order to deliberately teach distorted history designed to disrupt national unity. "A man of honest purpose has to concede there are important frictions existing between the Canadians of French and English descent. The differences of religion and language are, though they should not be, the fertile fields where the sowers of the seeds of discord work day and night, but mostly in the dark," he said, even quoting from *L'Emerillon*, which he described as the secret order's newsletter, forecasting "French domination in the more or less near future" in Ontario.

The speech touched off a firestorm of official outrage throughout Quebec and from many of his Senate colleagues, one of whom, Quebec senator Cyrille Vaillancourt said, "If there has been no revolution or any trouble in Quebec it is because we have had a clergy that gave us proper formation of character."

In the Commons, Justice Minister Louis St. Laurent, who would follow King as prime minister, refused to name a royal commission to study Bouchard's accusations, saying, "I am certainly not aware of the existence of a secret organization in Canada plotting to create a separate corporatist state." The Archbishop of Quebec, Cardinal Villeneuve, denounced what he termed as "insinuations against the Church and the clergy. . . . I must publicly disapprove such an insult to all what the French-Canadians love; to all their legitimate religious, social and political aspirations; to the authority of their bishops who are directly responsible for public education; and finally, to the teachings of the Pope and His Holiness' representatives in our midst."

Quebec premier Adelard Godbout, who became a senator himself in 1949, called the speech "absolutely unjustified and very damaging." While the leaders of several major Quebec unions supported Bouchard, André Laurendeau, leader of the Bloc Populaire, saw it as "a vast conspiracy by a large proportion of Liberal leaders, including members of the Godbout government, against the French-Canadian collectivity. . . . The pincer movement against our basic social, economic and educational institutions, already denounced by clear-minded persons, is being carried out in a systematic way and is being helped by certain French-Canadians. It is high time to oust all who may occupy leading positions." Throughout the controversy, Bouchard never wavered: "I will remind true patriots that when a fire is discovered the alarm is sounded at the start of the fire and not when the building is in ruins." More than fifty years later,

Jack Granatstein, a leading Canadian historian, in his book *Who Killed Canadian History?*, documented the harm being done to national unity by the pro-separatist bias of history being taught to Quebec students.

On April 15, 1945, King set a patronage record by appointing twelve new senators on the same day. One of those was John A. McDonald, fifty-five, of Upper Dyke Village, Nova Scotia, that province's sitting agriculture minister. That meant the upper chamber now had a total of two John MacDonalds and two John McDonalds and all of them, like the country's first prime minister, were John A. too. King's successor, Louis St. Laurent, matched the record November 12, 1953, appointing three women and nine men, all Liberals, and broke it July 28, 1955, with thirteen appointments.

Too bad Andrew Thompson wasn't around in December 1945 at the retirement of Senator E.D. Smith, of fruit-growing fame, on his ninety-second birthday. Smith, a former Conservative MP for Wentworth, spent thirty-two years in the Senate and, until the last session, when he was sick, attended every single session and rarely missed a day. "On only one occasion I drew my allowance for a few days' session," he said, adding, "and I never felt right about it."

Not all senators are sitting around collecting their pay and doing nothing to earn it. One active senator was Ontario Liberal W.D. Euler, who served as both revenue minister and trade minister in the Liberal government of Mackenzie King and fought for years to convince his colleagues to lift the ban on the importation, manufacture, and sale of margarine, a law designed specifically to placate the dairy farmers, particularly in Quebec, in the Dairy Industry Act of 1886. It may seem odd to Canadians today, but except for a six-year period at the end of the First World War, when butter was in short supply, margarine could not be sold in Canada. Euler lost his bid in 1946 by a 43–30 vote, and lost again by 35–21 in 1948, a vote that followed months of heated debate. In his fifty-five-minute speech immediately before the vote, Euler said the Senate itself was on trial, "not because of margarine, but because of the principle of a democratic right – the right to free choice, free enterprise, free competition. . . ."

Two years later the Supreme Court ruled that margarine could be sold, although some restrictions were allowed – for one, it couldn't be coloured to look like butter – and Euler then launched an attack on the eight per cent sales tax the government imposed in an attempt to discourage its use. The tax was not generally applied to food, but it was slapped only on margarine. Calling the tax unfair to housewives trying to fight the rising cost of living and "reprehensible in principle and absurd in practice," Euler said it would mean a three-cent-a-pound reduction in price, but Quebec senator Cyrille Vaillancourt, who owned a large maple syrup business, said it would also deprive thousands of farmers of incomes. Euler also wanted the Senate to recommend that the colouring of margarine no longer be prohibited, but Vaillancourt claimed that would only encourage people to eat more margarine and added that a Danish survey had discovered that people were "losing their sight" from "eating margarine too long."

The next day, Liberal senator J.W. De B. Farris, a Vancouver lawyer, quoted a U.S. scientist who also claimed that prolonged use of margarine caused eye defects. "The first generation can handle margarine all right," said Farris, "but after second and third generations defects begin to show up." Anyway, said Ferris, questions of taxation were for the government, not the Senate. He said the Senate could be regarded as "meddlesome and mischievous" if it tried to dictate taxation policy. Senator R.B. Horner, a Saskatchewan farmer, predicted that some day the manufacture and sale of margarine would be illegal again.

Once again, Euler's colleagues voted against him, but he still wasn't giving up. On March 6, 1952, he introduced a bill that essentially called for interprovincial free trade in dairy products. "Margarine may incidentally come into the question," he said, "[but] it has wide implications beyond the subject of margarine." Again, he didn't win. In April 1953 he was back at it, trying to remove what had become a ten per cent sales tax. A Senate committee had taken the unprecedented step of altering a government budget proposal by adding margarine to the list of the one hundred-odd foodstuffs exempt from the tax, but after another long debate that split along party lines, the Senate voted against Euler's move.

Euler's policy initiatives were not always quite so altruistic, however. An insurance executive from Waterloo, he stood in the upper chamber in January 1959 to introduce a private member's bill to grant federal incorporation to the Waterloo Mutual Insurance Co. Euler, in addition to his senatorial duties, was president of Economical Mutual Insurance Co. and a director of Dominion Life Assurance. He apparently saw no conflict in pushing a measure that could have a direct impact upon his own business. The company already was incorporated provincially, but wanted the federal stamp of approval so it could branch out into mortgage loans, many of which, no doubt, would be insured by Euler's firm. Not a single senator saw any conflict in this. It was, after all, just business as usual.

A bit of Canadian history was made August 18, 1949, when Mackenzie King's successor, Louis St. Laurent, appointed the first three senators from Newfoundland, Canada's newest province. A month later, St. Laurent announced by-elections for eight vacancies that had occurred since the election, three of them occurring that same day as the prime minister retired three veteran Liberal backbenchers to the comfortable confines of the Senate.

When seventy-five-year-old Walter Jones stepped down after ten years as premier of Prince Edward Island in May 1953, St. Laurent figured he'd make a perfect senator. Jones said his appointment to the upper chamber reminded him of a political song he learned in his youth:

> When our great statesmen get so old
> They don't feel their best,
> We send them to the Senate
> And they get a chance to rest.

On June 13, 1953, St. Laurent had two major announcements to make. First, there would be a general election August 10. And second, he named seven new senators, all but one of whom had been sitting in the Commons as a Liberal MP, giving the Liberals all but eight seats in the Senate. The lopsided nature of the upper chamber sparked rumours that St. Laurent was planning to take the almost unprecedented step of appointing non-Liberals to fill at least some of the vacancies.

On July 28, 1955, just eight of thirteen newly minted senators were Liberal, one was a Conservative, and the political leanings of four others were not clear. The new class included Hartland de Montarville Molson, the forty-eight-year-old brewery executive, who was one of Canada's wealthiest and most influential businessmen. His family was rumoured to have Conservative leanings, although he accepted the seat as an independent. The group also included former Ontario Liberal cabinet minister David Croll, who would go on to have a distinguished record in the Senate as a champion of humanitarian causes. Croll was the first Jewish senator in Canadian history and took his oath of office on a special Torah sent to him especially for the purpose by the Chief Rabbi of Israel.

For all the carping about the existing appointments system, not many people have been known to say no to the call. But on May 2, 1957, Canadian Labour Congress president Claude Jodoin turned down St. Laurent's offer to give labour a voice in the Senate, saying, "The CLC is opposed to non-elected legislative bodies and it would be quite impossible for me to hold a seat. I say this with all due respect for the senators." Forty years earlier, however, two prominent Canadians refused seats in the Senate on the same day. The late Col. Hugh Clark, parliamentary undersecretary for external affairs in 1917, had an office in the East Block right next to Conservative prime minister Sir Robert Borden's office. Borden had offered Senate seats to John Ross Robertson, proprietor of the old *Toronto Telegram* newspaper, and Huntley Drummond, a prominent Montreal businessman, whose father was a senator. In a 1954 letter to the editor of the *Ottawa Journal*, Col. Clark wrote, "I remember well his [Borden] coming in to tell me of something happening that day that never happened before in Canada – two men to whom he offered seats in the Senate had in the same mail that morning rejected his offer."

An even odder refusal was recorded in the early days after Confederation concerning the Power family from Halifax. S. Patrick Power, a Liberal MP, declined a Senate seat in 1877 so the appointment went to his son, Lawrence Geoffrey Power, who sat there until his death in 1921. For a time, the son was in the Senate at the same time his father sat in the Commons.

A more current refusal came in 1986, when one of Mulroney's most highly respected senior advisers, Charlie McMillan, decided he wanted to stop his weekly commute to Ottawa and go back home to Toronto to his wife and two daughters. Mulroney and his advisers were flying to St. John's, Newfoundland, for a planning and priorities meeting of cabinet and had stopped by New Brunswick on the way to pick up the prime minister's latest senior adviser – long-time Mulroney apologist Dalton Camp – partly to showcase his new acquisition to cabinet.

Things had not been going well. The Tories, trailing badly in the polls, had just struggled through the Sinclair Stevens mess – a senior minister involved in a series of conflicts of interest – and Mulroney, Camp, Bill Fox (Mulroney's communications czar), and some others were plotting strategy in their suite in the Hotel Newfoundland when McMillan told Mulroney he was, in his words, "going home to my girls."

"Is there anything you'd like to do?" Mulroney asked McMillan. "There's a Senate opening in P.E.I.," where McMillan and his twin brother, Tom (then Mulroney's environment minister), come from.

But before anybody could say a thing, McMillan looked Mulroney straight in the eye and said, "I don't want to go to the Senate. It's no goddamn good. You ought to abolish it."

Fox asked McMillan later why he didn't at least think about it first. "Charlie said because he believed that an unelected Senate was wrong and he didn't want anything to do with it. He had great intellectual honesty. He's not a guy for situational ethics." Ah, if only there were more Charlie McMillans in politics.

Back in the mid-1950s, the Liberals had been badly damaged politically by the 1956 pipeline debate, perhaps the most bitter parliamentary dispute in Canadian history. That set the scene for the June 1957 minority win by Conservative leader John Diefenbaker, and he wasted little time trying to change the political imbalance in the Senate. On September 20, Diefenbaker announced a three-way manoeuvre that gave him a new cabinet minister and opened the door for his external affairs minister, Sidney Smith, to enter Parliament. Diefenbaker appointed eighty-year-old Manitoban senator John T. Haig as government leader in the Senate and minister without portfolio. At the same time, he accepted the resignation of Hastings-Frontenac Tory MP George S. White, fifty-nine, naming him to the Senate and opening up the seat for Smith, who had stepped down a week earlier as president of the University of Toronto to become Diefenbaker's external affairs minister. The appointment of White gave the Conservatives thirteen senators, compared to seventy-eight Liberals.

During the 1957 election, Diefenbaker had promised to appoint for the first time a representative of Canada's 150,000 native Indians to the Senate. True to his word, on February 1, 1958, he named seventy-one-year-old James Gladstone, a Blood band member of Cree and Scottish ancestry. A former president of the Indian Association of Alberta, Gladstone was widely credited with bringing harmony between Alberta's two major Indian groups, the Crees and the three Blackfoot nations in the southern part of the province. Gladstone was one of the first group of boys enrolled at St. Paul's Anglican Mission school. A highly successful rancher, he and his two sons were running five hundred head of cattle and had eight hundred acres under cultivation at the time of his appointment. He was the first Indian on the reserve to buy a tractor, the first to use power machinery and chemical sprays, and the first to get electricity into his house. In 1937, one of his four daughters, a nurse, was one of two young women chosen to represent Canadian Indians at the coronation of King George VI in London.

During his maiden Senate speech, Gladstone, referring to his fellow senators as his "new tribe," spoke briefly in Blackfoot, his native tongue: "Eekoh-kinay-tames-tikee-kunay-apee unok-ohtayts-tseeh-pee mukiy-sitsip sukomoh-kee unok-see awk-aw-kee-tsee-maks. Nitowat-simoyeek-nukohk-okomot-ayhpo-wat-omohsah-ow." Translated it means: "The Indians of Canada are very happy to know they have someone in Ottawa to represent them in the government of Canada. I pray that I will be able to speak the right words for them."

Given the attitudes of the day – which still haven't improved all that much – Gladstone had his work cut out for him. During a Senate debate in 1950, for example, Senator T.A. Crerar, a former cabinet minister responsible for Indian welfare, said the "vast majority" of Canadian Indians did not want to become Canadian citizens, many of them because they would lose government aid if they did. To illustrate their "lack of self-reliance," Crerar told the story of an Indian trapper paid $600 for rabbit furs who squandered it within a few weeks. Other Indians, he said, employed during the war building an airfield at The Pas, Manitoba, drew their pay every two weeks and went out on a "binge." Some of them enjoyed spending their money driving around in a taxi all day. He said the Indian "problem" might be solved if they were compelled to accept citizenship, "but that would be a short-sighted policy. It would not solve the fact that Indians still are Indians." He said if the vote were given to Indians, "especially the primitive tribes, it might open the door to the greatest orgy of election bribery" Canada had ever seen.

When D.M. Mackay, director of Indian Affairs, said some white parents wouldn't allow their children to attend the same schools as Indian children, Senator John T. Haig, the Conservative leader in the Senate, said that one reason for that reluctance was that some Indian children had "things in their hair – and that is a serious objection." He said that by mingling with the white man, some Indians picked up all the white man's bad habits and dropped some of the "red man's" good ones.

Crerar finished the debate by suggesting the government discontinue the practice of building residential schools, a suggestion that, had it been taken, may have saved future governments and generations of native Canadians a lot of grief.

The Senate did not see its first Inuit member until Willy Adams, a forty-three-year-old native of Fort Chimo in Arctic Quebec, was named senator for the Northwest Territories in April 1977.

During a 1983 debate, Nova Scotia Conservative senator Richard Donahoe, the former provincial attorney-general, leaned over to Newfoundland Liberal senator Derik Lewis during a committee meeting studying a constitutional amendment on native rights and said there would be no problem "if they did just what they did in Newfoundland and shot them all." The reference, of course, was to the extermination of the Beothuk Indians of Newfoundland in the late eighteenth century by white settlers and Micmac Indians. Donahoe's remarks were overheard by a native CBC reporter and caused a stir both in the Commons and across the country. Donahoe said it was only a "joke" and turned down many calls for his resignation. In an interview the day after the incident, he said, "You have to admit that if in fact all Indians had been killed it would have made it easier."

Unfortunately, Gladstone accomplished little for his people, in part because he developed a serious drinking problem, adding fuel to the fire of Diefenbaker's critics who felt that the Senate was no place for Indians. There wasn't another Indian appointed, in fact, until Pierre Trudeau named Guy Williams in 1971. The long-time president of the Native Brotherhood of B.C., and chairman of Fisherman's Co-op and the Ucluelet Fish Processing & Cold Storage Company, Williams turned out to be an effective senator.

The first status Indian elected to the Commons and the first appointed to the federal cabinet was Leonard Marchand. He was given two portfolios by Trudeau in 1976 – small business and environment – and was named to the Senate by Trudeau in 1984. He started off fine, but near the end of his thirteen-year stay, ended up attending about fifteen per cent of the sittings, rivalling Ontario Liberal senator Andrew Thompson as the chamber's worst truant. In December 1996, Marchand announced he was stepping down, but Prime Minister Jean Chrétien talked him into staying another year. "He was the only native I had in the Senate," Chrétien said on a London, Ontario, radio talk show. "He's a good personal friend, so I wanted him to be around for the election." In fact, Chrétien was afraid that if Marchand resigned just before an election, Reform would create political problems for the Liberals in British Columbia by demanding an Alberta-style election to fill the Senate vacancy. Marchand resigned one week after the Senate suspended Thompson.

In January 1959, Diefenbaker appointed John Hnatyshyn, fifty, to the Senate. A Ukrainian-born Saskatoon lawyer and long-time personal friend of the prime minister, Hnatyshyn was so beloved by the people around Yorkton that he lost three federal elections and one provincial election. In the end, however, he did manage to win the one vote that counted most and he sat in the Senate until his death in 1967. His son, Ramon, would become a senior minister in the Mulroney cabinet and then serve a term as Canada's first governor-general of Ukrainian descent.

Two weeks after the appointment of John Hnatyshyn, Secretary of State Henri Courtemanche, forty-three, resigned from the Diefenbaker cabinet for "health reasons." Diefenbaker stood in the Commons that day and expressed his "personal regret and that of my colleagues that the state of his health had made it necessary for him to tender his resignation." Opposition leaders also joined in to express their concerns and wish the former minister well. Perhaps their good wishes and prayers worked, because Courtemanche apparently made a miraculous recovery. He was appointed to the Senate the very next day.

By November 1960, there were no Senate vacancies for the first time since 1945. The Tories were catching up, but they still trailed the Liberals twenty-six to seventy-three, with two independents and an independent Liberal rounding out the 102 senators.

Liberals, of course, have long viewed themselves as Canada's "natural governing party." And so it was that the Liberal-dominated Senate was growing increasingly unhappy over the fact that the great unwashed had been foolhardy enough to elect a Commons full of Tories. They decided it was time to flex their senatorial muscles.

On July 13, 1960, a defiant Senate turned down the government proposal to petition Westminster to write into the BNA Act a provision of mandatory retirement at age seventy-five for county, district, and superior court judges. The Liberal-dominated Senate, on an amendment from Senator David Croll, struck out all references to district and county judges, arguing that Canada could already retire those judges under the Judges Act of 1913. The move created an embarrassing problem for the government. Its resolution had already been approved in the Commons and passed on to the U.K., and as things then stood, the U.K. was being asked to enact two quite different constitutional amendments.

Diefenbaker, who was not amused, decided to accept the Senate amendment and re-introduce it to the Commons, where it was approved.

That little skirmish, however, was simply a mild precursor for what was to come in the spring of 1961 when Diefenbaker introduced a highly controversial bill to extend tariff protection for Canadian manufacturers, giving the government the power to increase customs duties on a wide range of products through a broadening of the definition of a class or kind of goods made in Canada.

The bill, which had been presented as a major initiative in the Tory budget, received third and final reading in the Commons on April 19 after nine days of vigorous opposition from the Liberals and CCF. It got off to a rowdy beginning in the Senate in May when Senator William Brunt, deputy government house leader, argued that the upper chamber had no right to change a bill dealing with budget and fiscal matters against the wishes of the elected representatives in the Commons. "If the government is wrong in this bill," he said, "there is a group that will correct it, namely the electors. That is their job, not our job." It was the first time anybody in the Senate had challenged the right of the Senate to amend government bills.

Through the years the Senate had rejected some Commons bills, including a private member's bill during the 1873–78 regime of Alexander Mackenzie for construction of a railway from Esquimalt to Nanaimo; a private bill during the Laurier regime for construction of a railway between Atlin, British Columbia, and Dawson City, Yukon; another bill during the Laurier regime for purchase of the Drummond County railway; a government bill during the Borden administration to amend the Railway Act; a highly publicized rejection of Borden's Naval Bill under which Canada would have provided financial aid to the British Navy; and an old-age pension bill sponsored by the Mackenzie King government in 1926.

Parliamentary rules provide that if the government majority in the Commons refuses to accept a Senate amendment, a Commons-Senate conference can be called. The so-called free committee is composed of three members from each House. That was last done in 1934 when a compromise was reached between the two Houses on an excise tax bill. There are no other steps provided for, but if a compromise can't be negotiated, the bill would likely just die.

Diefenbaker was governing with the largest majority in Canadian history at the time, but in the Senate, the Liberals held seventy-two seats, compared to twenty-five Tories, two independents, and one independent Liberal. The Liberal senators had already served notice that they intended to kill a major provision in the bill giving the minister arbitrary powers in some tariff rulings with no right of appeal. Brunt said if they persisted, it would lead to some unwelcome Senate reforms. Liberal senator Arthur Roebuck replied that he would not be "bullied or wheedled into abrogating my right to propose amendments . . . and will not be frightened by threats to abolish or liquidate the Senate." He said if Brunt believed what he said, "he might

as well pack his bags and return to his constituency of Hanover. . . .
He has no further purpose to serve by remaining here. If he believes
that, then he is all through and so are we, if we are to be hog-tied
hand and foot in that matter."

There was a bit more than parliamentary altruism at work here.
Senator Salter Hayden, the Bay Street tribune and chairman of the
Senate banking committee, felt the bill could harm some of his corporate interests and those of his corporate colleagues. He wasn't
alone. The committee then, as now, was dominated by lawyers,
bankers, and assorted corporate moguls. On June 7, the committee
rejected the key measure in the bill concerning ministerial powers by
a vote of 18–8 after nearly seven hours of heated debate. On June 14,
an amendment deleting the key point concerning ministerial powers
was passed 37–21 by the Senate then sent back to the Commons. On
July 6, Diefenbaker said there would be a general election "sooner
or later" on Senate reform unless the Upper House retracted its
amendment. "We will not take the amendment," Diefenbaker said,
thumping his Commons desk with his fist while the Conservatives
applauded and cheered.

Diefenbaker talked of a 1911 U.K. amendment that gave the
Commons the right to approve money bills without concurrence by
the House of Lords. The Commons voted 149–39 to reject the Senate
amendment. The Liberal senators went into a closed-door caucus
meeting to debate the issue. They announced that the Commons did
have the sole right to levy taxes, but claimed their amendment did
not infringe on taxation rights, so they were sticking with it. Pearson
dared Diefenbaker to call an election on the issue.

The eighty-three-year-old Liberal senator Arthur Roebuck, a
former Ontario attorney-general, rose in the Senate on July 10 and
challenged Diefenbaker to carry out his threats of Senate reform.
"Come on with your reforms," he said. "If, by the way, the threat
includes a general election, well, come along with that too." Roebuck,
who had been in the Senate since 1945, said he was prepared to "go
back to the hustings" to fight Diefenbaker. He said he was ready to
"stay here for a lifetime rather than agree to the department of

National Revenue being given the status of a dictatorship." Two days later, the Senate voted 38–17 to throw the bill back to the Commons and to insist on their amendment. On September 27, Diefenbaker said the government could not accept the amendment and said the legislation would be allowed to die with the end of the session. "Those in the Senate must accept responsibility for the economic consequences of this action, and the blame for the thousands of jobs which will remain uncreated," he said.

On January 22, 1962, Diefenbaker said he planned to set an age limit for senators, deprive the Senate of its remaining legislative jurisdiction over money bills, and set a given length of term for senators. "All will receive consideration," he said. He joked that former prime minister Mackenzie King's idea of Senate reform had been "Live Grits for dead Tories."

On April 8, Diefenbaker tabled a simple amendment to the BNA Act setting a mandatory retirement age of seventy-five for senators, to become effective after the next general election, expected that June. He said it would force the retirement of thirty-one senators, twenty-six of them Liberals. He said a pension was also included for senators. The bill passed first reading 143–7, with the Liberals voting with the government. In the end, the bill died on the order paper.

The other great fight during the tumultuous year of 1961 was the "Coyne Affair," which ran at times concurrently with the Senate battle over the tariff bill.

James Coyne, a boyish-looking Rhodes scholar, became the highest-paid public servant in 1955 when he accepted the $50,000-a-year post as governor of the Bank of Canada. But trouble was in the air. Coyne believed in a tight-money policy. Diefenbaker didn't. It didn't matter much the first two years with the Liberals in power, but during the 1957 election campaign Diefenbaker told a crowd at Truro, Nova Scotia, that "the little man – the farmer, the fisherman, and the small businessman – is being crushed by the Liberal government's tight money policy." He said that under a Conservative administration "tight money will disappear." Six weeks after making that promise, Diefenbaker became prime minister. During the short life of his first government, Diefenbaker and his finance minister, Donald Fleming, made it clear that the government intended to ease the bank rate further and assume direct responsibility for monetary policy. The Tories favoured increasing the money supply and implementing less restrictive interest rates to get Canada out of its recession.

But as the budgetary deficit continued to grow under the Tory administration after the 1958 election, Diefenbaker and Fleming began to retreat on their earlier claims and conceded that the Bank of Canada did not need instructions from the finance minister for everything it did.

Still, the relationship between Diefenbaker and Coyne, never entirely happy, took a turn for the worse in the fall of 1959 when Coyne, apparently buoyed by his own glowing press clippings, decided to take his message directly to the Canadian people. In an unprecedented series of public and highly political speeches, Coyne argued that Canadians were selling out control over their own destiny by living off the proceeds of foreign capital and selling too many of our natural resources to the Americans.

While the Conservatives were still trying to spend their way out of the recession, Coyne's annual report in 1960 said bluntly, "We must as a nation learn to live within our means." In his 1961 annual report, Coyne again suggested the government should cut the need for large foreign capital investment by regulating credit, distributing income, and even determining the amount of employment in particular industries or areas of the country.

That was simply too much for Diefenbaker. After all, he had been elected to run the country. Coyne hadn't been. On May 30, 1961, Fleming asked Coyne to resign. Coyne, whose term would have expired at the end of the year, refused. In Quebec City on June 13, the bank's board of directors voted nine to one to seek Coyne's resignation. Again, he refused, issuing a statement to Canadian Press saying, "I cannot and will not resign quietly," perhaps the understatement of the decade. He accused the government of having cast a "slander upon my own integrity."

Fleming, perhaps resorting to his pocket thesaurus, told the Commons that Coyne was defiant, provocative, rigid, doctrinaire, restrictionist, and guilty of making ill-considered public declarations that fell outside the realm of banking. Diefenbaker and Fleming also attacked Coyne, who was just fifty-one, for accepting a special bank pension of $25,000 a year on top of his regular $19,000 pension. Coyne at first denied the accusation, but it turned out to be true that on February 15, 1960, the board of governors, without telling the government, had raised Coyne's regular pension by $7,000 and his special pension by $13,000. Fleming accused Coyne in the Commons of "lacking in a sense of responsibility" for accepting the secret deal. By comparison, Diefenbaker pointed out that former prime minister Louis St. Laurent's pension was less than $3,000 a year.

The public feud continued back and forth. On June 23 Fleming introduced Bill C-114 in the Commons. It had one clause: "The office of the governor of the Bank of Canada shall be deemed to have become vacant immediately upon the coming into force of this act." Pearson and the Liberals attacked the government for not allowing Coyne "the justice" of a full hearing before a Commons committee. Coyne shot off an open letter to Fleming accusing him of "misrepresentation . . . blackmail tactics . . . and undermining the independence of the Bank of Canada." He demanded to be heard by a parliamentary committee. After a bitter and consistently unruly debate, the bill was approved 129 to 37 on July 7. Which is where the Senate entered the picture.

At the time, the Conservatives held 208 of the 265 Commons seats. In the Senate, however, it was 72–25 for the Liberals.

While the Commons refused Coyne a public hearing, the Senate banking committee seized the bill and asked Coyne to testify. In a 1971 feature article about the affair, veteran Canadian Press reporter Dave McIntosh described the Senate committee hearings this way:

"In the jammed, steamy Senate committee room, Coyne poured out his testimony at the rate of 9,000 words an hour for 13 hours in two and one-half days." He accused the government of using him as a scapegoat for its failed monetary policy. He conceded that he regretted "having said certain things and having done certain things," but concluded, "I shall be marked for life as a man, a citizen of Canada, declared by the highest court having jurisdiction in such a matter to have been proved unfit to hold high office of Parliament by reason of misbehavior in relation to the duties of that office.

"A verdict of not guilty will not prevent my immediate departure from office but it will permit me to retire honorably and to hold up my head among my fellow citizens."

With tears in his eyes, the normally icy-calm Coyne bowed to the chairman and walked out of the committee room. With their arms around each other's waist, he and his wife walked down the wide driveway in front of the Parliament buildings and away from the Hill.

The next day, on July 13, to Diefenbaker's great chagrin, the committee voted 19–7 to strike down the bill. The Senate itself upheld that decision by a thirty-three to sixteen vote. As promised, Coyne resigned as governor less than an hour after the Senate vote. Thus the Senate thwarted the will of the Commons while falling short of using its veto. The *Toronto Star*, having consistently sided with Coyne, proclaimed in a front-page headline the next day: "Cleared – Coyne Resigns."

While the Fathers of Confederation did not adopt the British system of peerages – Canada had no history of aristocratic privilege to draw on – there have been sporadic examples of a dynastic approach to filling Senate vacancies.

In 1960, Diefenbaker appointed Louis Philippe Beaubien of Montreal, whose father Charles Philippe had been a senator. When Senate Conservative leader John T. Haig retired in 1962, the seat was handed over to his son, Campbell, a Winnipeg lawyer, one of three appointments made by Diefenbaker during a cabinet meeting held on a Toronto-to-Hamilton train just three days before the June 18 election. Former Liberal senator James Gray Turgeon entered the Senate in 1947, three years after the death of his father, Onesiphore Turgeon, a senator from 1923 to 1944. Senator James Ham King, who died in 1954, was the son of George King, a senator from 1896 to 1928. And one of the last senators Lester Pearson appointed in April 1968 was St. John's, Newfoundland, businessman William Petten, whose father, Ray Petten, had also been a senator.

Retired senator Paul David of Montreal, a pioneer in cardiovascular care, died in April 1999, the only third-generation senator in Canadian history. He was appointed by Brian Mulroney in 1985. His father, Athanase, had been named to the Senate by Mackenzie King and his grandfather, Laurent-Olivier, was given a Senate seat by Sir Wilfrid Laurier.

Alberta Liberal senator Dan Hays, a Calgary lawyer, rancher, and farmer, inherited his father Harry's job as chief fund-raiser for the Alberta Liberal Party and his reward as a senator. Hays was one of the group of seven appointments made by Trudeau just days before he resigned as prime minister in 1984.

Author Larry Zolf wrote of the chamber, "The party connection in the Senate castrates the upper chamber; the business connection corrupts it; the grapes of froth sometimes debauch it. Still, there is no other museum a living fossil would rather be in than the Canadian Senate. In no other place can a Canadian live so long, be so well preserved and indulge in so many unsober second thoughts."

The pro-business "lobby from within," as political scientists have called it, was never more in evidence than in August 1962 when Diefenbaker – who would come to regret it – named corporate giant M. Wallace McCutcheon as both a Senator and a minister without portfolio in his new government. McCutcheon, who was rarely given to sober second thoughts, or sober thoughts of any kind, nonetheless was a mighty business figure. One newspaper headline at the time declared: "The name says it all." He was vice-president and managing director of Argus Corporation, then the country's most powerful holding company, and within four years would be working hard to oust Diefenbaker from his job and go after it himself. As a minister, McCutcheon said he would resign his numerous corporate directorships. Asked if he would also have to sell his stock shares, Diefenbaker said, "That is quite a different thing." Later, McCutcheon became Diefenbaker's trade minister but his career ended when he resigned from the Senate in May 1968 to contest the general election in Toronto's York-Simcoe riding. He lost.

One person who was not pleased by McCutcheon's appointment was constitutional expert Eugene Forsey – who also eventually became a senator – then the research director of the Canadian Labour Congress. Forsey argued it was "of very dubious constitutional propriety" for Diefenbaker to make major appointments before his minority government had won a Commons confidence vote. Forsey argued that both King and Meighen "followed the constitutionally correct course" in the topsy-turvy year of 1926. King made no senatorial appointments until he won a confidence vote and Meighen made none at all during his hundred days as prime minister. King wasn't quite so particular after winning another minority later the same year, however, when he appointed Paul Hatfield of Nova Scotia to the Senate a month before the new Parliament met.

Opposition leader Lester Pearson jumped into the fray, saying he agreed with Forsey. Pearson, however, lost his enthusiasm for constitutional purity just ten months later when, five days after winning his minority and weeks before the Commons sat, he appointed former Liberal MP Maurice Bourget of Lévis, Quebec, to the Senate and even elevated him immediately to Senate Speaker.

At 8 A.M. on November 22, 1962, Pete Robertson, a forty-nine-year-old railway worker like his father before him, was asleep in his freight train caboose on a siding in Ignace, 146 miles east of Kenora in deepest northwestern Ontario, when he was awakened to take an urgent long-distance telephone call.

His first thought was that something bad had happened at his home in Kenora where his wife and three young children lived. Happily, he was wrong. It was Prime Minister John Diefenbaker calling to offer him a Senate seat. The first thing Robertson did, after phoning home to tell his wife the news, was borrow a typewriter to bash out his acceptance and thanks. If Diefenbaker was seeking an "ordinary Canadian" instead of the usual representative of the country's business, legal, or social elite, he'd found him in Robertson. Mind you, the fact that Robertson was head of the local Conservative association may have played a minor role in the decision.

As suggested at the beginning of this chapter, some things don't change. One of those things is the direct connection between elections and Senate appointments. Both immediately before an election and shortly after one, every prime minister since Confederation has used the opportunity to load up the place with those who have served the partisan cause. With time running out on his regime, and all the political signs making it obvious he wasn't getting back in, the Chief gave one final taskless thanks to four lucky lottery winners.

On February 5, 1963, a delegation of eight Tory cabinet ministers met in Trade Minister George Hees's office in an effort to find a way to convince Diefenbaker to step down and allow a leadership race before it was too late. For the Tories, however, it already was too late. That same day, the House fell on a non-confidence vote, Parliament was dissolved, and an election was called for April 8, 1963, but not before Diefenbaker added four new Tory senators to the upper chamber. No appointment better illustrates the sense of utter chaos that had doomed the Diefenbaker regime than the very last appointment he made.

Those familiar with downtown Toronto's City Hall know that the huge public expanse in front of it is known as Nathan Phillips Square, named after the popular former mayor.

Figuring Phillips would make a good senator, Diefenbaker instructed his staff to take care of the details. The problem was, they thought Diefenbaker meant Orville H. Phillips, a dentist and undistinguished backbench Tory MP for the Prince Edward Island riding of Prince. And so it was that the thirty-nine-year-old P.E.I. dentist became Diefenbaker's final senatorial salute to the nation.

Despite the Chief's valiant efforts, however, the dreaded Liberals outnumbered the Tories 59–37 in the chamber of shameless second thought.

6

Rainmakers and Troublemakers

I T WAS, AS Yogi Berra was wont to say, déjà vu all over again.
It took the new prime minister, Lester Pearson, just five days
to appoint his first senator, former Liberal MP Romauld Bourque.
The seventy-three-year-old veteran MP, a former mayor of
Outremont, who in 1920 had co-founded *Le Nouvelliste*, a French-
language daily newspaper, was also named Senate Speaker at the
same time as a reward for stepping aside so that Secretary of State
Maurice Lamontagne could have a "safe" Liberal seat.

In July 1963, some prominent Liberal and Conservative senators
were pushing the radical notion that Pearson appoint former CCF
leader M.J. Coldwell to the Senate. The Upper House had three independent members, but there had never been a representative from
one of the fringe parties. Senator W. Ross Macdonald, the government leader in the Senate and a member of the Pearson cabinet,
joined other senators in saying, "We would like to see him here."
Coldwell, a resident fellow at Carleton University at the time, said,
"While the party to which I belonged was opposed to the Senate, I

have always felt that any Senate reform taken would have the best interest of the country at heart. The appointment of people to the Senate who believe in Senate reform would be beneficial." Everybody, it seems, thought it was a good idea – except Pearson. It would be Pierre Trudeau who broke the long-standing tradition against third-party appointments. Among the eight new senators appointed on October 7, 1970, were three from the splinter parties: former Quebec CCF leader Thérèse Casgrain, former CCF candidate Eugene Forsey, and long-time Alberta Social Credit premier Ernest Manning, father of current Reform leader Preston Manning.

What Pearson didn't hesitate to use the Senate for, however, was a refuge for cabinet ministers who got themselves into political hot water. In December 1963, after several months of controversy, Pearson announced that Justice Minister Lionel Chevrier was stepping down to take a diplomatic post while Post-Master General Azelus Denis was headed to the Senate. In the eight months since the twenty-six-member Pearson cabinet took office, Denis had drawn steady fire from the opposition for his blatant partisanship in handing out postal jobs. On several occasions he was accused of discriminating against war veterans by favouring non-veterans for the post. He even fired Betty Stewart as postmistress of Enterprise, Ontario. In place of this widow, veteran, and mother of five children, he gave the postal work to a local Liberal, prompting nearly everybody in town to sign a petition condemning the move.

While Denis was named to the Senate just to spare the Liberals from more embarrassment, Pearson had other things in mind in November 1964 when he rewarded Establishment big shot John Black Aird both for his efforts as fund-raiser in the previous six campaigns and his impeccable personal ties with Canada's business elite. In *The Canadian Establishment*, Volume One, author Peter C. Newman illustrates the kind of company Aird kept: "Paul Desmarais knows how to coddle the powerful," wrote Newman. "When John Aird, the Toronto lawyer who has become an important access to Establishment power, caught a bad cold in Montreal during the winter of 1974, Desmarais kept sending fresh handkerchiefs to his hotel room by Cadillac and telephoning to make sure he was comfortable."

Aird, forty-one at the time, was the perfect candidate to join Salter Hayden on the Senate banking and commerce committee. After all, his grandfather had been president of the Bank of Commerce and Aird himself was a director and member of the executive committee of the Bank of Nova Scotia. He was also the senior partner in the law firm of Aird, Zimmerman and Berlis, and was chairman of the board of Algoma Central Railway, deputy chairman of Reed Shaw Osler, and a board member of more than a dozen other large corporations, including Consolidated-Bathurst Ltd., Molson Companies Ltd., Eastern & Chartered Trust, and National Life Assurance Company of Canada.

The other noteworthy thing about Aird is that he was the last "lifer" appointed to the Senate, even though he left the upper chamber of his own volition in 1974. He went on to serve a term as Ontario's lieutenant-governor from 1980 to 1985, and was chancellor of two universities and holder of six honorary degrees.

NDP deputy leader Douglas Fisher of Port Arthur, now the dean of the Parliamentary Press Gallery, used the occasion of the 1965 debate over senatorial retirement to denounce the Senate as a front for big business. "One senator even has a stock ticker in his office," said Fisher, adding that a Senate appointment almost always amounted to a guarantee that the new senator would be named to boards of several companies that hoped to exercise "leverage" over legislation affecting them.

Of the nine senators appointed by Pearson, seven had been Liberal bagmen and two were MPs who stepped down to make way for new ministers. The "prize specimen" was Senator Louis Gélinas, chief Liberal fund-raiser in Quebec and a key figure in the Dorion judicial inquiry into the Lucien Rivard affair, a bribery and narcotics scandal. Fisher said the Senate banking committee, which blocked the incorporation of the Bank of B.C. a year earlier and held up two other "baby" banks for several months, included four senators who sat as directors of established banks, including Hayden, the committee chairman.

In a letter to the *Globe and Mail*, Senator John J. Connolly, another prominent Liberal bagman and newly named government leader in the Upper House, called Fisher's remarks "superficial and vicious," although he didn't dispute any of Fisher's facts. Connolly did say, however, that it was "significant" that attendance was seldom below sixty-five per cent: "This speaks very highly for the attention senators give to their duties here." Connolly said the Senate had dealt with a series of major issues, including a constitutional amendment providing for survivor benefits for the Canada Pension Plan and adoption of the new Canadian flag. It also passed 856 divorce resolutions. (At the time, neither Quebec nor Newfoundland had divorce courts, and the Senate acted in that capacity.) And while the 1964 pension and flag debates had been among the longest and most rancorous in Canadian history in the Commons, neither one lasted more than a few days in the Senate before being dutifully approved by the Liberal majority there. Connolly's ticket to the Senate, incidentally, had been purchased through his loyal service as national president of the party from 1961 to 1964, during which time he was credited with modernizing the party structure by hiring a full-time national organizer and nursing the Liberals back to health after their 1958 election debacle. Appointed to the Senate in 1953, he served as government leader in the Upper House and minister without portfolio from 1964 to 1968.

Diefenbaker had introduced a bill to make retirement mandatory at age seventy-five but it never got beyond the talking stage. In February 1964, Senator John Connolly announced that the government planned to introduce the retirement age and a pension of $9,000 a year, comparable to the MPs' annual pensions. Unlike Diefenbaker's approach – where everybody over seventy-five had to retire – the Liberals gave existing senators the option of either taking the pension or keeping their Senate seats. At the time, there were thirty-six senators aged seventy-five and over – thirty of them Liberals – and another fifteen between seventy and seventy-four years old. Four of them were at least eighty-seven.

In April 1965, the mandatory retirement issue was the first measure to come up for debate after the Easter recess. Diefenbaker dismissed it as a "sham . . . simply fiddling with Senate reform . . . a milk and water substitute." He said retirement should apply to incumbents as well as future appointments. Despite such opposition, however, the bill became law.

On June 7, 1965, Senator J. Wesley Stambaugh, an Alberta Liberal and senator since 1949, resigned his seat, becoming the first senator to honour the new retirement age. In a letter to Governor-General Georges Vanier, Stambaugh, the son of a Methodist minister, wrote, "I first advocated it [retirement at age seventy-five] before the national Liberal federation 17 years ago, and I have repeated it time and again in the Senate. I'm quite happy to be the first to retire. I'm practicing what I preached." Senators seventy-five and over had until June 1, 1966, to either accept the pension or stay on in the upper chamber. Twelve took the pension. Twenty-three stayed on.

The mandatory retirement rule quickly began to have a dramatic impact on the age of newly appointed senators. Pearson named ten lucky winners on March 4, 1966, the youngest being thirty-nine-year-old party operative Keith Davey, one of the more prominent senators in the upper chamber's history. Of the others named that day, five were in their forties and three in their early or mid-fifties. The only man over fifty-six – an age that was considered young for the job at the time – was former University of British Columbia president Dr. Norman A. MacKenzie. He was seventy-two. His other distinction was that he was the only one of the ten without direct Liberal Party ties.

In keeping with the traditional notion of the Senate as a handy repository for disgraced cabinet ministers, Pearson on April 7, 1967, named forty-nine-year-old Maurice Lamontagne to the upper chamber. Lamontagne, who at one time was seen as prime ministerial material, was Pearson's senior economic adviser from 1957 to 1962. He failed twice (in 1958 and 1962) to win the hitherto safe Liberal seat of Quebec East, but finally won in Montreal's Outremont-St. Jean in 1963. This was the seat that Romauld Bourque had vacated for him in return for Bourque's sinecure in the Senate. Lamontagne immediately became president of the Privy Council and then secretary of state, but was shamed into resigning from the cabinet in 1965 after news broke that he and another minister had bought thousands of dollars' worth of furniture from an upscale Montreal firm headed by two brothers, Max and Adolph Sefkind, without paying anything for it at the time. The firms later went bankrupt and Lamontagne's sweetheart deal was discovered during an investigation by police into a suspected mob-controlled bankruptcy scam.

Lamontagne was appointed to the Senate along with former Ontario Liberal leader Andrew Thompson, who would go on to make his own special mark on the upper chamber as the first senator ever booted out for poor attendance.

For his part, Pearson wanted to go out the way he came in, rewarding his friends to the last. Just in case there weren't already enough businessmen in the Senate, Pearson named two more three days before he left office in April 1968: William Petten of St. John's, Newfoundland, a customs broker and businessman, and Raymond Eudes, a lawyer and businessman who represented the Montreal area of Hochelaga in the Commons for the Liberals from 1940 until his retirement in 1965. That left Pearson's successor, Pierre Trudeau, to inherit a healthy majority in the Senate, with sixty-five Liberals compared to twenty-nine Tories, two independents, and a single independent Liberal, the vast majority of them, both Liberals and Tories, boasting of major corporate directorships. In 1969, the Senate banking committee approved amendments to government legislation to limit the ability of investment companies from competing with the chartered banks, all of which were represented by senator/directors on the committee. In 1971, a joint Senate-House committee, dominated by Senator Hayden and his corporate shills, spent nearly a year "studying" tax legislation that would have hurt business. The *Montreal Gazette* wrote that the senators "examined proposed income tax legislation and a raft of amendments, none of which were implemented. . . . During the study, the committee served as a forum for business interests that voiced opposition to the government bill." A survey of the 1973 membership of the Senate banking committee showed that its members held more than 130 corporate directorships, several of them with the major banks.

There are many reasons, of course, why particular party loyalists end up in the Senate. One of the more unusual entry fees was paid by long-time Liberal fund-raiser John Godfrey who told authors Robert Fife and John Warren that he won the job by getting drunk at the 1968 Liberal convention and proudly displaying a Trudeau sign. "The bar was full of people supporting Robert Winters or John Turner," said Godfrey, "so it sort of amused me to grab a Trudeau sign to show those buggers that at least one person was supporting Trudeau. My wife was absolutely horrified because she was for 'that nice John Turner.' She wouldn't even go into the bar with me when I was carrying the sign. I was the only person of any prominence in the business community who supported Trudeau at the time." Godfrey, of course, was much more than a hail-fellow-well-met, and turned out to be a hard-working and effective senator. At the time of his appointment, he was a senior partner in the prominent Toronto law firm of Campbell, Godfrey and Lewtas and was president of the United Accumulative Fund Ltd. and director of several other firms, including Montreal Trust Co., Canadian Admiral Corp. Ltd., United Investment Life Assurance Co. and Trans-Border Pipeline Co. Ltd.

Perhaps Trudeau's most bizarre Senate appointment came in October 1970 when he named teamsters' union boss Ed Lawson, an independent, who became labour's only senator. Lawson, head of the Canadian teamsters' union and a vice-president of the International

Brotherhood of Teamsters, had odd tastes for a union man: he seemed to enjoy hobnobbing with the high and mighty. In December 1981, for example, he waxed eloquently about enjoying a chat and a jellybean with U.S. president Ronald Reagan in Washington. His other oddity was that he liked Liberals, particularly Trudeau. In 1976, he was the only major labour voice backing Ottawa's wage guidelines. Critics noted at the time that Lawson himself had received a twenty-five per cent pay increase. In April 1982 he told the newly formed Canadian Federation of Labour it should offer a ten-year no-strike guarantee to get more major projects started. That's because Trudeau had said trade unions had failed to gain more influence in economic decision-making because they couldn't "deliver" their membership. Lawson said the labour movement should take "the challenge" seriously.

In July 1983, a dissident U.S. group called the Teamsters for a Democratic Union called the previously secret, six-figure salaries of sixty-five Teamsters leaders "shameful" and "completely out of line" with the current worker restraint. High on the list was Lawson, who was paid $147,956 (U.S.), not counting his senator's pay of $50,300 and an $8,200 tax-free expense allowance, making him by far the highest-paid union official in Canada. By comparison, Canada's second highest-paid union leader was Canadian Labour Congress president Dennis McDermott, who earned $74,058 Canadian in 1984, while secretary-treasurer Shirley Carr and two other senior CLC officers earned $67,326. Robert White, international vice-president and Canadian director of the 100,000-strong United Auto Workers, made a relatively paltry $64,261, while Jeff Rose, president of the 300,000-member Canadian Union of Public Employees, was paid $63,000.

Lawson made national headlines in November 1983 when he shocked the prestigious Canada Tomorrow high-technology conference, a three-day $650,000 federal seminar, with an off-colour luncheon speech. Instead of addressing the international gathering of thinkers, policy makers, and futurists on the impact of technological change on labour, Lawson delivered a string of tawdry jokes.

Lawson listed his own "Academy Awards" for fictitious movies, including one to Trudeau's estranged wife, Margaret, for supposedly turning her back on the limelight to "open up a half-way house for girls who won't go all the way." Another featured Liberal Party president Iona Campagnolo for her portrayal as a women's crusader and winning access to male locker rooms only to discover that "all men are not created equal." And he closed with a joke that cast British prime minister Margaret Thatcher in the role of deciding a Falklands War veteran's pension on the basis of the distance between two private parts of the male anatomy. Science Minister Don Johnson, the conference chairman, who had introduced Lawson, sat with his head in his hands for most of the speech. Lawson apologized the next day, admitting he might have "gone too far."

An editorial in the *Windsor Star* said Lawson's jokes "were dirty, offensive, and in extremely bad taste." Coming as they did just a few months after Nova Scotia senator Richard Donahoe was overheard making a casual slur against native Indians, the newspaper concluded, "Nobody expects much of the Senate. But surely Canadians have a right to expect more than this."

Well, they haven't received much more from Lawson. His attendance has been consistently poor, and for the longest time he refused to sit on any of the Senate's seventeen committees. In his first sixteen years in the Senate, Lawson missed 1,111 of 1,379 sittings. In 1987, he attended just twenty-two of the Senate's ninety-one sittings. Between 1970 and 1984, Canadian Press estimated Lawson averaged $1,673 per sitting. In 1988 the *Ottawa Citizen* reported that Lawson had attended fewer than half the sittings during the current session but had avoided fines after claiming twenty-four public days (that is, ostensibly devoted to public business). Lawson failed to return calls about his attendance and his office refused to reveal the nature of his public business. At one point, Senator John Godfrey devised what he called "the Lawson amendment," to increase penalties for non-attendance. Conservative senator Duff Roblin, a former Manitoba premier and, like Godfrey, another big business representative, said of Lawson's lack of attendance that "when you consider that senators are not elected, they're appointed, and that therefore they're really responsible to nobody, it behooves them to attend, does it not? That's the least they can do."

In July 1985, *Toronto Star* labour reporter John Deverell revealed that top Teamsters, including Lawson, who was expressing shock and anger in the wake of a major kickback and corruption scandal in Local 419 of the union's Toronto warehouse affiliate, knew about the scheme in advance. In the fall of 1982, Local 419 president Sean Floyd pleaded guilty to criminal charges in connection with the theft of goods worth $200,000 from a warehouse whose workers the union represented. He was sentenced to six months in Toronto (Don) Jail, but was allowed day parole, enabling him to stay in control of the union and draw his salary of about $800 a week. The *Star* revealed documents that showed Lawson had asked Flood to resign after he had admitted guilt, but when Flood refused, Lawson did not use his power to have the local put under trusteeship and remove Flood from office. Deverell wrote, "Lawson had always insisted that Teamsters corruption and criminality stopped at the U.S. border. He has claimed that the union's Canadian operations – however secretive and dictatorial – were clean." Yet despite knowing that Flood was involved in theft, Lawson and other senior officials did nothing to set the record straight for the rank and file when Flood ran for a second term as head of the local and won. Lawson did not move to put the local under trusteeship until after Deverell's story had appeared. He said in a news conference – which featured shouting matches with reporters – that "my primary concern is for the membership of [Local] 419 that have been cheated and robbed of the right to decent representation by their trade union." Lawson blamed Ontario Teamsters' boss Charles Thibault for protecting Flood and not taking action against him earlier. A subsequent *Globe and Mail* story said Lawson was paid more than $300,000 in 1984 according to the Teamsters for a Democratic Union. They used U.S. Labor Department data to compile the list, but conceded they couldn't be positive about additional union salaries Lawson received from the union in Canada because, unlike in the United States, there were no Canadian laws compelling disclosure. Lawson hotly denied the story.

In April 1986, the high-flying Lawson, who had a fondness for pinkie rings, Cadillacs, white wine, and fine clothing, was trounced in a union election in his home local by reformer Diana Kilmury, a well-known Teamsters' reformer and truck driver, who polled 1,243 votes compared to Lawson's 803. "What rank-and-file member of a union who has been out of work for three years or more is going to support some guy who is flying around all over the place in his own private jet airplane?" asked Kilmury. Lawson had also raised horses and was an above-average golfer. It was the first time in ten years Lawson had to face the membership in a ballot fight. Eleven delegate positions were open for the union's international convention in Las Vegas the next month, and Lawson finished seventeenth in a field of thirty-one candidates. It meant Lawson couldn't participate fully as a delegate to the convention and was not entitled to vote, but he was reappointed by the union brass anyway.

Lawson was in hot water again in June 1988 when the Teamsters leaders were described in a U.S. government civil suit as having made a "devil's pact" with the Mafia. Lawson was named as a defendant in the civil-racketeering suit. U.S. Attorney Rudolph Giuliani, now the mayor of New York City, had asked a federal judge to remove from office any Teamsters officer found to have violated federal racketeering laws. Lawson called the action a smear against Canadian Teamsters because "nothing has ever been proved in a Canadian court against our union." He added that it "raises serious jurisdictional questions as to whether U.S. law can extend its tentacles into Canada." Five weeks later, Lawson was ousted as the union's Canadian director and was replaced by Montreal's Louis Lacroix, head of Local 1999, although he retained his position as international vice-president and his right to sit on the union's eighteen-member executive board. Lawson, who had held the job for twelve years and still had three years remaining in his current term, said he was "very angry" at being fired. "It's not the kind of thing you'd expect a trade union to do." He lost his jet and a large chunk of his salary. In 1989, Lawson made an agreement with the U.S. government to support its effort against corruption in the Teamsters union in return for having his name dropped from the civil suit.

In February 1990, the *Globe and Mail* reported that Lawson's name had surfaced as a director of Boston Financial Group Inc., a comatose company whose share price climbed to $1.30 from ten cents in twenty trading days around the time he joined the board. Spread over about five million shares, that put a theoretical market value of more than $6.5 million on a company whose last published financial report showed assets of $23. The company, which has no connection to Boston, traded on the Alberta Stock Exchange and at one time ran a string of second-hand stores in the Vancouver area. In a brief interview with the *Globe* earlier that month, Lawson disclaimed any association with the firm before November. But his wife had been president since its birth in 1986, and their waterfront condominium in Vancouver served as company headquarters during much of 1989.

In June 1988, Lawson filed a lawsuit against Preston Manning and the Reform Party for putting him on their Web site list of the Senate's ten worst scandals. Reform said he gave slain stock promoter David Ward, who was connected to Boston Financial, rides on his Teamsters jet in return for equities. When Reform's statement of defence claimed a report of the "theft by conversion" had appeared in *B.C. Business* magazine, Lawson demanded publisher Peter Legge apologize and pay $10,000. Legge apologized and paid $5,000, which Lawson gave to the Vancouver Police Foundation Joe Cohen bursary fund. He joins Alberta Conservative senator Ron Ghitter, who is also suing Reform. In November 1988, Lawson told a cheering Senate that taxpayers should pay the cost of his and Ghitter's lawsuits to help defend the reputation of the beleaguered Red Chamber, in the same way they pay the costs for members of the Commons. Ghitter said later that Lawson's comments caught him off guard and he wasn't sure he supported the move.

As for Reform, spokesman Jim Armour said the party is covering its own legal fees. "If this is part of the Senate's public-relations campaign, you would think they could come up with better representation than Lawson and company," he said.

Nobody in the country packed more political punch during the 1960s and 1970s than Senator Keith Davey, the silver-haired, stoop-shouldered former advertising executive turned political pro. Like many senators before and since, Davey used his publicly financed sinecure more in the interest of the party than of the people. "Only in the senate could Keith Davey be a politician without having to be a legislator," wrote Larry Zolf. "Only in the senate could he work full-time and be fully paid by the taxpayers of Canada as the Liberal party's campaign director." But he did it so damn well.

Davey, an eternal optimist, baseball enthusiast, and for fifty-four days commissioner of the Canadian Football League, was at first resented by Trudeau. He spent the first term of Trudeau's regime on the outside looking in. Trudeau relied instead on such Quebec friends as Marc Lalonde, Gérard Pelletier, Michael Pitfield, and Jacques Hébert, but when he nearly blew his huge majority from 1968 and squeaked in with the teeniest minority in Canadian history in 1972 – defeating Bob Stanfield's Tories by two seats – the call once again went out to the old pro and his sidekick Jim Coutts to turn things around. For years, Davey took pride in a photo of Trudeau inscribed after the Davey-run 1974 election victory in which the Liberals regained their majority: "To Keith Davey, who made the sun shine. With a thousand thanks." Davey co-chaired that campaign along with Senator Gil Molgat and Transport Minister Jean Marchand, who would also become a senator.

At the 1957 Liberal leadership convention, Davey, already a veteran political organizer, had emerged as a key player in Lester Pearson's winning team and a charter member of the much-heralded Cell 13, a group of thirteen high-powered Toronto Liberals who helped guide Pearson to victory. As a reward, Pearson named Davey,

Daniel Lang, Andrew Thompson, and Richard Stanbury to the Senate. Trudeau appointed another member of the group, Royce Frith. In 1961, Davey was named national director of the party. A *Toronto Star* column the next day began, "Poor Keith Davey, Gone and lost, never to be seen again!" One of his first tasks was to go to Montreal to help twist the arm of a bright young lawyer whom Pearson felt had great political potential, a man named John Turner.

The closest Davey ever came to a personal scandal was in 1964 when Girard Girouard, MP for Labelle, publicly accused Davey of offering him a bribe to join the Liberals. Girouard, elected as a member of the Social Credit Party, joined the Tories instead. Davey denied he had offered the man a fat campaign fund to join the Grits, although he did admit to meeting with Girouard and four Liberal MPs in a hotel grill in Hull, Quebec. A Commons committee, reviewing the charges, made parliamentary electronic history when for the first time a tape recorder replaced high-speed shorthand reporters to record the testimony, but ultimately found "no evidence of bribery or attempted bribery." Girouard insisted that Davey had offered a large campaign fund for him to join the Liberals, but had testified he thought of it as an "inducement" or "temptation," not a "bribe." He called it a "gross personal calumny" for Davey to have called him a "Liberal reject."

Davey's most recognized non-partisan accomplishment was his Special Senate Committee on Mass Media, which reported in 1970 that Canadian newspapers were in danger of being dominated by a few owners. The report led to some legislative changes in the magazine industry, but had little real impact on newspapers other than serving as a reminder, looking back, that his predictions on the concentration of media ownership have come true. Davey likes to say, "I told you so." In 1970, sixty per cent of Canadian newspapers were owned by groups. Today, nearly all of them are. Then again, a big part of that stems from Davey-type, small "l" liberal policies restricting foreign ownership, supposedly to protect Canadian identity, but in reality restricting the competition and making newspapers ripe for the picking.

When Turner inherited the party from Trudeau, Davey at first was out of the loop. But in a desperate bid to turn his campaign around, Turner turned to Davey in mid-campaign for help. But it was too late, even for the man named "The Rainmaker" for his remarkable abilities to make anything happen. He retired from the Senate in 1996, one of the most able and best-liked people ever to grace the place.

Still, nobody's perfect, and Davey was a key player in one of the crassest exercises of political manipulation in Canadian history. And he lost. So too did his wunderkind protégé, Jim Coutts, the prime ministerial aide who had never been elected to anything (he lost an earlier election attempt in Alberta) but had visions of being the next prime minister. Davey & Co. decided that the downtown Toronto riding of Spadina would be a perfect launching pad for his grand ambitions.

It had been less than a year since Trudeau had made his miraculous return from the political dead to defeat Joe Clark and utter his famous election night victory line: "Welcome to the 1980s." And Spadina was about as safe a Liberal riding as you could find in English Canada, witnessed by the fact that the voters had elected the lacklustre Peter Stollery in 1972 and repeated the deed again in 1974, 1979, and 1980. Stollery, whose father owned an upscale haberdashery at the prestigious downtown Toronto corner of Yonge and Bloor, spent much of his youth in Bohemian pursuits, hanging around avante-garde bistros with painters and musicians or travelling around the world in sandals, shorts, and a T-shirt. Sometimes, as an MP, he moonlighted as a cabbie, to get closer to the people, he says. If Stollery could get elected in Spadina, the thinking went, what Liberal couldn't?

The problem was: what to do with Stollery to make room for Coutts? Stollery was first offered the chairmanship of the International Joint Commission but that didn't appeal. He was then offered the post of Canadian ambassador to Sweden – three times – turning it down every time. Finally, Stollery countered with an offer to Davey: he'd give up Spadina for a Senate seat. After some haggling, it was done. All of this was too much even for traditional

Liberal voters, and Coutts was defeated in the subsequent by-election by, of all people, Dan Heap, a surly Anglican priest running for the New Democrats. As for Stollery, the senator from Yonge and Bloor as he calls himself, he still has eleven more years to enjoy the spoils of Coutts's defeat at the expense of Canadian taxpayers. Perhaps his most memorable quote came in 1984 when he said, "The Senate can be boring too. But when it gets bad I can go off and do other things . . . or I can just go home."

During the 1970s, the Senate was so overwhelmingly Liberal that Trudeau felt compelled to appoint the odd Tory. In 1978, for example, he named former Conservative premier Duff Roblin and veteran Newfoundland Conservative MP Jack Marshall, who used his Senate seat effectively as an outspoken champion of veterans' rights. Trudeau also appointed Tory MP Claude Wagner, a former Liberal who finished second to Joe Clark in the 1976 Conservative leadership race. Wagner resigned his seat in the Commons and became a senator the same day. The Liberals hoped that with Wagner out of the way, the Liberal stood a better chance of winning his Quebec riding than the Tories did.

It had been four years since Trudeau swept back into power, but by this time he had fallen from the heights of Trudeaumania to the depths of Trudeauphobia. His party had disappeared from the charts in public opinion polling and he was under increasing pressure to call an election. The longer he waited, the worse it got.

In these circumstances, the Liberals were desperate for anything they could either protect for their own or, better still, snatch from the Tories. In early 1979, Allan MacEachen, the Celtic Sphinx from Cape Breton, dispatched veteran aide Neil McNeil to check into the Nova Scotia riding of Cape Breton-The Sydneys, where Conservative Bob Muir – called "Birthday Bob" for his penchant for sending every constituent a birthday card every year – had easily held the seat since 1957. MacEachen and the Liberals wanted to know how best to assist their up-and-coming young candidate, Russell MacClellan, who had no chance of defeating Muir. And so it was that two days before the election writs were issued, Trudeau invited Muir to join the Senate. Muir accepted; the Tories, without a candidate, were in disarray; and Cape Breton-The Sydneys went Liberal. It didn't help Trudeau defeat Joe Clark, however, as the Tories won a minority (only to lose it nine months later) but it began a career for MacClellan, who, after holding that seat until 1998, went back home to Nova Scotia where he was briefly (until July 1999) the province's premier.

When Clark unveiled his cabinet on June 4, 1979, he made up for his lack of Quebec representatives by appointing two senators from that province – Jacques Flynn as justice minister and leader of the government in the Senate, and Martial Asselin, minister of state for the Canadian International Development Agency – a technique Trudeau would later use to make up for his lack of western MPs. Clark also appointed Ottawa's Robert de Cotret to the Senate, then named him as minister of economic development and trade. In addition, Clark announced that his cabinet was incomplete and he was still scouring Quebec for "contemporary Francophones" to name first as senators and then as ministers.

Flynn had been mines minister in Diefenbaker's government but was defeated in 1962 and then named to the Senate. Asselin also served briefly in Diefenbaker's cabinet before being defeated in 1963. He was re-elected in 1965 and 1968 and named to the Senate by Trudeau in 1972. De Cotret was elected in a 1978 by-election in Ottawa Centre then defeated in the May 1979 general election. He was an economist and former president of the Conference Board of Canada. As for Trudeau, he promised that he would not press the seventy-one Liberal senators to use their huge majority in the upper chamber to vote against Conservative legislation passed in the Commons. In September, Clark rewarded Lowell Murray, chairman of the Tory campaign and a former aide to New Brunswick premier Richard Hatfield, by giving him a seat in the upper chamber along with two more faithful Tories.

Two weeks later, at a cabinet meeting in Quebec City, hoping to raise his party's profile in the predominantly Liberal province, Clark reversed himself and said he would not be appointing more senators to his cabinet after all. "My intention is to have future cabinet appointments from the House of Commons." In late September, Clark appointed three more senators, including chief Quebec fund-raiser Guy Charbonneau, who would play a key role in undermining Clark's leadership, paving the way for Brian Mulroney, and Arthur Tremblay, a strong Quebec nationalist and a father of the Liberal Quiet Revolution in that province. He agreed, however, to sit as a Conservative in the Senate. In just nine months, Clark managed to lard ten loyal Tories into the Senate, not bad for a guy who spent so much time in opposition attacking Trudeau for his partisan appointments.

Clark had also managed to fire Michael Pitfield, a close friend and senior adviser to Trudeau, who had been the highly politicized clerk of the Privy Council, the top bureaucratic job in Ottawa, making him the first top dog ever sacked by a prime minister. When Trudeau returned, so did Pitfield, summoned back from Harvard University. Trudeau also plucked Michael Kirby from the presidency of the Institute for Research on Public Policy in Halifax, to take the job as secretary to cabinet for federal-provincial relations. Both men would soon be headed to the upper chamber. Kirby, who for years was the public voice of the Liberals on various television talk shows, once boasted, "There are five hundred important people in this country and I know every one of them on a first-name basis." No humility there.

In their classic book *Trudeau and Our Times, Volume 1: The Magnificent Obsession*, authors Stephen Clarkson and Christina McCall wrote this about Kirby:

"Kirby unabashedly called himself 'Trudeau's son of a bitch.' Whereas [former Privy Council Office chief Gordon] Robertson had been trained to respect due process, Kirby's preference was to short-circuit them. . . . Kirby cared not a whit about proper procedure or how he treated people. Today's friend might be tomorrow's enemy. . . . Either was manipulable in the interests of achieving the prime minister's immediate goals." Kirby, who would spend much of his time working for pollster Martin Goldfarb and building up his own corporate directorships, was for a time one of Trudeau's most powerful advisers, particularly given the prime minister's obsession with Quebec and things constitutional. During the debates over the patriation of the Constitution, Kirby, as Trudeau's top point man, earned the nickname of the "dimpled Machiavelli," a sobriquet that speaks for itself.

Kirby was raised in Montreal, the son of an Anglican clergyman, although he tends to boast of his connections to Newfoundland – he's a fifth-generation descendant of an outport fisherman. He has a Ph.D. in mathematics from Chicago's Northwestern University and has taught at the university level in both Chicago and Halifax, and spent several years as an adviser to former Nova Scotia premier Gerald Regan.

When John Turner took over the leadership, Kirby was put in charge of running the party's federal election machine. A 1987 interview with Ross Howard of the *Globe and Mail* demonstrates one of the constant complaints people make about senators playing partisan politics at public expense. Some Liberals were criticizing Kirby for not being ready to fight the upcoming election, but Kirby said he was close to setting up the party's campaign advertising "structure" – organized around Red Leaf Agency, which Howard accurately described as "a shell company the party revives to house generous-minded advertising agencies during the campaign." For years, Red Leaf had been run by another senator, ad-man Jerahmiel Grafstein. The Tories, of course, were doing the same thing. It didn't take a genius to figure out what long-time political organizer Norman Atkins was doing in the Senate, not to mention Nova Scotian Finlay MacDonald or any number of senators, past and present, who, like Keith Davey, were there primarily to serve the partisan interests of their masters without so much as a nod to the propriety of the exercise. Like many senators secure in the knowledge that they hold considerable influence over the ultimate fate of Senate reform, Kirby, a recipient of a partisan gift, advocates an elected Senate and says he would be a candidate.

Of the eighty-one people Trudeau handed first-class passage to patronage paradise during his years in office, none caused more controversy than that of Pitfield in late 1982.

On December 22, on the last day of the parliamentary session before the Christmas break, the Commons approved a motion, passed by the Senate the day before, to set up a joint Senate-Commons committee to study reform of the Upper House and report back in a year.

That same day, however, Trudeau set off a firestorm by announcing that his old friend and right-hand man, Michael Pitfield, forty-five, a lawyer and university lecturer who had just stepped down as Privy Council clerk, was now a senator and would sit as an independent.

In theory, at least, the head of the civil service has traditionally been non-partisan. Pitfield's relationship with Trudeau, however, was highly partisan and personal. The two men went on private holidays together. In the mid-sixties, Pitfield, the youngest of seven children in a wealthy Westmount family, was a member of a small group of Quebec intellectuals organized by Marc Lalonde to debate Quebec affairs. This group, including Pitfield, was instrumental in encouraging Trudeau to first run for elected office and then go after the Liberal leadership. Peter C. Newman once described Pitfield as "the most formidable intellect to come to Ottawa in a generation," although others who worked closely with him argued that Trudeau was the brilliant one while Pitfield, in some respects, was benefiting simply by being in the great man's shadow. Both Lalonde and Pitfield were working as advisers for Lester Pearson when they joined a committee to review Quebec's controversial foreign policy in the wake of

Charles de Gaulle's infamous "Vive le Quebec Libre!" speech in Quebec City. The committee was chaired by Trudeau, and when Trudeau became prime minister he immediately made Pitfield deputy clerk in the Privy Council Office. Pitfield was the key player in the reorganization of the cabinet committee system that was supposed to streamline government work but ended up making policy decisions even more remote from the public, a factor in Trudeau's fall from grace during his first term.

Pitfield's mother came from a wealthy Quebec family and his father, who died when Pitfield was two years old, had struck it rich by founding Pitfield, Mackay Ross Ltd., which became one of Canada's largest brokerage houses. Journalist Judy Steed once described the young Pitfield as having "the aura of the Quebec, Anglo-elite in which he was raised, where they rode to hounds and played polo and controlled the economic wealth of the province." Through his mother, he is a relative of the Molson beer barons and the Prices, pulp-and-paper tycoons. His father was a business associate of Izaak Walton Killam and Lord Beaverbrook. Michael Pitfield was reputed to be antagonistic toward big business, opting for public service instead, but in 1984 he joined the board of directors of Cadillac Fairview Corp. Ltd., the Bronfman-owned Toronto real estate firm whose board chairman at the time was his senate colleague Leo Kolber. Pitfield said it was the first directorship of a public company he had accepted. It wouldn't be the last.

On the day he was appointed to the upper chamber, Tory leader Joe Clark – who should know, given his own experience – denounced it as "a partisan appointment." NDP leader Ed Broadbent said it "made a mockery of Senate reform," a topic that had been the subject of debate that very day.

Trudeau had tried to deflect some of the heat by appointing a big-name Tory operative to the Senate along with Pitfield, Ontario Big Blue Machine bagman Bill Kelly. This was in payment to then Ontario premier Bill Davis, Kelly's boss and close friend at the time – although they aren't speaking now – in return for Davis's undying support of Trudeau's constitutional initiatives. The wealthy Kelly, a former Consumers' Gas Co. executive and marina owner, was reputedly a ruthless and highly effective fund-raiser. His reputation may have been inflated, however, because when Kelly left, the Ontario Tories, who had been in power since 1943, found themselves with not much money in the till and many bills unpaid. Indeed, during the ongoing controversy over Pitfield's appointment, Kelly, safely ensconced in his own seat, was one of the few people who came rushing to Pitfield's defence, calling the attacks on Trudeau's close friend "cynical criticism." He said Pitfield's appointment "can only benefit the Senate. . . . He's a very, very able man."

Indeed, he is. And Pitfield's best work came a year later when he chaired a special Senate committee on Canada's internal security measures and expertly dissected a proposed Liberal spy agency bill, recommending it should be a civilian agency separated from the RCMP. Pitfield ended up recommending dozens of amendments to the government bill, nearly all of which were ultimately accepted, one of the rare instances where Senate committee work actually made a significant difference to government policy. Senate supporters constantly boast that their best work is done in committee, where senators have more time than the elected politicians to delve into issues. It's true they generally do take more time to study issues, and few bills pass through the Senate without some amendments being made. But overall, the history of special Senate committees has been that after the initial splash of publicity upon their release, Senate reports usually end up on a shelf in the Parliamentary Library.

A final word on Pitfield. At the time of his 1982 Christmas present from Trudeau, the *Toronto Star* hired an actuary to figure out what Pitfield's annual pension would be if he stayed there for thirty years until reaching the mandatory retirement age of seventy-five. His pension as a former civil servant and a senator, they estimated, would be about $368,000 a year. Since that time, of course, the Senate pay and pension benefits have increased. And yes, Pitfield remains a senator, although to his credit, he is one of the few who, despite suffering a debilitating illness that keeps him away from the Senate at times, pays the fines for his absences without complaint.

Just as Clark had little representation in Quebec when he won in 1979 and had to turn to the Senate for most of his Quebec ministers, so Trudeau faced a similar situation from 1980 on in trying to fill the western component of his cabinet. Jack Austin ended up being his sole cabinet representative in British Columbia after 1983 when Trudeau dumped former MP and B.C. Liberal leader Ray Perrault. Perrault, known as Senator Phogbound after the cartoon character in the Pogo cartoon strip, screamed bloody murder at the time, saying British Columbia had to have two ministers, not one. There was the small matter, however, of an alleged conflict of interest concerning Perrault who, as sports minister, created the sports pool lottery and, as a private promoter, was active in trying to get a baseball franchise for Vancouver. Professional baseball vehemently opposes lotteries of this type fearing they open the game up to gambling and may potentially lead to the corruption of players and the game itself.

As for Austin, he had never been elected to anything, and in fact was soundly rejected by B.C. voters when he ran for office. But never mind what the people think, Austin enjoyed the heady credential of having served as Master Trudeau's principal secretary. During the 1960s, as a lawyer specializing in international and commercial law, Austin had represented several western resource companies before going into business as a mining promoter himself in 1969. He had also served two years as executive assistant to Arthur Laing, then minister of northern affairs and natural resources. His appointment in 1970 as deputy minister of energy in Ottawa caused a stir as critics worried about conflicts of interest, but Trudeau said the appointment reflected "the government's desire to encourage leading men in industry and business to enter the government service." During his stint as deputy minister, Austin claims he came up with the idea of Petro-Canada. He joined Trudeau in 1974 as his chief political aide.

Because of his bloody-minded love of backroom wheeling and dealing, Austin has been credited with the classic Ottawa quip: "You can't be a virgin and have experience."

Perhaps not, but he had hoped to experience the joys of being Petro-Canada president when on August 19, 1975, Trudeau stuck him into the Senate instead, prompting veteran New Democrat Stanley Knowles to exclaim, "The prime minister is out of his mind." Knowles may have been right, because three days later Austin was named in a British Columbia Supreme Court suit alleging that he failed to deliver common shares of stocks in two companies. Nothing was ever proved against Austin, but a variety of accusations about his business and personal conduct did not exactly make him a hot political commodity. He had to bide his time in the upper chamber, which isn't the worst place to pick up high returns for low investments, until Trudeau turned to him as B.C. cabinet timber after the Liberals were completely smoked in British Columbia in the 1980 election.

At one point, Trudeau had four western-based senators in his cabinet. Besides Austin and Flynn, he named two CCF turncoats – Bud Olson in Alberta and Hazen Argue in Saskatchewan. Austin served as the minister responsible for the Canada Development Corporation, his own brainchild, which ended up costing Canadian taxpayers billions of dollars in propping up various Crown corporations, particularly Canadair and de Havilland. Later he was minister of state for social development, another department that fed his penchant for spending gobs of public money. Austin fell into another controversy in 1981 when he admitted that Canada did indeed enter a price "arrangement" with other uranium-producing countries when he was deputy minister of energy, mines, and resources in the early 1970s. The decision to join the cartel, which sparked a U.S. House of Representatives investigation, helped drive up the price of uranium ore around the world, dramatically increasing the cost of fuel for nuclear power plants.

When John Turner became prime minister in 1984, he booted Austin out of the cabinet. Mind you, Austin didn't suffer. Nor did his senatorial duties interfere with his 1985 appointment as president of the international division of the Bank of British Columbia, where board chairman Edgar Kaiser Jr. announced that "in addition to his Senate responsibilities, Senator Austin will be working to help Canada's Western Bank increase its activities in the bank's Hong Kong and London operations." Austin, who doesn't have to retire until 2007, has maintained his close ties with Trudeau, his major benefactor. In May 1996, Austin was the organizing chairman of a select group of twenty-five powerful insiders from around the world, called the InterAction Council, which is limited to former heads of state. When it met for four days at the Pan Pacific Hotel in Vancouver, guests included former French president Valéry Giscard d'Estaing, former German chancellor Helmut Schmidt, Poland's Lech Walesa, and former Chinese vice-premier Wu Xuegian. Trudeau chaired the meetings. They were not open to the public, Austin explained, "to allow the maximum amount of frankness and candour."

One of the weirdest and least-publicized results of Trudeau's surprise return as prime minister in 1980 – which came after he'd announced he was stepping down – was that between 1980 and 1982, Canada's main representative abroad was Senate Speaker Jean Marchand, the undiplomatic diplomat who once, over a glass or three, told the King of Morocco to "fuck off."

The problem was money. Clark became prime minister in June 1979, but when John Crosbie finally delivered his government's budget, it was defeated and an election ensued. When Trudeau returned in March 1980, the Liberals delivered an economic statement, but not a full-fledged budget. In essence, Canada went almost two years without a real budget, making spending tight, and diplomatic missions weren't exactly at the top of the list. What's more, foreign politics itself underwent a dramatic change when Ronald Reagan replaced Jimmy Carter. Carter had fallen into the habit of showing his disdain for many dictatorial regimes by sending an "ambassador in place" to represent the United States. Canada was happy to follow suit because it was cheap. Reagan, however, operated on the principle that the enemy of his enemy was his friend and decided to make a big show of American influence around the world. And so it was that his vice-president, George Bush, and a host of other senior officials – followed by a huge press corps – were constantly loading themselves onto Air Force One and charging off to the far-flung corners of the universe, where these major international events are extremely significant to the psyche and self-importance of the host countries.

The foreign affairs bureaucrats were in a complete frenzy, insisting that Canada, if it wanted to be an international player at all, had to be represented on the diplomatic circuit. But by whom? Canada already had a backlog of official visits that it owed various international leaders. The governor-general wasn't interested in travelling, nor was Trudeau at that time, although he became a world traveller three years later.

Marchand, as Senate Speaker, was on Canada's fourth level of protocol and also had a serious drinking problem. But since his Senate duties weren't exactly onerous, and he was one of Trudeau's closest personal and political friends – at his funeral years later, Trudeau said Marchand was "like a brother" to him – it seemed like a temporary solution to a vexing problem.

So off he went, often with his assistant Gordon Lovelace in tow. For the first several months both of them used their own VISA cards to pay for expenses. No private jets for them. On one trip to Togo for an international conference, they flew Air Canada to Paris then picked up a tourist charter flight from Marseilles that was jammed with drunken French tourists who hooted at the Canadian delegation because the plane had to be diverted to let them off at Togo. There was more than a little pathos in the spectacle of our two world-weary representatives lugging their baggage across a tarmac lined with expensive private jets, most of them owned by tinpot tyrants, many of which had been purchased with Canadian aid money. They had no hotel room, having been bounced because they had no money to pay the expected bribes, and ended up in a shabby hotel on the outskirts of town.

When the Three Wisemen – Marchand, Trudeau, and Gérard Pelletier – first emerged from Quebec, Marchand was considered the heavy hitter. The other two were relative unknowns. Marchand, a fiery public speaker, began his career in 1947 as a labour leader, who almost single-handedly transformed the low-key Catholic trade union federation into the aggressive Confederation of National Trade Unions and played a key role in Quebec's Quiet Revolution. Federalism itself was taking a real hit during the 1960s and the Liberals needed him badly. He agreed to help, but insisted on bringing Pelletier and Trudeau with him. It was Marchand who was expected to go after the leadership when Pearson stepped down. Pearson put Marchand into his cabinet almost immediately in 1965 as citizenship and immigration minister. In 1967 he took on added responsibilities as Pearson's Quebec lieutenant and manpower minister. But over dinner with Pelletier and Trudeau at Montreal's Café Martin in early 1968, Marchand told his two dearest friends that he wouldn't seek the leadership and that Trudeau would be a better choice. Without that endorsement, Trudeau would not have sought the job, at least not in 1968. Marchand resigned as leader of the Quebec wing of the party in March 1968 and announced he was backing Trudeau, then justice minister in Pearson's cabinet.

Marchand served in a host of senior cabinet positions for Trudeau, including the job of Quebec lieutenant, which he quit again in 1975. In August 1975, he was convicted of failing to remain at the scene of an accident, fined $200, and prohibited from driving for one year. In May 1976, the *Toronto Sun* reported that Marchand, environment minister at the time, had conveniently had his suspension lifted by the parole board. In the Commons, then solicitor-general Warren Allmand denied charges that he used his influence in the case. Allmand did admit that Marchand had asked him how he could get his driver's licence reinstated and that he, Allmand, had merely asked for information from parole board chairman William Outerbridge.

A month after that story was published, Marchand resigned from the federal cabinet, citing his disagreement over the government's handling of the bilingual air traffic dispute, but he stayed on as MP for Langelier. In July, Marchand and federal supply minister Jean-Pierre Goyer were charged with slander and libel in separate actions launched in the Ontario Supreme Court. Andrejs Berzins, an assistant Crown attorney in Ottawa, filed a writ against Marchand for saying he had been cheated by Berzins during his trial for leaving the scene of an accident. Marchand had told the *Globe and Mail* that the prosecutor had reneged on a negotiated deal that would mean a fine but no licence suspension. Two years later, Marchand apologized to Berzins. In August 1976, Marchand filed a $25,000 damage suit against Montreal radio station CKAC and commentator Roger Delorme saying they made injurious, defamatory, offensive, and false statements against him.

In October 1976, Marchand left the Commons, ostensibly to crusade for federalism by running in the November Quebec provincial election in the riding of Louis-Hébert against separatist Parti Québécois heavyweight candidate Claude Morin. Trudeau had offered Marchand a Senate seat, but Marchand declined, saying "I'm still alive enough to fight." He lost and, forty-five days after turning down the first offer, accepted Trudeau's new offer of a Senate seat. He entered the upper chamber along with retiring Saskatchewan Liberal leader Dave Steuart. Marchand said he had hesitated because the Senate "had not been my objective," but he took the job because it gave him a chance to remain active. "There are useless senators like there are useless MPs," he said.

In November 1977, Marchand had his driver's licence suspended again, this time for nine months, and was fined $300 after pleading guilty to charges of impaired driving and refusing to take a Breathalyzer test. In March 1978, Marchand was implicated in the massive Hamilton and Toronto dredging scandals when the former president of a dredging company testified that a $25,000 payment was made in 1972 to the re-election campaign of Marchand, then federal transport minister, after Ottawa awarded a $2.7-million contract for dredging near Trois-Rivières, Quebec. Marchand told the Senate the next day that he had never intervened in the contract and had never received the $25,000 cheque. Marchand said he wasn't even minister of transport at the time of the dredging scandal, a case in which eleven executives and their nine companies were charged with defrauding the federal and Ontario governments of about $4.2 million. Six weeks later, a copy of a federal Treasury Board document signed by Marchand and authorizing the contract was introduced as Crown evidence at the trial. The topic of the document was "Authority to enter contract." The handwritten words "Original signed by J. Marchand" appeared at the bottom. Horace Rindress, former president of J.A. Porter Co. Ltd. of Montreal, had testified that the contract was awarded after he had asked Jean Simard, a vice-president and director of Richelieu Dredging Corp. Inc., to approach Marchand over the contract. Simard, one of the accused, was convicted on three counts and given a three-year prison term at the end of the longest case ever tried by a Canadian jury.

In August 1979, in the wake of Clark's election victory, Marchand resigned for the third time as president of the Quebec wing of the federal Liberal Party. Three weeks earlier he had attacked "opportunists" who were guilty of "back-stabbing" and "foul play," saying he would stay on to fight them. In March 1980, after the Liberals defeated the Clark Tories, Trudeau named Marchand as Speaker of the Senate, replacing Ontario Conservative senator Allister Grosart. In 1983, four days before Marchand's sixty-fifth birthday, Trudeau announced that his friend had resigned from the Senate to become chairman of the Canadian Transport Commission. Nova Scotia Tory MP Patrick Nowlan said Marchand's appointment "will destroy the credibility of the transport commission. The trough just isn't big enough for these people."

In July 1988, Marchand was taken to Laval University Hospital Centre in Quebec City suffering broken ribs after falling twenty metres (sixty-five feet) from the roof of his summer cottage at nearby St.-Augustin. He had been painting a pole on the roof when he fell about ten metres, then slid another ten down a steep incline beside the cottage. A passing neighbour found him lying on his back. A month later he was dead. He was sixty-nine. The coroner's office said he died of a ruptured aorta, the main artery leading to the heart, and it was probably unrelated to the fall from the roof.

At his August 31 funeral service at the ornate, centuries-old Quebec Basilica in the heart of the old city, Trudeau said, "He brought me into politics and he made me prime minister. . . . [Marchand] could have been prime minister if he hadn't been so modest. He was the greatest democrat we ever had in this province and had a giant heart that beat only for justice."

There were only two wise men left then, Trudeau and Pelletier, who arrived at the funeral together. Pelletier, the former editor of Montreal's *La Presse*, one-time secretary of state and communications minister for Trudeau and Canada's ambassador to France from 1975 to 1980, died in Montreal on June 22, 1997, leaving Trudeau to walk alone.

Two days earlier, Conservative John M. Macdonald, ninety-one, the dean of the Senate and the last senator appointed for life, died in North Sydney, Nova Scotia.

The Trudeau era ended in 1984 with an obscene outburst of patronage pay-offs to Trudeau's friends and colleagues.

It began December 23, 1983, when Trudeau appointed Ian Sinclair, chairman of Canadian Pacific Enterprises; Charlie Watt, a Quebec Inuit leader; and Leo Kolber, a powerful Montreal businessman, chairman of Cadillac Fairview, and director of several boards, including the Toronto-Dominion Bank and Seagrams.

On January 13, 1984, he appointed five more loyal Liberals: Michael Kirby, then vice-president of Canadian National Railways; Nova Scotian John Stewart, a former Liberal MP and then professor at St. Francis Xavier University; Anne Cools, a social activist and the first black appointed to the Senate; Jerry Grafstein, president of Red Leaf Communications Ltd., the Liberal advertising agency; and Philippe Deane Gigantes, a Greek-born journalist, failed Liberal candidate, and former director of communications for the Liberal Party and its federal caucus.

Eleven days later, Liberal Lorna Marsden, a Liberal Party policy adviser and vice-provost of the University of Toronto, became the ninth new senator named by Trudeau in the past month. Marsden, a sociologist and former president of the National Action Committee on the Status of Women, had been a Liberal vice-president from 1975 to 1980 and chairman of the Liberals' standing committee on policy since 1980, but she laughed off the suggestion that any of this partisan work was a factor in her appointment. "I'm a professor at the University of Toronto and have been for ten years," she said. "And that is, of course, my major interest in life. You may be interested in the politics, of course, but that's what I do as a hobby." During the September election campaign, her "hobby" took her to the Northumberland Liberal Association in Trenton, Ontario, where she told the party faithful that Mulroney's promises of sweeping change would bring "chaos" to Canada should the Tories win. "It won't be change Mulroney brings. . . . It will be an act of terrorism . . . not a government of change but one of old reactionary ideas."

After her appointment, Mulroney, echoing a theme that would help him win that election, said the political pay-offs were, "solving the unemployment problem for the Liberal party. But it's not doing much for the one and one-half million Canadians who are out of work when every other night a couple more Liberals are heaved into the Senate."

The onslaught of patronage appointments even caught the interest of the *New York Times* and the *Christian Science Monitor*. The Ottawa correspondent for the *Times* wrote that nine prizes had just been "awarded including yearly payments of $61,425 until the age of 75, office staff, free postage, free haircuts, free massages, travel allowances, subsidized lunches and tax exemptions. These are not the payoffs in a Canadian lottery; they are the benefits that go with appointments to the Senate." *Monitor* writer Fred Langan wrote, "American Senators just don't have it this good, and they have to deal with such exercises as elections."

On Saturday, June 16, 1984, John Turner defeated Jean Chrétien by five hundred votes on the second ballot to take over the Liberal leadership. The next day, moments before Turner arrived at 24 Sussex Drive to discuss the transition of power scheduled for June 30, Trudeau told reporters that he wanted to fill "some" of the twelve Senate vacancies before he stepped down as prime minister.

On June 29 and again on July 9, Turner, clearing the decks for the September 4 election, announced that a total of twenty-three Liberal MPs had been given Senate seats, judgeships, ambassador-ships, or other plum patronage jobs.

Mulroney branded the appointments as "vulgar" and "scandalous" and said any government he led would choose only high-calibre people for such jobs.

The new senators were Eymard Corbin, MP for the New Brunswick riding of Madawaska-Victoria, Tom Lefebvre from the Quebec riding of Pontiac-Gatineau, and Charles Turner of London East, government whip in the Commons. In an interview in the *London Free Press*, his local paper, Turner said, "I just got my reward." He certainly did. He and almost one-sixth of Trudeau's former Liberal caucus.

It was over this issue during the televised election campaign debate in July that Mulroney scored his famous knock-out punch on Turner, when the struggling Liberal leader tried to explain that he had "no option" because he had to sign an agreement with Trudeau to make the appointments after he became prime minister or else the appointments would have been made before Trudeau left, leaving Turner without a majority in the Commons. Mulroney told him he did have an option. He could have said no. It was the defining moment in the campaign and arguably the most direct political hit in any campaign debate in Canadian history.

In a 1999 interview with me, Turner said, "Christ, Trudeau had already done them [the appointments] before I got there. I was presented with a done deal. If I hadn't agreed to do it, all those guys would have left and I wouldn't have had a majority and the governor-general may not have come to me to form the government.

A real sweetheart, eh?" he said, meaning Trudeau. "So I thought I had no option. Looking back, which is easy to do, I probably would have been better off to refuse and provoked an immediate election. I couldn't have been hurt any more than I was.

"But I underestimated the patronage issue then. Everybody in the party did. That's the way it was always done and we didn't see it as something that would stick," said Turner. "But the guy who profited from it, Mulroney, turned out to be better at it than Trudeau was."

7

THE RED CHAMBER GUERRILLAS

I N HIS *Maclean's* magazine Business Watch column shortly after
the 1984 federal election, Peter C. Newman wrote this of Liberal
leader John Turner and the Liberal-dominated Senate:

"One of the more cruel anomalies of Turner's current situation is
that because of the reduced House of Commons contingent, senators
will play a much more significant role within the Liberal caucus.
They will prevent Turner from dismantling any of the policy initiatives that originated during the Trudeau years. By filling the Senate
with his ideological soul mates, Trudeau has, in effect, perpetuated
his own retroactive government in the Upper House."

Trudeau's Liberal Senate, in fact, would come to dominate
much of the political landscape during the late 1980s and early
1990s in a way no other Senate ever has. But it wouldn't be fighting
Turner's notion of Liberalism as opposed to Trudeau's. Rather, it
would be engaged in prolonged hand-to-hand combat with Brian
Mulroney and his majority Conservative government. The fight
culminated in the 1990 GST battle and Mulroney's controversial

Senate-stacking ploy through an obscure and never-before-used constitutional provision.

Turner, who has long favoured an elected Senate, announced shortly after the 1984 election that the unelected seventy-three Liberal senators – compared to twenty-one Conservatives – would not be held as a club over the heads of Mulroney's elected Tories, who had surpassed Diefenbaker's 1958 sweep to become the largest majority in Canadian history. Indeed, Diefenbaker also faced a predominantly Liberal Senate, but with few exceptions, that Senate managed to respect the tradition that the unelected chamber should bow to the will of the elected one. That was certainly Turner's view. He reminded everyone, including his own Liberal senators, that the Commons "is the chamber elected by the Canadian people with a massive majority and . . . the government has the confidence of the Canadian people."

Turner didn't count on the Celtic Sphinx.

Invariably described as wily by every journalist who mentioned him, the bloody-minded Cape Bretoner Allan MacEachen was also recognized as the most tendentiously partisan zealot in Ottawa. He too had seen the enemy, but unlike the cartoon character Pogo, it was not himself he saw, but anybody who was not a Liberal. As Liberal leader in the Senate, the veteran cabinet minister set out from day one to punish the dreaded Tories for the unforgivable sin of getting elected. How dare they displace Canada's natural governing party.

MacEachen, as Trudeau's finance minister in 1980 and 1981, authored arguably the worst budgets in Canadian history. Completely consumed by politics, he had all the warmth of a mother bear protecting her newborn cubs. MacEachen understood one thing for sure: the Senate had power – real constitutional, legislative power – that it rarely used. He intended to use it.

Who cares what the public wants? Certainly not MacEachen. He had a higher calling: the Great God Liberal Party. All hail the Liberals!

Born in Inverness, Nova Scotia, in 1921, MacEachen and two brothers were raised by his mother and coal miner father. He was a deeply religious man. Before entering politics, he was a professional academic, who taught first at St. Francis Xavier University, then the University of Toronto, then the University of Chicago and the Massachusetts Institute of Technology, before returning home to St. Francis Xavier as a professor of economics. Except for the 1958 Diefenbaker sweep – when MacEachen lost by eighteen votes – he won every election from his first in 1953 until he quit to join the Senate. But he wasn't just another tough guy from the neighbourhood. Except for his 1980s budgets, he was good. As labour minister in the 1960s, he was credited with introducing a federal minimum wage, and he was the health and welfare minister who introduced both medicare and the Canada Pension Plan. Diefenbaker, not a man given to praising Liberals, once called him the best Liberal parliamentarian in the House, and Pearson, under pressure by reporters one time to define specifically what he meant by a cabinet consensus, replied, "Sometimes MacEachen and I are a consensus." He is also credited with keeping Trudeau's minority government afloat from 1972 to 1974 and of engineering the 1979 defeat of Joe Clark's short-lived government.

In his maiden speech as leader of the opposition in the Senate in December 1984, MacEachen said the upper chamber should not "usurp the leading role" of the Commons or "systematically obstruct the will of the majority in the elected body of Parliament. . . .

"However . . . there is an important question of mathematical strength. We do have numbers on this side; we have a strong Liberal majority. . . . Of course, the difference between us [and the Tories] is not just in numbers. We differ in political philosophy. We are Liberals on this side of the chamber, and we have a distinctive approach to public questions. . . . We cannot become Tories just to make life easy for ourselves and our colleagues on the other side."

MacEachen wasn't the only Liberal senator stirred up by Mulroney's landslide victory. Even Keith Davey, who lived at the other end of the geniality scale from MacEachen, and saved his best efforts for backroom dealing, stood in the upper chamber in November 1984, his first speech in several years, to announce he was "prepared to describe myself as a born-again senator," flaying Mulroney's thirty-nine-member cabinet as "the largest and most over-stocked cabinet in Canadian history." And London Liberal senator Charlie Turner said, "If I think [the Tory legislation is] wrong and a majority of the senators think it's wrong, absolutely, that's the job of the Senate, to vote against it. If I think it's wrong, I'll do everything in my power to prevent it."

The first serious skirmish came in February 1985 when the Liberal senators disregarded the tradition that the Upper House would not hold up money bills and tied up a routine borrowing bill for two months, prompting Mulroney to denounce them as a "bunch of Liberal rejects . . . [and] political discards" – a pejorative that apparently didn't apply to all the Tory rejects he had been appointing at every available opening. Mulroney also got tentative agreement of all provinces except Manitoba and Quebec for a constitutional amendment to place a limit of thirty days on the hold-up of money bills and forty-five days on other Commons legislation. The resolution, which also called for a federal-provincial conference on Senate reform by the end of 1987, eventually died on the order paper. Over the next five years, MacEachen either delayed or completely derailed a dozen pieces of Conservative legislation.

Meanwhile Mulroney, who had promised to clean up political patronage, continued to plug the Senate with his friends and supporters. In March 1985, he appointed veteran *Globe and Mail* editor Richard (Dic) Doyle to the Senate. Editor for twenty years until being named editor emeritus in 1983, Doyle wrote a column on Senate reform just three weeks before his own appointment in which he slammed "the beached whales of Liberal fame who have been using the forum of sober second thought to obstruct and harass an elected Parliament" by blocking the borrowing bill. He added, "If the Senate did not exist, we might well not invent it." In 1963 he had attacked the Senate as "decaying and dispirited, a haven for has-beens." In 1966 he wrote, "It is election to the Senate that provides the payoff for a host of party bagmen and party organizers, as well as cabinet ministers and other MPs who have become a nuisance or an embarrassment to their party leaders." In October 1970, he wrote, "There are 18 empty sets in the Senate at present. Really, there are a great many more, if one is talking in terms of useful occupancy."

Things change. A year after Doyle joined Canada's most exclusive and best-paid patronage club, the man who alternately felt the Senate should be "abolished, elected or hung out to dry," said he now agreed with Sir. John A. Macdonald that the Senate serves as a forum for sober second thought on legislation that may have been rushed through the Commons, and he criticized the Parliamentary Press Gallery for ignoring the Senate and clinging to the "mythology" that it is a pasture for overpaid geriatrics with little to contribute to running the country. He retired in 1989.

In July 1986, Mulroney appointed veteran Tory political organizer Norman Atkins to the Senate. Atkins had been co-chairman of his 1984 election campaign and one of the over-rated engineers of Ontario's Big Blue Machine, which orchestrated four winning elections for Bill Davis, two of them minorities, in a province that had been easily controlled by Tory majorities since the Second World War. Atkins was named to the Senate just in time to join Joe Clark in blocking the offer of a Senate seat from Mulroney to recently defeated Ontario Tory premier Frank Miller. Clark, one of the pettiest political practitioners in Canada, still held a grudge against Miller who, as Ontario treasurer in 1979, had criticized Clark's ill-fated federal budget. Judging by the results of the subsequent election, Miller wasn't alone in opposing Clark's eighteen-cent-a-gallon gasoline tax proposal. Atkins, a pink Tory, opposed Miller on ideological grounds. He didn't want right-wingers to get patronage plums that could be more happily dispensed to his ideological fellow travellers. As for Miller, who has prospered without the Senate sinecure, he says he "would have been happy" to join the Senate. "I

was feeling down at the time and uncertain about my job future."
Atkins, whose easy-going style belies a ruthlessness in things political, is the Tory equivalent of Liberal Keith Davey, precisely the type
of purely political appointment that Mulroney had so angrily
denounced when the Liberals did it.

Atkins had taken extraordinary pains to secure his own
appointment. In a 1999 interview with me, Mulroney explained
that he appointed Atkins as a result of a persistent Senate "campaign organized by and on behalf of Norman Atkins. . . . It was the
biggest campaign of solicitation for a Senate seat in my experience,
the one with the most intensity," he said. "You go from that
extreme to people who have never mentioned an appointment,
Marjory LeBreton for example. Marjory did most of the calls for
me to the people . . . yet she never mentioned her own name for a
possible appointment. Never.

"Not everybody wants it, you know. Some people decline the
Senate. Bill Davis turned it down. Peter Lougheed is another. Jean
Beliveau and [former Mulroney public works minister] Stewart
McInnis said no. Sometimes they don't have the time, some don't
have the interest, others don't want the exposure that goes with the
appointment, and many find that it's just not a place of influence, so
they're not interested."

Atkins was certainly interested. For some people, apparently,
prospering at the expense of taxpayers is a tough habit to break.
Atkins's pursuit of a public paycheque is not surprising for a man
who spent almost his entire career living off the avails of advertising
and consulting contracts from politically friendly governments. His
main contribution as a senator, although not his only work, has
been as a partisan labouring loyally on behalf of his party. Just four
weeks after he became a senator, Mulroney named him chairman of
organization for the federal Conservative Party, once again raising
the legitimate question of why the public, and not the political
party, should be paying the salary of party workers. And the beauty
of it all is that under election expenses rules, the pay of full-time

Senate partisans doesn't count as an expense against the legislated spending ceilings.

On July 2, 1986, the Liberal-dominated Senate approved a major amendment to a Tory bill designed to tighten up mandatory supervision, the controversial program for the early release of prison inmates. The Liberal senators argued that the bill was a denial of basic rights because it gave the National Parole Board the power to keep dangerous offenders behind bars for their entire sentence, a power the Liberals said should only be in the hands of unelected judges. Solicitor-General James Kelleher – who was also destined for the Senate – had appealed for speedy passage without amendment so it could be passed into law before the Commons adjourned for the summer. The government was responding to some high-profile heinous crimes committed by dangerous offenders on mandatory supervision, and Kelleher cautioned that any delay would leave the public unprotected from dangerous offenders, about forty of whom were scheduled to be released over the next three months. But MacEachen and his Red Chamber guerrillas cared more about flexing their legislative muscles. They passed the amendment 23–17 and then immediately adjourned for the summer, delaying passage of the bill until the fall and forcing Mulroney into recalling the House on July 24 for an emergency one-day sitting so they could re-approve the parole bill. It was the twelfth time since Confederation that Parliament had been recalled between normal sittings, the first since Trudeau did it in October 1980 to debate the Constitution.

In early December 1987, immigration minister Benoît Bouchard told the Senate's constitutional and legal affairs committee that he was prepared to consider minor changes to his emergency refugee bill to meet their concerns that it violated the Charter of Rights. But he wasn't ready to weaken the bill in any way. "I will be happy to consider any amendment that gives lawyers less to argue about," he said, "provided such an amendment does not weaken the operation of the bill." This did not sit well with Liberal senator Jerry Grafstein, who argued that the upper chamber had a "duty" to reject the bill and send it back to the Commons with amendments to make sure it conformed to the Charter and to international obligations. The bill was introduced in the wake of a controversy over the unannounced arrival by ship of 184 Tamils, most of them Sikhs, to Nova Scotia that summer. It would allow the government to turn boats carrying bogus refugee claimants away from Canadian shores and to keep refugees in detention while their identities and security status were checked. It also provided for fines of up to $500,000 and ten-year jail sentences for refugee smugglers. A companion bill called for more stringent screening of refugees in order to reduce the number of illegal claimants clogging the immigration system.

When the bill was introduced in September 1987, MacEachen promised the Senate would not stall the bill, although Liberal senator Jacques Hébert called it "fascist and racist" and demanded a major overhaul. Hébert, a close friend and long-time travelling companion of Trudeau, made his mark, such as it was, when he went on a specious twenty-two-day hunger strike in 1986. He camped out in the lobby in front of the Red Chamber to protest, of all things, the Tory decision to cut Katimavik, a program for young Canadian volunteers aged seventeen to twenty-one to engage in make-work projects in various parts of the country, ostensibly to increase their understanding of Canada's diversity and environment. It was the millionaire Hébert's favourite Liberal-government-sponsored, $50-million-a-year, summertime project for a few thousand privileged youths. It was cut off by the Tories after a review found a host of serious problems. In addition to reports of drug abuse and sexual escapades, Katimavik's $2.1-million training centre in Quebec, complete with swimming pool, had a $116,980 operating loss, mainly because it had an occupancy rate of only forty-four per cent. In the final two years of the program, administration ate up almost thirty per cent of the cost. It also had a dropout rate of more than thirty per cent, and a survey of more than four hundred Katimavik "graduates" found that almost half of them said they had not learned any skills useful in their work, the main reason for the program. It was supposed to cost $20 million a year, but ended up costing $50 million.

Hébert, who had devised the program ten years earlier and sold the idea to his pal Trudeau, had long been an ardent advocate of government-funded programs. He certainly practised what he preached. For two years before Trudeau gave him a Senate seat in 1983, he was co-chairman of a federal committee studying Canadian culture. For ten years before that, he was a commissioner on the Canadian Radio-television and Telecommunications Commission. He had pledged to refuse food until Katimavik was restored, but he gave up his fast when Jean Chrétien, who was then out of elective politics, put together a committee to seek public and private funding for the program. His fast had brought him considerable publicity, with high-profile visits from Trudeau and musician Bruce Cockburn. On the day he quit, he said, "As of today, I know that Katimavik will live." It didn't.

Meanwhile, back in the Commons, the refugee bill received third and final reading on September 14, 1987, with ninety-two Conservatives supporting it against fifty-two Liberals and New Democrats, after which it was sent to the Senate where MacEachen's earlier promise of reasonable cooperation was quickly forgotten. The Senate's banking, trade, and commerce committee had already recommended in May that Ottawa and the provinces should abandon a deal brokered with the United States to replace the controversial export tax on lumber with higher provincial fees for timber-cutting. The government wasn't thrilled with the deal either, but had agreed after the Americans had moved to impose a punitive duty on Canadian lumber that would have devastated British Columbia's largest industry.

In addition to the refugee bill, the Commons had proposed controversial amendments in May to the Patent Act concerning prescription drugs. The legislation was designed to encourage more drug research in Canada by increasing patent protection for new brand-name prescription drugs and delaying the introduction of low-cost generic copies of those drugs.

MacEachen and his crew held up the drug bill for six months. They agreed to approve it only after Quebec Liberals, both senators and MPs, pleaded with him not to kill the bill because it would cost their province millions of dollars in economic benefits. During the fall of 1987 and into the spring and early summer of 1988, the Senate also held up the government's copyright legislation, despite pleas for its passage from much of Canada's artistic community. The bill, intended to bring the sixty-four-year-old copyright laws into the age of computers, photocopiers, and compact discs, strengthened the right of artists to control their works. The Senate bounced the refugee and immigration bills back to the Commons four times with the result that they weren't given Royal assent until July 21, 1988 – almost a year after their introduction.

In an interview with Linden MacIntyre for CBC Radio's *Sunday Morning* program in the fall of 1987, MacEachen – who had also turned his sights on studying Mulroney's treasured Meech Lake Accord – wasn't making any apologies for his unrelenting campaign of obstruction.

"I believe that the Senate, if it is to justify its existence as part of the constitutional system, must be more visible and more active," he said, "so that the Canadian people will know and see what the Senate is doing. I do not believe that an invisible body has any place in a democratic society, and if it is invisible, it will be irrelevant. And therefore, I hope that, as appropriate and when justified, the Senate will continue to be a visible participant in the legislative process."

Senator Pietro Rizzuto, a millionaire road builder and Trudeau loyalist, made himself visible in 1988. Rizzuto, the Liberal campaign co-chairman and chief Quebec fund-raiser was fired by Turner in May after publicly telling the Liberal leader he should quit. Rizzuto, who had been leading an underground anti-Turner campaign for some time, came out into the open in late May when he presented Turner with letters signed by twenty-two MPs calling for his resignation. "I feel I did what I had to do," said Rizzuto. "Unfortunately, it turned out badly because it leaked out and became public. Personally, if it was to be done over again, thinking it would not go public, I would do the same thing." In fact, Rizzuto himself had been leaking anti-Turner tidbits to journalists for months and made sure they knew in advance about the letters to Turner. Rizzuto and a significant group of Liberals felt that Turner could not defeat Mulroney in the next election and believed the Liberals would stand a better chance with a Quebec-based leader such as Chrétien. Just as Mulroney had used his loyalists to undermine Joe Clark's leadership after the 1980 election, so too had Chrétien been involved in quietly double-dealing against Turner, who had defeated him for the leadership in 1984. Many Liberals disagreed with Turner's support of the Meech Lake Accord – which Chrétien had openly opposed. Many of the party's business-oriented MPs and senators were unhappy with Turner's opposition to Mulroney's proposed free trade deal with the United States.

Rizzuto's actions demonstrated again that the Senate is most conspicuously misused as a taxpayer-subsidized backroom for partisan shenanigans.

The Senate made history on June 7, 1988, by splitting a bill already adopted by the Commons and, in the process, overruling a decision by Tory Speaker Guy Charbonneau, something Charbonneau would remember and make them pay for in the great GST debate two years later.

Liberal senator Alasdair Graham, a former Liberal president, in a move widely seen as setting the stage for a Senate debate of free trade legislation, moved to dramatically change several sections in a Tory plan to establish the $1-billion Atlantic Canada Opportunities Agency (ACOA) – essentially a huge pre-election Tory slush fund for the Atlantic region. ACOA had already doled out $180 million in grants to the region since its inception in June 1987 even though the bill had not yet become law. Graham, a MacEachen disciple, wanted the sections of the bill dealing with money-losing Cape Breton

Development Corporation (Devco) separated from the rest of the bill. The Tories were proposing to roll Devco into a new entity reporting to ACOA. Graham's motion was unprecedented and Charbonneau at first ruled it unconstitutional. A day later, in a lengthy decision, Charbonneau revisited the issue, ruling that because the bill involved money matters it should not be split by the Senate. The Liberal senators then used their majority to overrule his decision, something that had happened in the past, but rarely.

An hour later the Senate reverted to debating the original Graham motion and adopted the change. MacEachen said the senators "broke some new ground and I think it is important that we edge a bit forward in the way we do things." Tory House leader Doug Lewis said the delaying tactics threatened the entire ACOA bill, but MacEachen and Graham, both Cape Bretoners, didn't seem to care. Both had a strong personal interest in Devco. MacEachen, as the cabinet minister in charge at the time, had created it. And Graham, before he left the job to become a senator, was vice-president of Devco.

After Commons Speaker John Fraser ruled that the Senate had violated the privileges of the Commons when it split the bill, MacEachen announced he would take another, long look at the original bill. "We will have to go back to the drawing board and start over again," he said. In his ruling against the Liberal senators, Commons Speaker Fraser said the Senate "should have respected the propriety of asking the House of Commons to concur in their actions." Fraser, in an unusually blunt message for a Speaker, added that "the Senate should view with more respect the financial prerogatives given this House in money matters."

It was the first time the Senate had split a bill that originated in the Commons, and both the Conservatives and the New Democrats in the Commons argued that, if allowed to stand, it represented an unprecedented attack on the ability of the Commons to make laws.

In March 1982, the Senate committee on foreign affairs released a 155-page report two years in the making recommending that all trade barriers between the United States and Canada be torn down by the mid-1990s. Rather than being a threat to Canada's independence, it said, free trade is the only way the country can maintain its standard of living and keep its economy productive.

The committee chairman, Liberal senator George van Rogen, a corporate lawyer noted for his suspenders and black horn-rim glasses, said that the recent multilateral tariff agreements left Canada "in the worst of two possible worlds." Tariffs were too low to be an effective protection but at the same time Canada was the world's only major industrial country without free access to a market as large as those of its major trading competitors.

As enthusiastic as van Rogen and his committee were, however, the chances of free trade becoming a reality were remote. For one thing, the Liberal government wasn't impressed. Trade Minister Ed Lumley rejected the idea out of hand, saying it might work in some specific sectors, such as automobiles, but would be "impossible on an all-encompassing basis" and could affect our political sovereignty. External Affairs Minister Mark MacGuigan said dismantling our trade barriers would not be in Canada's best interest, citing the danger faced by relatively small Canadian industries having to compete openly with their larger U.S. counterparts.

Then there was Canada's political history on the issue. In 1878, Sir John A. Macdonald ran against Liberal Alexander Mackenzie, an avowed free trader, on a national policy of self-reliance and won. Wilfrid Laurier lost in 1891 on a campaign of "commercial union" with the United States and in 1911, as prime minister he negotiated a "reciprocity agreement" with the Americans allowing a free exchange of a wide range of products. Robert Borden, fighting against the plan, easily defeated Laurier and the agreement was never ratified.

Arthur Meighen defeated Mackenzie King in 1925 by running on a policy of high tariffs. Lester Pearson adopted a sectoral approach in the 1960s, signing the immensely successful Auto Pact in 1965, and a year after the Senate study recommended removal of all barriers, Trudeau initiated some tentative talks on removing barriers in specialty steel products, mass-transit vehicles, computer services, and agricultural equipment.

Historically, Conservatives had always been opposed to free trade. With Liberal popularity plunging in 1982 and the Tories coming on, the likelihood of a Canadian free trade initiative developing was bleak. During the 1983 Conservative leadership convention, Newfoundland's John Crosbie came out strongly in favour of free trade. Mulroney, the victor in that convention, ridiculed him, saying it would be like sleeping next to an elephant: "It's terrific until the elephant twitches, and if it ever rolls over, you're a dead man."

A few months later, by 1984, however, safely ensconced in power and having held a summit with U.S. president Ronald Reagan, an ardent free trader, Mulroney, always anxious to please the Americans, had changed his mind about the dangers of sleeping with elephants. In a November 1984 economic statement, Finance Minister Michael Wilson spoke of "opportunities to pursue trade liberalization on a bilateral basis with the United States. . . . The question is how best to capitalize on this advantage, while managing the adjustment that freer trade would entail."

Reagan already had approval from the U.S. Senate to enter into "trade agreements that provide for the elimination or reduction of any duty imposed by the United States." Only two countries were listed as eligible: Israel and Canada. Within two years, Canada and the United States were in serious negotiations to remove trade barriers on their $170-billion two-way trade. And by 1988, Liberal leader John Turner, beset by internal divisions in his own party, and being genuinely appalled by free trade in any event, decided that this was the issue on which he would stand or fall.

In an absolutely stunning move, Turner announced on July 20, 1988, that the Liberal majority in the Senate had been ordered by him to block legislation for the free trade deal until Canadians could vote on the issue in an election.

"Call an election and let the people decide," Turner told Mulroney in the Commons, to which the prime minister responded by accusing the Liberal leader of "hijacking the fundamental rights of the House of Commons."

At an earlier news conference, Turner had rejected the idea that the Senate, not free trade, would be the issue in the next election. "The Senate is not the issue here. I am the issue," he said. "I have asked the senators to do this and I will take the responsibility." MacEachen, barely able to contain his glee, said he would make sure Turner's threat was carried out. "We support the position of Mr. Turner. And we're working on how to carry through that position."

By this time, the Commons had already given approval in principle to the trade bill, which required amendments to twenty-seven federal statutes, and a committee was giving the legislation detailed study.

A Gallup poll sponsored by the right-wing National Citizens' Coalition (NCC) concluded that Mulroney could not win a majority in the next election on the issue of free trade. NCC president David Somerville said the issue should be settled by a national referendum where it would "likely pass," but if Canadians were forced to vote for Mulroney's Tories in order to get free trade, "it will likely be lost." The Gallup survey of 1,018 Canadians said forty per cent would be less likely to vote Tory if passage of the free trade deal depended on re-electing the Conservatives. Twenty-six per cent said they would be more likely to vote Tory.

On August 31, with Canadian flags displayed on the desks of MPs on both sides of the Commons and opposition members singing the national anthem in protest, the Conservatives outvoted the Liberals and New Democrats by 177 to 64 to pass their omnibus free trade bill. The vote came after months of heated debate in the Commons. The bill would now go to the Senate. Government officials hoped optimistically that some of the sixty Liberal senators would break ranks and vote with the government, but with only thirty-one Tories and six independents, it would take more than a few to help their cause.

Trade Minister John Crosbie, who had crossed swords with MacEachen for years, said the Senate was on a deliberately "obstructive course." He even accused MacEachen of "lacking patriotism," saying he was a "gnome down in the crevices of the Senate who appears to be out to sabotage a legitimate elected government."

MacEachen said the Senate had no intention of killing the bill, just delaying it so the people would have a chance to vote. "I would think not twice, but twenty times before I would recommend the Senate kill the trade bill in one plunge of the dagger," said MacEachen. "If we killed the bill in September, there would not only be a trade issue but I think a constitutional issue. And do we want to have a constitutional issue created by the Senate defeating a bill of this importance?"

On September 13, MacEachen said Liberal senators would abstain from voting on second reading – approval in principle – so the legislation could go to a committee. Two days later, twenty-seven senators, primarily Liberals, did abstain and Conservative senators approved the bill in principle by a 19–0 vote. This meant it would now go to a committee for detailed study, which included the Liberal plan for cross-country hearings on the issue. Senate Tory leader Lowell Murray said, "The appointed Senate must have a role secondary to that of the elected House of Commons. I would die of embarrassment to be associated with the quaint idea that in 1988 an appointed body has equal influence with the elected representatives of the people."

To what extent Turner's tactics helped him or hindered him in the November 21, 1988, election, nobody really can say. But there was no doubt that Mulroney's majority – making him only the second Conservative this century to enjoy back-to-back majorities – cancelled any authority the Senate had to delay free trade any longer.

Royce Frith, deputy Liberal leader in the Senate, announced the day after the election that the Senate would keep its promise and pass the legislation quickly. On December 30, just two days before the treaty was to begin tearing down trade barriers in the world's largest two-way trading partnership, the bill received Royal assent.

The ceremony in the Senate chamber was presided over by Supreme Court Justice Antonio Lamer, and witnessed by just ten MPs and fewer than thirty senators. The Senate had given final approval in the upper chamber earlier that day on an unrecorded voice vote in which most of the Liberal senators abstained to let the bill pass.

And so ended one of the most protracted debates in Canadian history.

And now, the main event.

The election results might have instilled just a touch of humility in less partisan hearts, but MacEachen and his fellow Liberal senators were undaunted. For its part, the government wasted no time in showing that it was prepared to do whatever it took to perform end runs around the Senate.

In early May 1989, the Commons approved the government's $33-billion supply bill, a relatively routine procedure that, despite the amount of money involved, usually involves debate but rarely sparks much heat, since governments, like households, need the money to pay their bills. In the course of the debate, rookie Liberal MP Peter Milliken of Kingston objected that the government's use of special warrants for about $8 million issued by Governor-General Jeanne Sauvé between sessions had affected his right as an MP to scrutinize public spending. Speaker John Fraser did not agree. MacEachen did.

The Tories had gone to Sauvé before the House was recalled and got some governor-general's warrants, which are then approved by cabinet, in order to keep the government running. This procedure is in the books to be used only in emergencies. There was no emergency here. The procedure had only been used twice since Confederation in similar circumstances, yet the Tories did it four times in early 1989. Three warrants worth about $1 billion had been issued to meet expenditures between January and the end of the fiscal year in March. Another for $6.2 billion was issued April 1, just two days before Parliament reconvened for the first time since the election.

Senator Eugene Forsey, long recognized as one of Canada's leading constitutional authorities, declared flatly that it was unconstitutional because Parliament, not just cabinet, must approve spending. He said the Senate should kill the supply bill and force the Tories to introduce a new bill stating explicitly that the use of the warrants is "retroactively legal." Otherwise, he said, the situation could be used as a precedent and government would not have to bother getting Parliamentary approval for its spending in the future. The Senate approved the supply bill, but added an amendment saying the controversial warrants "shall be deemed to be legal."

This time, the Senate actually had a point, but after the previous four years of guerrilla warfare, the government wasn't interested in accommodation. Justice Minister Doug Lewis said the government had no intention of admitting any wrongdoing and unless the Senate ended its "bizarre game" the government would not be able to issue cheques to pay 135,000 veterans' pensions. Lewis said if the impasse wasn't sorted out "we will give any veterans who call the phone number of Senator Allan MacEachen."

On May 15, the government rejected the Senate's amendment and demanded that the supply bill be approved as it was originally passed in the Commons a week earlier. Treasury Board president Robert de Cotret sponsored a resolution rebuking the Senate, accusing the Liberal senators of being irresponsible. Mulroney predicted the Liberals would pay a political price. "The Canadian people have had it up to the teeth with a bunch of Liberals who don't understand they are appointed and not elected. . . ."

Back in the Senate the next day, the government plea was rejected but senators voted 41–26 to refer the issue to their finance committee and call de Cotret and Lewis to appear before it. But MacEachen did suggest his party would allow the bill's passage in time to pay its sixteen thousand RCMP employees that week. "The Liberal Senate will not prejudice any payment owing to any individual," he said.

On May 17, the Senate finance committee recommended that the Senate pass the supply bill without amendment. The committee also sent a message to the Commons calling the government's use of warrants "wrong and abhorrent." The supply bill was approved in the Senate with twenty-four Conservatives voting for it and thirty-three Liberals abstaining.

During this period, Mulroney had decided to appoint senators under the terms of the Meech Lake Accord, which hadn't been ratified; the accord called for the prime minister to choose candidates from lists provided by each province where a vacancy occurred. The first winner in this new lottery was Newfoundland's former energy minister and House leader Gerald Ottenheimer, a lawyer and former provincial Tory leader. He was appointed December 31, 1987, bringing the Senate Tory numbers to thirty-two, exactly half the Liberal strength. There were five independents.

On June 21, 1989, the government introduced Bill C-21, legislation designed to overhaul the $13-billion-a-year Unemployment Insurance Act, slashing $1.3 billion in benefits and cutting $3 billion the government was paying into the program each year. About $800 million of the savings would go to new job-training initiatives and the rest to improve sickness and maternity benefits. The legislation would make UI harder to get by lengthening the qualifying period for benefits from ten to fourteen weeks of work, depending on regional unemployment rates. The government said this would mean a loss of benefits for about thirty thousand people a year, but critics said at least twice that many would be cut off. The government wanted the new law approved quickly so that the changes could take effect January 1, 1990. It wasn't to be.

In November, after the Commons approved the bill, Senator Royce Frith, the deputy Liberal leader, said the senators were planning cross-country hearings. He conceded that would likely jeopardize the government's January 1 deadline. Asked if the Senate was digging in for another knock-down fight with the government, Frith replied with a smile, "I wouldn't put it that way, but I suppose you might."

In mid-December, Mulroney again denounced the Liberal majority in the Senate for refusing to move quickly on the bill. "They are non-elected senators who take anti-democratic positions against the interests of Quebec and Canada," he told reporters outside the Commons. At one point he said the senators "have no right to do such a thing," but quickly amended that to say they do have a right "if they are prepared to accept the consequences." The next day, the Senate announced it was extending the committee's public hearings until the end of January to hear more of the 250 witnesses who had asked to speak. Committee chairman Senator Jacques Hébert said the government could pass an interim one-page bill extending lower qualifying periods in high jobless areas if it wished, pending the outcome of the debate on the full bill. "It's not the Senate's fault, but the government's stubbornness and their will to blackmail the Senate once again," he said, apparently in earnest.

MacEachen's next move was to introduce his own bill, S-12, and ask the Commons to approve it. His bill would extend provisions of legislation already in effect allowing easier access to benefits for people in areas of high unemployment, such as his own area of Cape Breton. It duplicated legislation passed each December in the Commons that spells out the poorer regions in which people can receive benefits after fewer than fourteen weeks of work. But that legislation was contained in the larger government bill, and the Tories claimed if it wasn't passed by January 6 those most in need of benefits would suffer. To nobody's surprise, the Conservatives in the Commons defeated MacEachen's bill. "We don't intend to blink on this," said Doug Lewis. "We don't even intend to wink." With that, the Commons began its Christmas break.

The big concern was the impact the delay would have on the thousands of jobless people who were already suffering from the devastation of the east coast fishery. NDP employment critic John Rodriguez supported the Senate bill, saying, "If I have to go to bed with the devil to get benefits for unemployed Canadians in Atlantic Canada, I'll even go to bed with a senator."

Throughout January, while the government stewed and many

unemployed people were in danger of losing their benefits, the special seven-member Senate committee chaired by wealthy Trudeauite Jacques Hébert continued its methodical clause-by-clause study of the bill and its protracted public hearings. MacEachen continued to claim that the delay was for the long-term benefit of the unemployed and asked them to "be patient." Easy for him to say. On January 19, at the committee hearings at the Radisson Plaza Hotel in St. John's, Newfoundland, Hébert upped the ante, threatening to kill the UI bill completely if the government rejected the Senate amendments.

On February 5, Employment and Immigration Minister Barbara McDougall angrily told the grim-faced senators at the committee hearing in Ottawa, "Your approach to this plan, I'm afraid, has brought no credit to the Senate. [If there are] any hardships that result, you must bear the responsibility." The Liberals, rather than pepper the minister with questions, opted instead for stony silence. McDougall was simply dismissed at the conclusion of her fifteen-minute presentation. Knowledgeable onlookers said it was likely the only time in Senate history that a minister had been dealt with that way. MacEachen told reporters later, "I didn't find anything the minister said had produced any possibility for a question."

On February 14, the Senate lobbed the bill back into the government's lap, calling it "a demolition operation designed to destroy the present unemployment insurance plan" and demanding a host of changes. Responding to the proposition that the Senate should not block bills passed by elected MPs, Hébert said, "If we don't like it [the Senate], let's abolish it. But as long as we have it, we have to understand it has some powers and it has some duties." Speaking to a Canada-U.S. trade group in Toronto the next day, International Trade Minister John Crosbie said, "We're not going to have this unelected coterie of Trudeauites decide what the policy of Canada is to be in 1990."

In March, Mulroney appointed Tory bulldog Harvie André government house leader in the Commons, a sure sign he wasn't interested in adopting the tactics of gentle persuasion. When the

Commons rejected Hébert's proposals on March 13, André thundered that the Senate had no constitutional right to amend financial aspects of the bill. In his usual style, yelling in the Commons about the Liberal-dominated Senate, André echoed the equally excitable Crosbie, saying, "What deity bequeaths to these has-been Trudeauites the right to decide the agenda of this country?" The Canadian Labour Congress president said the Tories would pay "at the ballot box" for their bill, adding, "I'm still hoping that the Senate will kill the bill." Sounding reasonable by comparison, MacEachen said he wouldn't recommend killing it: "We're going to continue trying to improve the bill."

And so it went, recriminations and threats were lobbed back and forth between the two houses throughout March and into late April. Both sides then claimed to be vindicated by a ruling from Speaker John Fraser that the government was procedurally powerless to stop the Senate's fight against the bill. The Liberal senators said that was a victory for their side. Fraser also said, however, that the Commons had moral and democratic principles on its side and warned that the Senate could be provoking a constitutional crisis.

MacEachen said reconciliation would come only if the government backed down from its hard-line position and negotiated a deal, either informally or through the rarely used "conference" method between the two chambers. On May 7, the government blinked, backing down from its demand that the bill be passed without amendment and said it would accept some of the Senate ideas. But Employment Minister McDougall accused the Senate of being "caught in a historical time warp. . . . We believe that the use of that power by the Senate is unconscionable on moral and democratic grounds and that it is unacceptable on policy grounds," she said. "If we blindly accept the message from the Senate . . . the powers of the House of Commons will be eroded – for partisan political tactics."

On May 9, the Commons voted 112–83 to ask the Senate – for the third time – to pass the UI legislation. Hébert, enjoying the spectacle of having the government on the run, made it clear the senators would not cooperate until the government agreed to maintain at least some of the $3 billion it contributed each year to the unemployment insurance fund. "It's really no surprise," said Hébert, ". . . we are going to insist on the government's contributions. . . . It was the most important thing in our [committee] report."

On May 22, MacEachen called again for a meeting with the Commons to break the UI deadlock. Speaking in the Senate, he said, "I believe we are on solid ground to insist on the time-honoured normal practice of negotiation and discussion." Given the circumstances, however, Mulroney wasn't interested in the public humiliation of having to plead with MacEachen for passage of a major piece of legislation, so once again, MacEachen's call went unheeded.

On June 28, Parliament adjourned for the summer, leaving behind the collapse of the Meech Lake Accord and three important bills in limbo: the Senate still refused to approve the seven per cent goods and services tax (GST), a bill to "claw back" social benefits, and the UI bill.

Finally, when they returned in the fall, the Tory government and Liberal senators struck a deal to pass the UI bill while suspending the other major battle over approval of Mulroney's controversial GST proposal. On October 22, while Liberal senators cried, "Shame, shame," Bill C-21 passed by a vote of 53–40, helped by the infusion of eight new Tory senators appointed by Mulroney under an obscure clause in the Constitution. The appointments gave the Tories a 54–51 edge over the Liberals in the Senate. The bill took effect November 18, 1990.

Throughout the UI battle, ferocious as it was at times, there was constant speculation that it was viewed by MacEachen and his troops as simply a trial run for the big fight – over the dreaded GST. Indeed, when he announced that a deal had been reached on the UI bill, MacEachen said he was not prepared to filibuster over the UI legislation because blocking the GST remained the primary goal. "This is a battle against the GST . . ." he said. "We regret that [Bill C-21] will pass. We certainly won't vote for it. But there's no prospect now that the government would negotiate with us because it would undermine the whole basis for their eight [additional] senators."

And so, the Mother of All Senate Battles was joined.

THE TAX MAN COMETH

O N APRIL 10, 1990, after eight months of bitter debate in the Commons, the massively unpopular seven per cent goods and services tax, or GST – designed to replace the hidden 13.5 per cent manufacturers' sales tax, was approved by a 144–114 Commons vote and sent to the loaded-for-bear, Liberal-dominated Senate. The government intended to have the tax up and running by January 1, 1991.

Public opinion polls showed that both the tax and Mulroney's government were extremely unpopular. The Tories had sunk to a record low of fifteen per cent support in the polls. The GST wasn't doing much better. Not that you expect any tax to be popular, but these polls suggested the GST was opposed by almost eighty per cent of Canadians.

The Senate wasn't exactly a public favourite either, but that did not matter to Allan MacEachen – who had just orchestrated an eight per cent increase in the Senate budget from $37 million to $40.1 million, despite restraint being placed on everybody else. MacEachen was fully aware, as was Mulroney, that the Liberals commanded fifty-four seats and could count on at least two of the five independent senators, while the Tories trailed far behind at thirty-four senators. On the other hand, there were eleven vacancies, and it didn't take Mulroney long to begin filling them with loyal Tory hacks and flacks. But even if he filled them all – which he did – that would still leave the Tories with fewer senators than the Liberals. So even then there was speculation that Mulroney would invoke Sections 26–28 of the BNA Act, which allows a prime minister to increase the number of senators from the normal maximum of 104 to 112. The section, intended to cover a dire emergency that crippled the government's ability to govern, had never been used in Canada's 123-year history. The country's second prime minister, Liberal Alexander Mackenzie, had tried in 1873, but Queen Victoria refused her consent on the grounds that no such emergency existed.

The other issue under serious dispute was just how much power the Senate has constitutionally to change money bills, which the GST clearly was. Nobody disputed the fact that the Senate's powers were almost equal to those of the Commons. The major exception is that the Senate is not allowed to originate money bills. No law, of course, can become law until it is ratified in its final form by both the upper and lower houses.

To no one's surprise, MacEachen's position was that the Senate had the power to defeat or amend money bills. But the classic text on the matter, *The Government of Canada* by Robert MacGregor Dawson, revised in 1987 by Norman Ward, says this: "The Constitution is clear enough about which House may initiate money bills but it says nothing about whether the Senate can amend or delay them, and the point has frequently been challenged." Indeed, the issue had long been a matter of dispute. The Commons rule book quotes a British resolution of 1678 suggesting that only the Lower House can initiate "aids and supplies granted to the sovereign," and adding that such bills "are not alterable by the Senate." Dawson and Ward note that "almost the only attention the Senate has given to this grand assertion is to ignore it."

The Senate's argument is that if the Constitution was designed to limit its power over money bills, it would say so, but it doesn't. What's more, Senate supporters say the upper chamber can't do its job as a protector of provincial and regional rights if it can't change money bills. Given that the Commons has, on numerous occasions, accepted Senate amendments on money bills, the senators were on solid ground. Dawson and Ward concluded that despite the constitutional ambiguity on the issue, the precedents would allow the Senate to "amend a money bill out of all recognition so that, in effect, the bill was rejected."

This kind of argument is usually reserved for legalistic, professorial, academic debate. But by the end of the GST battle, it became far more than just a theoretical dispute among constitutional scholars.

Exactly a week before the Commons approved the GST, Liberal leadership candidate Paul Martin – later to become Canada's finance minister – told members of the *Montreal Gazette*'s editorial board that his Liberal colleagues in the Senate should drop their opposition to the controversial unemployment insurance bill "and dig their heels in on the GST. . . . I would abolish the GST," he said. "The manufacturers' sales tax is a bad tax but there's no excuse to repeal one bad tax by bringing in another one." Martin's major leadership rivals – Jean Chrétien, who won, and Sheila Copps – also professed their absolute opposition to the GST and promised to abolish it. In the subsequent 1993 election, Chrétien made several explicit promises to kill the GST and replace it with another tax. For all that, of course, the GST is still with us.

Two days after Martin's war cry his Liberal colleagues announced plans for cross-country hearings. Saskatchewan Liberal senator Sidney Buckwold, chairman of the Senate banking, trade, and commerce committee, advised reporters to "tell the people they're going to get a chance to be heard," as if he was really interested in what people had to say. Buckwold, a one-time mayor of Saskatoon, had been handed his first-class ticket to patronage heaven by Trudeau in November 1971 after the people in his riding had spoken and said they didn't want him representing them in Ottawa. As former Privy

Council boss Gordon Robertson wrote, "In the United States you have to win an election to get into the Senate. In Canada, it is more effective to lose."

For all the talk about listening to what the public had to say, Buckwold made it clear the day after the Commons approved the GST that the Senate had already made up its mind. "It may be in the view of Canadians that this tax is so outstandingly bad that it should be completely rejected – and that's what we'd recommend," he said. Buckwold said he understood a move to change or reject the tax bill could lead to a constitutional crisis, "but we're proceeding with the view that we do have the constitutional authority to make amendments or even to reject the whole thing." With that, the Liberal senators decided to take a three-week recess.

In his 1991 book on the GST called *Hoods on the Hill*, Liberal senator Royce Frith asserted that "despite government and some editorial rantings about 'systematic obstruction' the 'liberal-dominated senate' had passed more than 95 per cent of Mulroney's legislation without amendment. It had amended only a few bills – and defeated none." Frith's claims are misleading at best. Sure, they passed lots of routine, uncontroversial legislation, particularly in Mulroney's first term. But since the Tory re-election a bad situation had grown much worse. The outrageously obstructionist Senate forced every major Tory initiative to pass muster through MacEachen's megalomaniacal gauntlet. The only thing that stopped the public from rising up and rebelling against it was that both Mulroney and the GST itself were even less popular at the time than the Liberal senators.

Look at the facts. Between 1965 and 1984, under Liberal rule in the Commons, the Liberal majority in the Senate did not contest a single measure proposed by their governing colleagues, including the much-hated National Energy Program. Between 1980 and 1984, still under a Liberal government, just nine bills were detained in the Senate for more than a month, the longest for eighty-three days. But between the 1988 election and the 1990 GST fight, when Mulroney was in power, twenty-three bills were held for more than a month in the Senate – including seven that still hadn't been passed by the end of September 1990.

While we're on the topic of conflicting principles, the NDP, which has consistently called for the abolition of the Senate and railed against its undemocratic nature, cheered MacEachen on to kill the GST. Leader Audrey McLaughlin told the Liberal senators, "You have a majority in the Senate. You have a chance to kill the GST bill. Use your majority in the Senate. Don't miss this chance. Kill the bill. Stop the GST." And Lorne Nystrom, who in 1999 joined with back-bench Liberal Roger Gallaway in a national campaign to abolish the Senate, told the Liberals to kill the GST before Mulroney packed the Senate with Tories. "Liberal senators must act quickly on the GST while they can still win votes," he said.

The collapse of the Meech Lake Accord on June 23 was a blow to Mulroney's constitutional ambitions, but made it easier for him to begin packing the Senate because it freed him from having to consult the provinces first. By mid-August there were fourteen vacancies. They didn't remain vacant for long.

On August 30, he appointed five prominent Tories to the upper chamber: Consiglio Di Nino, fifty-two, president of Cabot Trust Co. of Toronto and head of Harbourfront Corp.; Pat Carney, fifty-five, a veteran federal cabinet minister from British Columbia; Mario Beaulieu, sixty, a Montreal lawyer and businessman, chairman of Simard-Beaudry Inc., a construction company, one-time Quebec finance minister, and Mulroney's Quebec campaign chairman in the 1988 election; Nancy Teed, forty-one, a New Brunswick business-woman and former provincial Tory cabinet minister, Canada's youngest senator at the time who was tragically killed in a car accident near Fredericton in January 1993; and Gerald Comeau, forty-four, an accountant, associate professor at the Université Ste. Anne in Church Point, Nova Scotia, and a former Tory MP for South West Nova, defeated in 1988.

Mulroney said he had no apologies to make for naming the five Tories. "We are going to get the GST through and I'll do whatever is appropriate and democratic to get it done," he said. "We're elected. We have a mandate from the people of Canada and that mandate cannot be frustrated by a group of appointed people from a holdover regime."

On September 7, Mulroney made three more appointments: Don Oliver, a senior partner in the law firm of Stewart, McKelvey, Sterling and Scales, the largest law firm in Atlantic Canada, and a former vice-president of the federal Conservative Party; John Sylvain, head of the United Provinces Insurance Co. Ltd., a director of the Canadian Development Investment Corp., and campaign manager in the riding of Lachine-Lac-St. Louis then held by former Tory cabinet minister Robert Layton; and former Conservative New Brunswick premier Richard Hatfield, who ran his province from 1970 to 1987 before he was defeated in the worst electoral landslide in Canadian history, when every single seat went to the Liberals under Frank McKenna. It took the New Brunswick Tories twelve years of living in the political wilderness before upstart leader Bernard Lord led them to a surprising majority victory in 1999.

Hatfield, a colourful, jet-setting politician, was greatly admired by the media because of his affable style and his penchant to blab to reporters about secret meetings. A man dubbed Disco Dick, he once responded to criticism that he spent more time in New York bars and Moroccan beaches, often at public expense, than he did in New Brunswick by saying he was elected to govern New Brunswick, not to live there. When he died of brain cancer in 1991 at age sixty, eulogies poured in from across the country. He certainly did make a considerable contribution to Canadian politics, but many who have attempted to elevate him to sainthood have tended to ignore the seamy underbelly of his so-called eccentric lifestyle – a bachelor, he lived alone in a small house full of collector dolls. Throughout his career, particularly given the socially conservative nature of New

Brunswick, there was always an undercurrent of uneasiness about him that periodically went beyond whispers and flared out into the open. During the 1978 provincial election, for example, when Hatfield accused Liberal leader Joe Daigle of lacking originality, Daigle snapped back, "I'd rather be a secondhand rose than a faded pansy." In 1985, after Hatfield was acquitted on a marijuana charge – officials had found the stuff packed in his suitcase when he was travelling with, of all things, the Royal tour – two young men spoke out publicly of a night of drugs and booze with Hatfield followed by a trip to Montreal on the government airplane. And a year after his death, an unidentified young man said that in the 1977–79 period Hatfield sexually harassed young men whom he had hired from a local group home to do odd jobs around his house. He said local authorities, including the police and social services officials, were told about it, but nothing was done.

Throughout the Mulroney years, no premier in the country was more consistently compliant toward the prime minister than Nova Scotia's John Buchanan, the Conservative premier for twelve years. And no individual appointment Mulroney made during his Trudeauesque orgy of patronage in 1990 provoked more public anger than his decision to bring the fifty-nine-year-old Buchanan to the Upper House on September 12. Why? Because Buchanan, who loved to campaign as "Honest John," was under an RCMP investigation over allegations – which were never proven – made against him by a former top civil servant concerning kickbacks and patronage abuses.

On July 20, the RCMP in Halifax announced they were conducting an inquiry into allegations levelled in June by Michael Zareski, the former deputy minister of government services, including the charge that Buchanan (who was not publicly named) personally intervened in issuing government contracts to ensure they were awarded to his friends and supporters. Zareski also suggested that Buchanan was to receive a kickback from a deal involving Canstone, a company set up to restore the legislature building. In addition,

Halifax police announced they were re-opening an earlier investigation into the charge that Buchanan's health minister David Nantes released confidential medical information about Zareski in an effort to discredit him.

Asked by the opposition in the provincial legislature if he intended to resign in the wake of the investigation, Buchanan said, "Why should I? I'm not even mentioned in the [RCMP] statement. There have been many allegations made over the last month." That, of course, was the point.

On September 12, however, Buchanan resigned as Canada's longest-serving premier and his former deputy, Roger Bacon, was sworn in as interim premier in a secret ceremony attended only by Buchanan, Lieutenant-Governor Lloyd Crouse, and the province's senior civil servant. (Six months later, Pictou County dairy farmer Donald Cameron became premier, but the ruling Tories were demolished by Liberal John Savage in 1993.)

Moments after Buchanan resigned, Mulroney caught everybody by surprise – not to mention shock and horror – by announcing that Buchanan was headed to the Senate. With him went Noel A. Kinsella, a New Brunswick public servant and academic, who helped organize Mulroney's successful 1983 Tory leadership campaign. Kinsella, a former chief commissioner of the New Brunswick Human Rights Commission, had appealed to New Brunswick premier Frank McKenna in December 1988 to get rid of patronage by making it illegal. Kinsella said it might be done by adding a clause to the provincial Human Rights Act.

As for Buchanan, after twenty years as party leader, all but eight of those as premier, there was no public ceremony to mark his departure from office, a graphic demonstration of what those who knew him best thought of him. Bruce McKinnon, the *Halifax Chronicle-Herald*'s political cartoonist, depicted him fleeing Nova Scotia in a get-away car driven by Mulroney. And when Buchanan returned home to Spryfield, the working-class area in his former riding, he was booed by a small group of protesters. In February 1991, the party faithful kicked off their three-day leadership convention with a perfunctory farewell, but that was it. Buchanan himself used to turn up his nose at any talk about a Senate seat, saying he didn't like Ottawa and had no interest in being there. But that was when he had other options. During the Meech Lake Accord discussions, Buchanan had offered to give up at least one of Nova Scotia's Senate seats to accommodate western demands for more. Had that been accepted, ironically, the seat he took might not have been there for him.

Buchanan's appointment, given the outstanding accusations against him, was universally condemned. An *Ottawa Citizen* editorial called it "the Mulroney government's most contemptuous and appalling act of patronage – a dubious achievement indeed. . . . Is Mulroney no longer politically astute enough to realize the degree of outrage this appointment would provoke? Has he given up? . . . Buchanan's obvious willingness to abandon his government while it's under the cloud of criminal investigation shows the kind of principles and talent he will be bringing to the Senate. Remember, Buchanan was the premier who said the goods and services tax is 'wrong in every way . . .'."

The *Montreal Gazette* agreed. Its main editorial was headlined: "An insult to the Canadian people: Sending Buchanan to the Senate is an outrage." It accused Mulroney of sullying Parliament by such "wildly unsuitable appointments. . . . In naming Mr. Buchanan a senator before the allegations against him are disposed of, Mr. Mulroney has insulted Parliament and the people of Canada." And *Gazette* columnist William Johnson wrote, "Legally, Buchanan is innocent until proven guilty. Politically, though, Buchanan is tainted; and so the people of Nova Scotia have recognized. In a recent poll he received the favor of only 13 per cent of the sample," which made him the only political leader in the country who was lower in the public opinion polls than Mulroney.

To add insult to injury, Buchanan ended up making more money as a senator than the $97,000 he made as premier, all at public expense. That's because his basic Senate pay of $62,100 (it has gone up since) would be augmented by his $60,000-a-year provincial pension.

In April 1991, Buchanan, already facing two RCMP investigations, was hit with new allegations that he may have violated the provincial Conflict of Interest Act by accepting and keeping secret payments made to him as premier of Nova Scotia beginning in 1978. When the story broke, Premier Don Cameron revealed that Buchanan had accepted $3,300 a month on top of his $97,000 salary in 1988. Provincial NDP leader Alexa McDonough – now the federal NDP leader – laid a formal complaint, seeking a judicial review under the act, saying that while both the Tory party and Buchanan have acknowledged the payments, "the source of these funds is not known to the people of Nova Scotia." Under the act, passed by Buchanan's government, all MLAs are required to disclose details of financial dealings and money they received outside of their provincial salaries. The legislation allows only the commissioner in charge of the act to review those statements. During the 1988 election campaign, Buchanan did reveal a disclosure document filed under the act. In the space where he was asked to show the source of any money he received besides his salary were the letters "n.a." Cameron said he was "more concerned about the allegation of how the money was raised for that fund than who it was being paid to. . . . I feel sorry for [Buchanan], he's been through a lot, but he'll have to take responsibility for his own actions." Between April 1985 and January 1989, twenty-four donations totalling $216,300 from fifteen sources were made to the trust fund. The money was then used to pay Buchanan's debts, incurred mainly by bad real estate deals.

In August 1991, Mr. Justice Alexander MacIntosh of the Nova Scotia Supreme Court ruled that his hands were tied because the provincial law applied only to current members of the legislature and Buchanan no longer qualified. That prompted Attorney-General Joel Matheson to promise that the government would immediately close the loophole that prevented an inquiry into Buchanan's secret income. The next month, the RCMP announced that Buchanan would not face criminal charges into allegations by Zareski of kickbacks and patronage abuse. "There is no evidence established to support any criminal wrongdoing by Senator Buchanan," the RCMP statement said. Buchanan said he was "relieved" to see the end of a "difficult, vicious year." Two of Buchanan's former officials were charged in the Zareski case.

In a January 1991 interview, Buchanan said he had no regrets about stepping down as premier but was having some difficulty adjusting to life in Sleepy Hollow. "Quite frankly, I don't have enough to do," he said. "When you are trained at doing something for over 20 years, you don't change overnight."

He did say, however, he was prepared to accept board director-ships to help him while away his time.

On September 23, 1990, the day before Senator Buckwold's Liberal-loaded committee recommended that the upper chamber simply not consider the GST legislation, and in effect kill the bill, Mulroney named five more senators, bringing the number of appointments in two weeks to fifteen. The standings were fifty-two Liberals, forty-six Tories, four independents, one independent Liberal, and Reform Party senator Stan Waters.

Typically, the new senators had both big-time political and business ties. One of them was Trevor Eyton, fifty-six, a Toronto lawyer, president, and chief executive officer of Brascan Ltd. and director of several other major corporations, including General Motors of Canada Ltd., M.A. Hanna Co. of Cleveland, John Labatt Ltd., Royal Trustco Ltd., and Coca-Cola Canada Ltd.; his main contribution to the Senate has been as a serious rival to disgraced former senator Andrew Thompson in the race for worst all-time attendance records. Along with Eyton, Mulroney also named Claude Castonguay, sixty-one, a former Quebec provincial Liberal cabinet minister, now a Montreal business executive; John Lynch-Staunton, sixty, chairman of de Kuyper Canada Inc. and a key member of former Montreal mayor Jean Drapeau's administration; Mabel DeWare, sixty-four, of Moncton, a long-time member of the Conservative government of former premier and newly minted senator Richard Hatfield; and James Kelleher, a fifty-nine-year-old Sault Ste. Marie lawyer and former federal solicitor-general who was defeated at the polls in 1988.

In the Senate, Buckwold announced that the GST "is a very bad piece of legislation that Canadians by the millions asked the Senate to reject and we've acted accordingly." That prompted Tory senator Jean-Maurice Simard to call on Mulroney to "swamp" the Senate with eight extra Tories under the never-used constitutional provision. The move would need the approval of Governor-General Ray Hnatyshyn, hardly a challenge since Hnatyshyn was not only the son of a former Tory senator but had served as a senior Mulroney cabinet minister before getting his vice-regal sinecure.

On September 27, Mulroney used the constitutional clause to stuff eight new GST senators into the Upper House, prompting British Columbia to say it would challenge the constitutionality of the extra seats. Saying it was his "duty to defend the rights of the House of Commons and its supremacy over appointed senators," Mulroney also orchestrated the early retirement of seventy-four-year-old Alberta senator Martha Bielish and immediately replaced her with Walter Twinn, an Alberta Indian chief and businessman.

The new standings gave the Conservatives fifty-four senators, still three seats short of an absolute majority, but two ahead of the Liberals. There were also four independents, one independent Liberal, and one Reformer.

The "GST Senators," as they will always be remembered in infamy, were:

- Michael Meighen, a millionaire lawyer, former national Conservative president, and grandson of former prime minister Arthur Meighen.
- Normand Grimard, a Quebec lawyer and businessman with Tory ties. He was vice-president of the Quebec Chamber of Commerce in 1959.
- Janis Johnson, a Winnipeg consultant, former national director of the Conservative Party, close friend and shopping companion of Mila Mulroney, and ex-wife of former Newfoundland premier Frank Moores.

- James Ross, a wealthy Fredericton lawyer and chairman of Ross Ventures Ltd., which had holdings in industrial, residential, and commercial real estate, broadcasting, and aquaculture.
- Michael Forrestall, a former journalist and twenty-three-year Tory MP who was not only enjoying his generous parliamentary pension at the time but was also revelling in a Mulroney gift of a patronage post on the Veterans' Appeal Board.
- Thérèse Lavoie-Roux, former Quebec Liberal health and social services minister, a social worker, and professor at the University of Montreal.
- Eric Berntson, former Saskatchewan deputy premier and businessman who was convicted in 1999 of fraudulent use of provincial funds while in office there.
- Wilbert Keon, Canada's foremost cardiac surgeon, the most surprising appointment of all given his high standing in the community and his complete lack of partisan ties. People expected more from Keon than that he would lend his name to such a tawdry exercise. Keon was pursued by protesters, his office was picketed, and he was deluged with mail. He received threatening calls at work and at home. "I was frightened for my own personal safety," he said later. "It shook me up. And I'm not easily shaken. I found myself questioning my own judgement and my own conscience." Too late, alas.

Since the Senate had resumed sitting on September 25 following the summer break, the Tories in the upper chamber had been staging a filibuster in order to give Mulroney time to name the additional senators and tip the balance of power in their favour. The "royal stackers," as Liberal senator Royce Frith called the GST Eight, were actually sneaked through an old underground tunnel, stooping to avoid low-hanging water and heating pipes, from the East Block to the Centre Block, where the Red Chamber is, near a stairway that went up to Tory Senate Speaker Guy Charbonneau's office, where they were sworn into office in a clandestine ceremony instead of the usual swearing-in performance in the Chamber itself. As the Tories continued their lengthy tributes to retiring senator Martha Bielish, Frith called for the Speaker to put the question "that strangers be order to withdraw," a move that is designed to protect senators from interlopers and that must be called without debate or amendment. This was the start of an unbroken three-month war by the Liberal senators to kill the GST bill. Their efforts were thwarted in part by the dictatorial rulings of the supposedly neutral Senate Speaker, Guy Charbonneau, a Quebec Tory, who interpreted the rules his own way, broke several agreements he'd made with the Liberals, and simply ran roughshod over them when it helped the Tory cause. At one point, Charbonneau even locked the chamber doors and called a vote when there were no Liberals in the Upper House, leaving fifty-two Tories and two independents to vote down an opposition move and put an end to their delaying tactics. He even ignored the Senate tradition that the Speaker doesn't vote, siding with the government senators on every single vote.

While the Liberals were, of course, outraged by Charbonneau's contempt for the chamber's rules and traditions, they themselves had long gone over the line of legitimate debate. At this point, it was difficult to cheer for either side.

In what must be by any measure the low point in the entire history of the Senate, Liberal senators were reduced on October 5 to a twenty-four-hour filibuster in which they blew kazoos, rang cowbells, shouted obscenities, and generally obstructed Senate business. MacEachen, who was travelling in Europe on private business for the Bank of Montreal, had left his deputy, Frith, to organize the Liberal troops. The floor of the Red Chamber was in complete disarray, with papers strewn about, chairs jolted out of place, and other papers flying across the aisles. Liberal senator David Steuart, seventy-four, pressed his finger into a Tory senator's chest and called him an "obscene bugger." Senator Philippe Deane Gigantes, once the secretary-general to the King of Greece and a former Greek culture minister, blew a raspberry and later produce a pea whistle. After that, he began reading the Lamentations of Jeremiah in his deep, mellifluous voice. Senator Roméo LeBlanc, our future governor-general, wandered around the chamber tooting an old-fashioned bicycle horn with a rubber bulb, while his Liberal colleagues continued to create a hellish din by banging the lids of their wooden desks. Senate Conservative leader Lowell Murray kept trying to read a motion to get business started, but Liberal Peter Stollery had moved his chair to what was described as a "confessional position," directly in front of Murray's microphone. Whenever Murray began to speak, Stollery drowned him out.

At one point, Chrétien appeared in the public gallery, looked down at his Liberal colleagues, and simply smiled.

Liberal House leader Jean-Robert Gauthier accused Mulroney in the Commons of using Nazi-like tactics to push the GST through the Senate. He said the Tories had been putting "the jackboot to Canadians."

And so it went. Demands and counter-demands, recriminations, stalling tactics, a round-the-clock filibuster by the Liberal senators. At one point Senator Jacques Hébert accused Charbonneau of acting like a "Nazi," an unfortunate accusation against a man who fought the Nazis as a captain with Les Fusiliers Mont-Royal. The only fighting Hébert did during the war was in the nature of deep philosophical disagreements while he and his good pal Pierre Trudeau sipped tea at Montreal cafés. Mulroney meanwhile accused the Liberal senators of "legislative terrorism" and attacked media coverage of the stand-off for being too "soft" on the Liberals.

By mid-October, the Ontario Court of Justice had ruled that Mulroney's Senate stacking was legal, rejecting a challenge by Liberal senators against the appointment of New Brunswick's James Ross. MacEachen scoffed at the notion it was a setback. "I've said from the beginning that our battle with the GST didn't hinge on court rulings, the judging on the law. We're judging on a tax."

Things returned to relative normality around that time when the senators called a temporary truce to resume other Senate business – but not debate the GST – to clear a backlog of legislation. By the last week in October, Chrétien conceded that Liberal tactics were hurting his party when a Gallup poll showed the NDP surging ahead to become the top choice with voters. It showed the NDP at thirty-eight per cent, Liberals at thirty-one, and Tories, fifteen. But that didn't stop Chrétien from declaring on October 28 at a Montreal fund-raiser that the GST would not pass. "I am opposed to the GST," he said. "I have always been opposed to it and I will be opposed to it always."

The all-night sittings and tactical warfare resumed on October 30. Senator Philippe Gigantes, sixty-seven, announced he was out to smash the record of sixteen uninterrupted hours, the longest non-stop parliamentary speech in Canadian history delivered by Amor de Cosmos, a member of the colonial legislature in British Columbia in 1866. In the spring of 1990, Ontario NDP MPP Peter Kormos had spoken for about seventeen hours while in opposition but had taken the odd break. Earlier in the GST debate, Gigantes had spent eight hours, much of it reading from one of his books. He was accused by Quebec Tory Paul David of doing it so that he could get a free translation from *Hansard*, the daily written reports of speeches in both official languages. Gigantes spoke for seventeen hours and forty-five minutes, touching on everything from take-out pizza to the political philosophy of Machiavelli. According to the Guinness record keepers, the world record for speeches, including seven stops, is forty-three hours set by Texas state senator Bill Meier in 1977.

The round-the-clock battle continued. At 5 A.M. on November 30, Liberal senator Earl Hastings, sixty-six, collapsed in his chair after speaking for several hours. GST senator Wilbert Keon, the heart surgeon, rushed across the aisle to help Hastings, who had a history of heart problems. Keon checked his condition, sat with him while he regained his strength, then took him to the Senate's clinic. Fortunately, the collapse was not a heart attack, but was caused by a combination of stress, exhaustion, and taking cardiac medication on an empty stomach. On December 5, while Senator Joyce Fairbairn was approaching the six-hour mark in her filibuster speech, Justice Nicholson McRae of the general division of Ontario Court rejected a constitutional challenge to Mulroney's appointment of the extra senators. The Liberals, despite their Herculean efforts, were running out of both time and tactics. Finally, on December 14, the Senate voted 55–49 to approve the GST bill, just in time for it to take effect on January 1, 1991.

MacEachen, who had called Senate Speaker Charbonneau a "gangster" for allowing the vote after only eleven of the fifty-one Liberal senators had debated it, said the final vote was "a dirty launch to a dirty bill." He vowed never to cooperate with the government on future business. Not that he had been cooperating anyway.

On June 6, 1991, the Conservative majority in the Senate proposed sweeping rule changes for the Upper House that make it impossible for a repeat of the GST battle. "The lack of adequate rules has led to a shameful waste of time," said Tory senator Brenda Robertson, head of the Senate rules committee. "You come and you expect to work and you don't work. It's really very discouraging."

The new rules eliminate a number of the Liberal stalling tactics, such as the endless reading of petitions on a name-by-name basis, make government business the top priority each day, and limit senators to fifteen minutes of debate. The seventy-eight-page package parallels similar changes adopted in April by the Conservative majority in the Commons. The Liberals had refused to participate in Robertson's committee, so the committee of eight Tories and independent Hartland Molson rewrote the rule book without them.

The rules limit daily question period to thirty minutes – previously, there was no time limit – and make Senate committee meetings – except those dealing with personnel matters and labour relations – open to the public. They give the Speaker the power to interrupt debate to enforce the rules. They also make it easier for the ruling party to shut off debate and force a vote.

In a story by *Toronto Star* reporter William Walker in April 1992, both the Tory Senate leader, Lowell Murray, and his Liberal counterpart, Royce Frith, conceded that the new rules allowing the majority party to invoke closure and force a vote have taken much of the starch out of the place. Senate attendance "is worse, I think it's fair to say," Murray admitted. Frith said the upper chamber had reverted "to the old mouldy fig club. That's what it is, only worse. It's just worse. . . . The Senate is now just the footstool of the government. The only thing the Senate can now do is rubber-stamp legislation. It's really very frustrating, even depressing."

One thing Mulroney was determined to do before his retirement on June 25, 1993, was to make sure he crammed as many Tories into the upper chamber as it would hold.

On March 25, 1993, Mulroney appointed Ron Ghitter, fifty-eight, a Calgary lawyer and former Alberta MLA, who was also chairman of the federal Tory election campaign committee for Alberta; and Terrance Stratton, fifty-five, a partner in AirWest Air Charter Service in Winnipeg and a vice-president of the national Tory association. Those appointments came a couple of weeks after he named former Liberals Jean-Claude Rivest and Raynell Andreychuk, both of whom, like good little boys, agreed to confess their earlier sins and sit in the Senate as Conservatives.

Trudeau's patronage machine had cranked into high gear the closer he got to retirement, but Mulroney's machine made it look slow. Mulroney charged into a frenzy of patronage pay-outs, which is at least part of the reason why Canadians remember him, even now, with revulsion. On May 26, he named four more senators: Fernand Roberge, an old Mulroney crony and former inn keeper at Montreal's Ritz Carlton Hotel; Leonard Gustafson, a nondescript Saskatchewan MP who had been Mulroney's parliament secretary; and Duncan Jessiman, a longtime party fund-raiser from Winnipeg. He also named veteran Liberal MP Marcel Prud'homme, who agreed to sit as an independent. The new senators replaced three Tories who stepped down early – E.W. Barootes, Jean-Marie Poitras, both of whom were several months away from mandatory retirement, and

James Ross, fifty-five, one of the infamous GST senators – along with independent Hartland Molson, eighty-five, one of the two remaining senators-for-life. (The other was Nova Scotian John M. Macdonald, who died a month later at age ninety-one). Mulroney's strategy was clear. The more he could get rid of aging senators and pack the Senate with younger ones, the longer the Conservatives could maintain power in the Senate.

On June 18, Mulroney elevated Marjory LeBreton, the patronage queen herself, to the upper chamber, along with Pierre Claude Nolin, former chief of staff to Mulroney minister Roch LaSalle, also a PMO aide, lobbyist, and fund-raiser. LeBreton, who is one of the nicer people in politics, was nonetheless a natural for an appointment. As Mulroney's deputy chief of staff, it was her job to coordinate the roughly three thousand patronage jobs available to the prime minister for doling out. Having faithfully served her master, LeBreton was in the perfect position to organize herself right into the best patronage job of all.

Five days before Kim Campbell began her short tenure as Canada's first female prime minister, Mulroney rewarded Montreal lawyer David Angus, a major businessman and chairman of the PC Canada Fund. In the previous two weeks he had appointed three more loyal Tories: Jean Desmarais, sixty-nine, a retired Sudbury doctor whose major credential was that he is the brother of Mulroney's old friend Paul Desmarais, founder of Power Corp.; Erminie Cohen, sixty-six, a Saint John businesswoman and long-time Tory; and David Tkachuk, forty-eight, a Saskatoon businessman who served as principal secretary to former Saskatchewan premier Grant Devine until the provincial Conservative caucus rebelled over his prickly personality and forced Devine to bounce him.

And on June 23, 1993, with just two days left in his job as prime minister, Mulroney took a moment to name former B.C. MP and national party president Gerry St. Germain as his final lucky lottery winner.

Since announcing his resignation plans in February, Mulroney had named twelve senators. All but one – Prud'homme, the former Liberal turned independent – were Tories, leaving the Senate with fifty-five Conservatives, forty-one Liberals, five independents, and three vacancies.

As for MacEachen, a man so tight-fisted he used to travel with his own bread and sometimes asked restaurants to toast it, he found it hard to break a lifetime of living off the avails of the taxpayers. He formally retired from forty-three years of public life on June 19, 1996. But, being MacEachen, he wasn't quite finished. His own regal sense of entitlement outweighed the small matter of the mandatory retirement age of seventy-five.

On May 28, 1998, two years after he officially retired, MacEachen dismissed Tory criticism concerning the three-room office suite he still occupied at public expense in the newly renovated East Block of the Parliament Buildings. He claimed he had been given the office to work on his "papers" in keeping with the "tradition" established by the late Eugene Forsey.

He had quietly commandeered a fully equipped first-floor government office. According to fellow Cape Breton Liberal senator Al Graham, the government leader in the Senate, it was perfectly appropriate because MacEachen was a "national resource," who, like Forsey, could be used by all parties, an absurd claim that provoked derisive laughter from Conservative senators.

John Lynch-Staunton, the Senate opposition leader, said he had agreed in 1996 with the Liberal government that MacEachen could keep a small office in the Victoria Building, west along Wellington Street, to get his papers in order, "beyond the two months" normally allowed for retiring senators. "It was in deference to his many years in Parliament. But we were never, never, never asked for approval for him to move to the East Block."

Graham denied that MacEachen was also enjoying the services of government-paid staff, even though he was in fact using their services. Graham claimed one of the two young men was a volunteer. The other, he said, actually worked for Graham but was in MacEachen's office because of a shortage of space.

The Liberals then tried to compare MacEachen's suite with a small desk being used by former Tory senator Jack Marshall to work on veterans' files. Marshall, a long-time activist for veterans' rights, was simply using a table in the corner of Senator Brenda Robertson's office two days a week to work on non-partisan requests for help from veterans across the country. Liberal House leader Don Boudria – a charter member of the former Liberal opposition "Rat Pack" – argued that "the point is not the size of the office the former senators use. The fact is that other members of other parties, including the Tories, were accorded the same kind of benefits."

In a short interview with the *Ottawa Citizen*, MacEachen said he was reconsidering his situation in view of the fuss being made by the opposition parties. "Thanks for the memories," he quipped. "It is an occupational hazard, isn't it? It's like the old days, I was struggling for obscurity and I get all this attention."

And he loved every minute of it.

9

AIRPLANES, HOCKEY STARS, AND
OTHER STRANGERS

I T SURE MADE the headlines. And garnered votes.

Liberal leader Jean Chrétien, campaigning in Toronto on October 6, 1993, attacked the Conservative government for what he charged was a sweetheart deal to reward Tory developers by giving them a $700-million contract to privatize Toronto's Pearson International Airport. Under the terms of the deal Pearson Development Corp., a private consortium, would lease Terminals 1 and 2 for fifty-seven years and keep the profits in return for $700 million in renovations. Chrétien turned the issue into a potent symbol of Tory patronage and the influence of paid lobbyists in the outgoing regime. Elect him, said Chrétien, and he'll review the deal.

The next day, Prime Minister Kim Campbell signed the deal with the consortium. Eighteen days after that, Chrétien won a majority, reducing the governing Tories to two seats. Three days later, as promised, Chrétien appointed veteran Liberal soldier Robert Nixon, a one-time Ontario Liberal leader, to conduct a thirty-day review of the deal. The government released Nixon's shoddy, superficial four-teen-page report on December 3. It criticized lobbyists and political aides for fashioning a deal that gave the private consortium "excessive profits." Nixon – who was subsequently rewarded for his loyal service by being made head of the Atomic Energy Board of Canada – recommended that the deal be cancelled.

Nixon conveniently ignored a Transport Canada briefing paper that concluded that the contract process was fair. It also said that Deloitte & Touche, as independent consultants, concluded the fourteen per cent annual rate of return projected by the developers was "reasonable." In addition, Price Waterhouse said the net value of the contract to the government was $843 million – "considerably better" than the $595 million the government could earn by operating Terminals 1 and 2 themselves. In short, the experts, studying the facts, said it was a good deal. The Liberal politicians, playing politics, said it wasn't.

The original contract was won in December 1992 by Paxport Inc., a firm headed by former Conservative Party president Don Matthews. But when it couldn't raise the necessary money, it merged with Claridge Properties Ltd. to form Pearson Development Corp. Claridge, which owned sixty-five per cent of the consortium, was headed by Liberal senator Leo Kolber on behalf of Charles Bronfman. In other words, both main parties were directly involved in the deal, but despite this, Chrétien and the Liberals continued to insist throughout the long controversy that it was all a Tory patronage plot hatched by Mulroney to reward his friends.

In April 1994, the then justice minister Allan Rock tabled legislation that, incredibly, took away the right of the consortium to sue the Crown for lost profits. Instead, the government offered $30 million for the company's out-of-pocket expenses, a tad less than the $454-million the company said it would lose. The right to sue is a matter of basic justice. It doesn't mean you'll win your case. That's up to the courts to decide. But even if the Pearson deal was a patronage pay-out – although the Liberals are hardly in a position to offer moral guidance on that, either – it was indefensible to unilaterally remove the consortium's right to sue for damages.

The manifestly unjust bill was approved by the Liberal majority in the Commons on June 16, but it ran into a wall of opposition in July from the Conservative majority in the Senate. The worm had turned.

The Tory senators used their majority to amend the bill and send it back to the Commons.

Prime Minister Chrétien, who had openly cheered when Allan MacEachen and the other Liberal senators obstructed the Mulroney Tories, now railed against the Tory senators, accusing them of abusing their power.

In late September, Transport Minister Doug Young angrily rejected the Senate amendments, charging that the consortium wanted to sting the Canadian public for more than $400 million. By December, the Liberals had calmed down enough to agree to some minor amendments to the bill. Later on, Rock offered to permit the consortium to sue the government for defamation and allow claims for legal and other expenses. But the government would not drop the provision that prevented the company from suing for lost profits or lobbying fees.

In January 1995, Ontario Court Justice Stephen Borins ruled that the Liberals had breached a contract when it cancelled the Pearson deal after the election. This cleared the way for a damage suit from the consortium. On May 2, the Liberals reluctantly caved in to the Senate demand for a Senate inquiry into the deal. The government lost its appeal of the court ruling on May 23.

The standoff showed no sign of coming to an end in December when the Senate's $250,000 inquiry issued a report following eight weeks of testimony and sixty-five witnesses. The seven-member Conservative majority on the committee – chaired by Nova Scotia Tory senator Finlay MacDonald – refused to approve the Liberal legislation and accused the government of wasting millions of dollars to make a political point.

While railing about Tory patronage, of course, Chrétien had been using every available opportunity to load the Senate with more Liberals. His first appointment came in August 1994 when he named Jean-Louis Roux, seventy-one, a well-known Quebec actor, writer, and director. The next month he appointed three prominent Liberal women: Sharon Carstairs, a former Manitoba Liberal leader; Lise Bacon, a former deputy premier of Quebec; and Landan Pearson, a daughter-in-law of former prime minister Lester Pearson and well-known children's advocate. In November, veteran Ottawa Liberal MP Jean-Robert Gauthier and New Brunswick businessman and Liberal enthusiast John Bryden became senators. The same day, Chrétien named his old friend Roméo LeBlanc, then Senate Speaker, as Canada's new governor-general. In March 1995, Chrétien named two more women: former federal fitness minister Céline Hervieux-Payette of Montreal and Rose-Marie Losier-Cool, a former teachers' union leader and women's advocate from Bathurst, New Brunswick. In September, Chrétien brought the Liberals within one seat of the Tories by filling four more vacancies: William Rompkey, a veteran Newfoundland MP; Doris M. Anderson, a one-time home economics professor from Prince Edward Island; Lorna Milne, a local political activist from Brampton, Ontario; and Marie-Paule Poulin, a former CBC vice-president and senior federal bureaucrat from Sudbury.

When Conservative senator John Sylvain retired in January, the Liberals and Tories were tied at fifty seats each. About the same time Chrétien was grabbing a protester by the throat in Hull in February, he was also shipping former Quebec Liberal MP Shirley Maheu into the upper chamber, giving the Liberals a one-seat edge, with three independents. He maintained that edge in February when he sent Alberta Liberal Bud Olson back home to be lieutenant-governor and replaced him with former Alberta Liberal leader Nick Taylor. Taylor had been instrumental in pushing the idea of elected senators in Alberta. As an appointed senator, he quickly made his mark by chalking up $105,000 in travel expenses, which included the cost, at public expense, of flying eight of his nine children to Ottawa for his induction.

The Pearson bill died after Parliament prorogued in February, but the Liberals re-introduced it in April. It was defeated in the Senate on June 19 on a 48–48 tie vote when one Liberal voted against it and two were absent. Saskatchewan's Herbert Sparrow stunned the Liberals by siding with the Tories. "They went just too far in trying to prohibit anyone who may be damaged from taking it to court," he said. Former Ontario Liberal leader Andrew Thompson, naturally, wasn't around, and gadabout Colin Kenny was in Europe freeloading at a meeting of the Canada-Europe interparliamentary union. The Liberals were so anxious to pass the bill that Jean-Robert Gauthier was brought to the Red Chamber in a wheelchair and Shirley Maheu turned up despite recent heart-bypass surgery. By this time, the developers were suing the government for $660 million. Transport Minister David Anderson was furious, saying, "All I can assure you is this, that we are not going to allow the Conservative senators to thwart the will of the Canadian public as expressed in the election and provide up to $600 million in totally unearned profits to the developers."

Chrétien vowed to bring back the bill. "There will be a bill, I'm telling you. I've not changed my mind about it. We do not intend to pay all the money that is asked of us."

In September the government took a different tack, trying to negotiate an out-of-court settlement with the developers. A proposal by the consortium was rejected.

At the same time, throughout most of 1996, Madam Justice Donna Haley of the Ontario Court's General Division heard evidence from the consortium that it was owed between $523 million and $662 million in lost profits. The government began its defence of the charges in late January 1997 when justice department lawyer Ivan Whitehall said, "Our position is, very simply, that they overstated the amount of money they would have made."

On April 17, 1997, the government agreed to a complicated out-of-court settlement that cost the government $245 million. The deal was contingent on the sale of Pearson's Terminal 3 for $719 million to the non-profit Greater Toronto Airports Authority. Donald Matthews, the former Conservative Party president whose involvement in the deal sparked the whole affair, said he was glad the process had cleared his name, adding that the government move was "purely political" because of the anticipated upcoming election. "I think the government recognized they were in the wrong here," he said. "And when you're in the wrong you don't want to be involved in an election campaign trying to defend what's wrong." Eleven days later, Chrétien announced a June 2 general election

After winning his second majority in 1997, Chrétien continued to ignore the moralizing in the Liberal Red Book – the party's formal election platform – and appointed party loyalists to the Senate at every opportunity.

One of those who caught the attention of Reform leader Preston Manning was a millionaire businessman and party organizer from Kelowna, British Columbia, Ross Fitzpatrick, who was appointed March 6, 1998, and was soon appointed Chrétien's B.C. lieutenant. Fitzpatrick's friendship with Chrétien dated back thirty-five years. In 1987, when Chrétien was out of elected politics briefly, Fitzpatrick sold Chrétien, who was then a director of Viceroy Resource Corporation, 10,000 shares of his (Fitzpatrick's) corporation for $8 each, although the fast-rising shares were selling for $12.75 that same day on the Toronto Stock Exchange. A week later, Chrétien sold 5,000 of the shares at $17.125, for a neat $45,625 profit. "In other words," said Manning, "the prime minister appointed a long-time party activist, personal friend, and financial benefactor to the Upper House. A reasonable person operating on the general information available to the public would conclude that this was first and foremost a 'patronage appointment.'" Reform MP Bill Gilmour said, "It looks like payback time. It has a bad smell to it."

On March 18, Chrétien threatened to sue Manning if he repeated accusations outside the Commons that Fitzpatrick had bought his Senate seat. Manning didn't bite, but continued to describe the appointment as "smelly."

On June 12, 1998, former NHL hockey star Frank Mahovlich appeared in a large advertisement in the *Globe and Mail* wearing a Harry Rosen suit. Mahovlich, on his way to take his seat in the upper chamber, figured he might as well get something else to supplement his newly acquired $65,600 salary plus $10,300 tax-free expense allowance.

Roger Gallaway, the Sarnia Liberal MP who is campaigning to have the Senate abolished, said of Mahovlich and another new senator, fashion designer Vivienne Poy, "They make it even more difficult to make the thing work. People who cannot just get up and speak have to have everything written for them. I suppose they're less likely to do things they ought not to do – but it makes them less likely to do anything."

In an interview with *Hockey Night in Canada* producer Jim Hough, Chrétien said it was "a way to recognize all the hockey players who make a great contribution not only in the so-called entertainment of hockey but in their private life. There are many of them who are very available to help kids and all sorts of other organizations that are dedicated to making a better society. So, having to choose one, I picked up Frank Mahovlich because he has a great personality and he's very popular in the caucus because, you know, for us we all have our stars in sports."

Actually, Mahovlich was retired senator Keith Davey's pick. Chrétien and Mahovlich had met only briefly at three social functions over the years, but Davey, a dedicated jock and incurable political fixer, figured the Big M would be a popular choice.

There are many old hockey players around who can actually speak in complete sentences without having it written down for them, as was Mahovlich's maiden speech on a bill to ban tobacco sponsorship of sporting and artistic events. There are many others who have worked long and hard in various volunteer activities to make it a better society. Mahovlich is, well, a hockey player. A damn good one, but little more.

In a March 1999 *Saturday Night* magazine feature on Mahovlich by Allen Abel, Manitoba's Sharon Carstairs conceded that Mahovlich and Poy, to name two, "are somewhat bewildered," but she was conducting seminars for them.

Barry Cooper of the University of Calgary saw the appointment of Mahovlich as just about the last straw for the upper chamber. "I think his exact quote when he was named was, 'I'm going to sit there and keep my mouth shut.' Well, that's really not what the Senate is for, even in its current incarnation as a patronage holding tank," said Cooper. "The PM can say what he says about why he chose Frank Mahovlich, but I don't believe him for a minute. Just because he talks funny doesn't mean he's stupid. He's got an agenda for the Senate. To pick Frank Mahovlich or a fashion designer is his way to diminish any authority the Senate has left."

As if to prove Cooper's point, Mahovlich's next three-minute speech was about Frederick W. Schumacher, the Ohio cough-syrup magnate, mine owner, and philanthropist, after whom Mahovlich's northern Ontario hometown is named. He spoke about how all the kids in town got Christmas presents from Schumacher – who could no doubt afford it given the back-breaking work of their fathers in the mines – and said one year he got a Detroit Red Wings hockey sweater and a pair of socks and immediately changed his allegiance from the Toronto Maple Leafs to the Red Wings.

Abel writes, "What the monologue has to do with the course of Canada's ship of state is rather indistinct, but when it concludes, members on both sides of the aisle thump their desks and shout huzzahs and it may even be that they mean it."

In his April 20, 1998, attack on the Senate, Preston Manning claimed that over the past thirty years the taxpayers had paid out $1 billion to keep the place going, an expense that far outweighed any benefits that may have accrued. According to Manning, senators' salaries in that time have cost $354 million; their travel, $133 million; office expenses, $72 million; and administration and services, $441 million.

A word of praise for independent senator Doug Everett, the Winnipeg businessman who retired on January 20, 1994, at age sixty-eight after twenty-two years in the Senate, several of them as chairman of the finance committee. For his last six years Everett did not accept any salary, saying he could "no longer devote the time necessary" to be an effective senator, so he didn't deserve the money.

In 1867, the entire government was run for $451,810, and $96,580 of that was used to keep the Senate in business. By 1963–64 the Senate budget was still a relatively modest $1.85 million, and ten years later was just slightly over $2 million.

It wasn't until the Trudeau crowd began moving into the Senate from the Commons and the PMO, where the living was easy and all the perks were in place, that the cost of servicing their demands began to push the Senate budget beyond reason. By 1981–82, it had mushroomed to $19 million, jumping to $26 million in the 1984–85 public accounts, and passing $30 million by 1987–88. It shot past $40 million in 1990–91, hung around there during the Liberal cost-cutting days, but shot up again to $44.7 million in the 1998–99 estimates.

And these figures don't show the real cost of the place. When former auditor-general Kenneth Dye studied the 1989–90 budget – over the serious objections of the senators themselves – he concluded that the Senate enjoyed other services at public expense valued at $11.5 million that did not show up in the $42-million budget. These services come out of Canada Post, public works, secretary of state, treasury board, RCMP, and the Library of Parliament and brought the public cost of each senator to well over $500,000 annually. Since that time, administration costs alone have more than doubled, to $22 million, a fairly heavy load for an institution where the inmates sat only for sixty-six and one-half days.

In his 1989–90 audit, Dye's major concern was the lack of overall accountability for public money spent, a problem that still hasn't really been resolved. Dye noted that the personal staff of the senators receive more generous pay than other government workers, part of which he attributed to the large number of family, friends, and other faithful retainers working in their offices. Dye called the number of relatives on the senators' payrolls "inconsistent with the spirit of the Parliament of Canada Act which states a Senator cannot have a direct or indirect interest in a contract funded with public money."

Dye also criticized the senatorial phone bills – which were averaging $10,000 a year – and wondered why salaried *Hansard* reporters and transcribers who record the deathless Senate debates were paid as full-time employees even though they worked only between 100 and 150 days a year. Indeed, the senatorial practice of taking advantage of the system extends to their staff as well. In a November 1993 article in the *Ottawa Citizen*, reporter Greg Weston discovered that a dozen full-time Senate reporters with nothing to do for the previous five months had been earning about $300 a day moonlighting for other federal agencies while at the same time collecting their $60,000 government salaries. Since the Senate convened for only forty-three days in 1993 – one of which was to vote themselves a $6,000 pay raise – the transcribers spent much of their time getting paid for doing nothing. And so, with the blessings of their Senate managers, they began renting themselves out to private firms with lucrative government contracts. Three of them, for example, were earning $300 a day transcribing for public hearings being conducted by the federal government's Radio-television and Telecommunications Commission, a practice that Weston characterized as "double-dipping on a grand scale."

Before the Trudeau years, the Senate was a relatively frugal place. At one time, for example, Senator Hartland Molson, one of the richest men in the world, shared an office and one secretary with two other senators. Until around 1984, if a senator wanted, say, a new fax machine, he had to buy it out of his $9,000 expense allowance.

Enter Senator Colin Kenny, widely known as "Colonel Klink,"

a mocking reference to the bumbling commandant in the TV series *Hogan's Heroes*, stemming from the days when he organized the luggage and other things for Trudeau's election tours. Kenny, who runs a tanning salon in Ottawa and has the personality of an injured bear, has consistently argued that senators are underpaid – he's serious, really – and has done everything he could to get them more money and perks. Kenny, a high roller, is fond of custom-tailored shirts with the "JCRK" monogram and his vanity licence plates, SEN101.

In 1984 the senators started a totally discretionary Senate research fund out of which each senator was given a budget of $15,000 a year to do with as he or she wished. Actually, a sub-committee of the internal economy committee, meeting in camera, added another $30,000 per senator. They did not advertise the fund among all the senators, particularly the non-Liberal senators, so what was little more than a Senate slush fund was made selectively available. For the first few years, it wasn't even put in the annual spending estimates, appearing only when it was renamed as the Senators' Office Budget. One former insider said, "A lot of unemployed Liberals were hired during this time. There were a lot of them around after 1984, and the slush fund was used to hire them."

In addition to hiring their friends, of course, senators could use the fund to pay for the things their expense allowance was meant for – overnight accommodation, meals, that sort of thing – so their average take-home income went up without it being shown to have done so on the official books.

In 1987, Kenny proposed to a closed committee meeting that each senator be given an extra $52,000 a year to hire research staff and spruce up their offices. All eleven Liberals on the committee voted for it. The four Tories said no. Kenny also wanted senators to go on full pension after fifteen years, instead of twenty-five, and better pay for senators who act as whips and committee chairmen. He also wanted the tax-free allowance of $9,200 to balloon to $19,100, and added that senators be given $100,000 a year to hire personal staff. His proposals would have increased the Senate budget by a full twenty-five per cent.

In March 1990, the Gentleman Usher of the Black Rod, René Gutknecht, resigned after complaining that Kenny blocked changes to end the honour system under which senators had operated since Confederation. He said Kenny repeatedly acted to bar administrative changes that would govern a senator's use of facilities, staff, supplies, and services. Kenny denied it by saying, "Did we bog him down? It's not a question of us bogging him down. The Black Rod works for the Senate. We don't work for him, he works for us."

Kenny was also active in a brazen attempt by the senators in June 1990 to give themselves an additional $153 a day just for showing up. While the first ministers were debating Senate reform as a way of possibly breaking the Meech Lake Accord deadlock, the Senate quickly and quietly passed this per diem proposal motion without debate. They would have got away with it except for a protest by Tory backbencher René Soetens, who insisted in the Commons that it was a back-door money grab that could be allowed only through legislation approved by both Houses. "The process of paying someone extra money to show up to do a job that they are paid to show up and do is wrong," said Soetens. Speaker John Fraser agreed with him and shot it down.

Not discouraged, however, Kenny was behind the 1991 approval of a $2-million renovation project for new Senate offices and committee rooms. Each of the eleven new offices in the Victoria Building was given a private bathroom and separate offices for secretaries and researchers. Senator Michael Kirby's secretary actually had workmen raise the floor in her office by three inches. Why? So she could get a better view out of the window, which, incidentally, led her to complain about the pigeon droppings on the window sill. Kenny had commissioned a report in 1989, which concluded among other things that senatorial offices should be sound-proof and that the senators needed a fully equipped exercise room, a private dining room, and a lounge for the female senators, complete with a kitchenette. They backed off when the secret report was leaked to the

Ottawa Citizen. But Kenny was just in a holding pattern. In March 1991, his internal economy committee, in a closed meeting, approved spending $29,200 for a fitness centre in the Victoria Building. That was in addition to the three gymnasiums that already existed on Parliament Hill. They also built a women's lounge in the Centre Block and hid it in the official budget documents by calling it a "women's cloakroom."

Authors Bob Fife and John Warren also wrote about Kenny hiring a university student to prepare a document listing the decisions of his internal economy committee. He then got the Senate to spend $8,000 to hire the same student for a quarterly update, something that could have easily been done by paid staff. The committee also approved free food in the reading room near the Senate chamber, along with cellular phones, faxes for their homes, personal laptop computers, stereos, cameras and video cassette recorders, the latter so senators could use them for speech training. Kenny also proposed the Senate spend $185,658 to install "duress alarms," silent alarms under the desks of senators and their staff. The committee also approved an additional $20,000 to rent a second grey minibus to carry senators the half block from the Victoria Building to the Senate door, despite the fact the Commons had nine shuttle buses circling the same route at the time.

In February 1998, Kenny was outraged at a new proposal from the Commons that would mean that MPs, for the first time, would be paid more than senators. Kenny, who, in fairness, actually does put in long hours in his job, said, "Senators work as hard as members of the other place. I don't have any difficulty looking anybody in the eye and saying that I am worth whatever a member of the House of Commons gets." In fact, Kenny has argued for years that senators should get the same pay as high court judges, more than $125,000 a year. Mind you, this was the same year that the Senate took a three-week hiatus at Easter, when its workload had diminished to the point that senators sat for only twenty minutes on April 1. Just before ending the June session for an extended summer break, they voted themselves an annual two per cent raise for the next four years, plus a new $9,000 annual housing allowance. Then, having just returned from their exhausting summer break, they took an additional two-and-one-half-week Thanksgiving vacation. The Commons sits five days a week for more than 150 days a year. The Senate sits for three days and averages about sixty-five days a year. Some senators and MPs also spend extra time in committees.

The senators constantly claim they spend many, many extra hours in committee work. Well, some of them do, but many of them don't. And even when they do, most of their reports end up collecting dust in the library. A March 1999 survey of Senate committees by *Hill Times* reporter Mike Scandiffio put the lie to the constant claims of heavy workloads for committees. Scandiffio reports that the Senate Privileges, Standing Rules and Orders committee met on average 11.4 hours a year for the past eight years, while the Senate Fisheries Committee put in just 14.2 hours a year over that time. The Senate Aboriginal Peoples Committee logged about 16.9 hours a year since April 1, 1991, and dealt with a grand total of two bills.

The busiest committee was the prestigious Banking, Trade and Commerce Committee, which met an exhausting 75.9 hours a year – less than one week out of a full year – followed closely by the Legal and Constitutional Affairs Committee, which put in an almost equally gruelling schedule of 74.6 hours per year. Third busiest – if we can use that term – was Social Affairs, Science and Technology, with 70.2 hours, followed by Transport and Communications at 52.4 hours; Agriculture and Forestry, 37.7 hours; Internal Economy, Budgets and Administration, 35.4; Foreign Affairs, 34.3; National Finance, 33.9; and Energy, Environment and Natural Resources, a paltry 26.9 hours. Put another way, the twelve standing committees of the Senate put in an average of 40.3 hours a year, which is about what most people put in each week. Even Senator Kenny conceded, "We are talking about an embarrassingly light workload." New Brunswick Tory senator Brenda Robertson, vice-chair of the Standing Orders Committee, said the party has problems getting senators to attend committees and in four years may not have enough members to fill the seats. "According to my math," she said, "in about four years we will have about twenty-five active members in the Senate."

Senators frequently say that they are off working for the good of the people on what are called "public business" days, which they claim to avoid being fined for excessive absenteeism. But that often means they are either working on their own private interests – in 1997, for example, Senator Trevor Eyton claimed "public business" days for attending a Toronto SkyDome board meeting and international chamber of commerce meetings in Paris – or they are travelling at public expense in the faithful service of their particular political party. In an October 1997 story by *Ottawa Citizen* reporter Jack Aubrey, for example, Saskatchewan Tory senator David Tkachuk, co-chairman of the federal Conservative election team, explained his $100,000 air travel bill for the year by saying, "As campaign chairman, I had to travel all over the country for the party before the election. The Senate allows party activities as public business." Later, he telephoned Aubrey to say that much of his expenses came from travel between his home and Ottawa, although some of those trips were for election meetings in the capital. He said Liberal senators do the same thing, which is true, but hardly justification for charging the public for what should clearly be a political party expense.

The question of senatorial ethics – which some people consider an oxymoron – has been floating around the upper chamber forever. The Mulroney government introduced a new ethics package in March 1988. Under the terms of the package the senators would have been required to declare their interests, including corporate directorships, shareholdings, family financial arrangements, and fees charged for private consulting and other outside interests, to an independent ethics commission. "There are very few of us who have no outside interests," conceded Tory senator William Doody. Needless to say, the reform package was never put into effect.

Senators are regarded as valuable lobbyists for private interests because of their access to senior politicians and bureaucrats and their own role in the legislative process. They get to see draft legislation and amendments to bills before the public does. The same week that the reform package was introduced, for example, Tory senator Jean-Maurice Simard learned "from Ottawa sources" that the federal government was going to bail out *Le Matin*, a Moncton French-language newspaper for $75,000. He called the cabinet decision "blatant interference with the press." Simard was upset because he wanted to take over the newspaper himself. In exchange for a five-year contract, he claimed he could generate $250,000 in private-sector backing for the paper. *Le Matin*'s publisher, Adelin Blanchard, wanted the paper to merge with the rival *L'Acadie Nouvelle*, but Simard won control of the paper in March, only to admit defeat in June when he resigned as publisher.

At about this time, the Senate Banking, Trade and Commerce Committee had just finished reviewing the fundamental regulations governing financial institutions and put forward amendments affecting all bankers, trust companies, insurance firms, and brokers. The senators on the committee, in addition to supposedly protecting the public interest, also represented the corporate interests through their own directorships on just about every major corporation affected by the regulations. Among the firms that were represented by senators who were their board members were the Toronto-Dominion Bank, Bank of Montreal, Investment Dealers Association of Canada, First City Financial Corp. Ltd., Mutual Life Assurance Co., Mutual Fund of Canada, Alliance Global Fund, Canadian Investment Fund Ltd., Savings and Investment Trust, Savings and Investment American Fund Ltd., and Savings and Investment Corp.

Committee chairman Senator Ian Sinclair dismissed suggestions that these corporate senators have a conflict. He told the *Ottawa Citizen* that "if you own $1 million-worth of stock in Canadian Pacific, that's a flea bite." A senator would have to be on a company board and executive committee and own about twenty per cent of the equity "to enable the accounting profession to determine that you have significant influence."

Senators have long been prohibited from voting on any question in which they have "a pecuniary interest, not available to the general public," but the actual vote on an issue is just the final stage in a process that involves a lot of arm-twisting and discussion during which senators are free to exercise whatever influence they can.

A November 1998 survey of the banking committee by the *Ottawa Citizen* found that eight of the twelve senators who were drafting an important report on merger proposals by the major banks had direct ties to the financial-services sector, while another one, Senator Leo Kolber, had just stepped down from the board of the Toronto-Dominion Bank after twenty-seven years, citing the "perception" of a conflict of interest. He continued to sit on the committee.

Committee chairman Liberal senator Michael Kirby was on the advisory board of the Commercial Capital Corporation, which arranges term loans for small business. He had also conducted market studies for insurance and banking firms in the past. A week earlier, Conservative senators James Kelleher – a board member of Banco Commerciale Italiano – and Michael Meighen – Deutsche Bank Canada – had to withdraw after witnesses from these "Schedule 2" banks appeared before the committee to testify.

Kirby did set a precedent earlier in 1998 by asking committee members to file letters with the Senate law clerk revealing any business relationships they have with the financial-services sector. However, when the *Citizen* requested full disclosure from the law clerk, the request was only partially fulfilled.

Corporate directors usually are paid between $10,000 and $25,000 a year plus per diems of between $500 and $1,000 for attendance at each board meeting. A 1996 survey of 1,400 Canadians asked how acceptable it was that a senator "who has no other outside employment agrees to serve as a corporate director for a small fee." Fifty-five per cent said it was unacceptable, and only twenty-seven per cent said it was acceptable. Maureen Mancuso, a political science professor at the University of Guelph and one of the authors of the study, told the *Citizen* that Canadians wonder that even if the public interest is never harmed, would a senator have been appointed to the board if he or she had not been a public official?

Kirby said that senators with outside interests such as director-ships "were put there precisely because they would give expertise – they understand the business." Asked about the Liberal Red Book election promise to restore integrity to Parliament Hill, Kirby said, "That book is so long ago, I can't remember what is in it." Kirby also dismissed the poll's findings by noting that the Senate fares badly in most opinion polls. Perhaps he should ask himself why.

While the banking committee is the one most often cited in this regard, it's certainly not the only place you'll find blatant conflicts. A 1993 survey of the Energy and Natural Resources Committee, for example, found the following corporations represented by senators/ directors: Petro-Canada, Argyll Energy Corp., Abitibi Price, Central Mine Supply Co., Colonial Oil and Gas, Comaplex Resources International Ltd., the Saskatchewan Mining Development Corp., IPSCO Inc., and Producers Pipeline Inc.

During debate on the government's bill to limit tobacco sponsor-ship of arts and sports events, Tory senator Bill Kelly didn't vote, but he warned his colleagues that the legislation was "seriously flawed constitutionally." Senator Kelly, coincidentally, was chairman of Rothmans Inc. and had been a member of the board of directors of Rothmans, Benson and Hedges for fifteen years. Senators Michael Kirby and Roch Bolduc were absent for the vote in the upper chamber, but both of them had corporate connections with the tobacco companies as well.

In 1998, shortly after the internal economy committee approved a new $181-a-day tax-free housing bonus for senators who actually show up in Ottawa, a Senate committee fired off an angry letter to the Toronto airport authority to complain that the airport had taken away their long-standing free parking passes. Adding to the insult, the generally wealthy senators whined, Toronto-area MPs retained their free parking. Steve Shaw, an airport official, said the authority could only "justify" giving free parking to "elected" MPs. Anyway, he said, the senators are reimbursed for parking fees so they don't lose any income as a result. Senator Pierre Claude Nolin, committee chairman, said, "We expect the airport to reconsider their position. It's not a priority or anything, but we are pursuing it."

The year before, after winning re-election in June, Toronto Liberal MP Tom Wappel parked his car in his usual spot in a lot near the East Block only to discover when he came back out again that his car had been ticketed. "I looked up, and that's when I noticed the Senate sign," Wappel told freelance journalist Tim Naumetz. It seems the unelected senators took advantage of the election, when the MPs were out getting themselves re-elected, to steal some of their free parking spots. Parking was at a premium because of massive renovations and construction on the Hill, and several spots were taken away to make way for gravel trucks, cranes, and tractors. After MPs complained, the Senate signs were quickly taken down and replaced with tow-away signs for everybody. Senators got an extra couple of days by placing green garbage bags over the tow-away signs, but those bags quickly disappeared too. Senator Colin Kenny waded in to negotiate a compromise and Commons officials ultimately agreed to pave a lawn behind the Centre Block to give the senators ten spaces away from the truck traffic. They also agreed to add twenty-eight spots outside the East Block, and in July Ottawa fire officials complained that they had been delayed twice while responding to alarms because delivery vans and other vehicles were blocking the single lane that was left after the Senators had taken up more than half the roadway with their new spots. In 1999, perhaps as retribution for critical media coverage, the Senate took over a collection of prime parking spots directly behind the Centre Block which until then had been used by members of the Parliamentary Press Gallery.

The senators themselves are aware that their public image stinks, but they are unwilling to make any significant changes that might improve it. Instead, they're constantly developing schemes to make it appear as if they're worthy of public support.

In 1997, Jack Aubrey wrote a series of hard-hitting articles in the *Ottawa Citizen* in which he revealed that one-fifth of the senators had missed a majority of meetings, while other senators were charging travel expenses for politically partisan activities. In November, Ontario senator Marie-P. Poulin, chair of the Liberal caucus, responded to Aubrey's revelations and the negative publicity they caused by sending her colleagues a secret memo of so-called "talking points." The plan was to stick to generalities and focus the blame on a few bad senators. The memo also suggested that senators handling calls from the public should stress that the taxpayers are getting good value for the then-$42 million a year spent on the upper chamber. Aubrey also broke the story about Poulin's secret memo.

"There have only been a couple of examples of flagrant absenteeism," wrote Poulin. "Otherwise our attendance in the Senate is equal to, or better, than that in the Commons." Actually, twenty senators missed more than half the meetings of the Upper House.

Under the heading, "We All Know," the memo said: "That while pay and benefits for parliamentarians are not popular among the public, fair remuneration is vital to our democracy. . . . We should not hesitate to stress our contribution to the progress of our country." The memo argued that the per capita cost of the Senate is $1.50 compared to $7.13 for the Commons. Even if it were the same size as the Commons, the Senate would cost only $4.50 per Canadian. This is more than a little misleading, since, as Auditor-General Kenneth Dye had pointed out years earlier, the Senate benefits from several million dollars' worth of public services that are charged to the Commons and not to the upper chamber.

The senators launched another offensive in October 1998 when they invested $3.3 million of the taxpayers' dollars on a public relations campaign to convince those same taxpayers that their money is well spent. Most of the spending was directed at publicizing the work of the committees. Part of the spending was covered by a $1.27-million surplus from 1997–98. A big part of the Senate plan is to have senators firing off angry letters to the editor whenever they don't like a news story. Senator Pierre Claude Nolin also announced the Upper House was buying more television equipment to broadcast committee meetings – to whom, one wonders? As part of a pilot project, they did televise a few committee meetings throughout 1988, but there is still no talk of televising the sittings in the Red Chamber where the television lights might keep some of them awake. Liberal MP Roger Gallaway, who wants to abolish the Senate, said, "If they ever did allow it to be televised, it would be only a week before the public would rise up and abolish it. It would happen very rapidly."

So what has the Senate learned as a result of all this public scrutiny? Nothing, apparently. Construction had begun in the summer of 1998 on a $1.4-million tunnel to link the East Block with the Senate entrance to the Centre Block – a monumental distance of 101 metres, or roughly 140 paces, which the East Block's twenty-four senators, along with seven cabinet ministers and four backbench MPs felt was just too far to walk in Ottawa's biting winter months. Reform Party whip Chuck Strahl said the project is "the kind of thing that drives people nuts." Yup.

And in August 1998, freelance journalist Tim Naumetz visited the plush new Senate cafeteria in a renovated 1910 wing of the East Block featuring light dimmers that cost at least $1,000 each, a carpeted floor, hanging lamps made of brass and oyster-shell glass, and French windows opening onto the serene confines of a bricked courtyard. The kitchen's walk-in cooler and the wall-hung refrigerators were humming away, as they had been for seven months, but the cafeteria remained vacant. An old cafeteria in the East Block had been closed several years earlier to save money when a massive cafeteria was expanded in the West Block. The Commons had also announced plans to open a cafeteria in the nearby Confederation building to serve MPs and senators during renovations of the West Block, so there was no pressing need for an East Block cafeteria at all.

The cafeteria – along with the Senate's spiffy new $3-million committee room – was certain to interest Auditor-General Denis Desautel. Desautel had just announced he was launching an inquiry into Parliament Hill's massive renovation and construction projects, expected to cost more than $800 million, nearly double the original estimates.

During 1998 and 1999 the Senate increased its spending by sixteen per cent, a jump of $3 million in one year alone, having already overspent their 1998 allocation by $3.3 million. New Democrat MP Lorne Nystrom, who along with Gallaway has mounted a public campaign to kill the Senate, says it shows "they are accountable to no one. Where does the buck stop?" Liberal senator Bill Rompkey said the six per cent increase was needed to keep up with personnel costs and for upgrading the Senate's computer technology. In 1998, the Senate budget was bumped up by ten per cent. The House of Commons, meanwhile, was proposing a budget increase of just two per cent in its operations and capital budget, and just three per cent overall. Rompkey claimed the public was getting good value because the Senate filed seventeen major reports that year. The 1999–2000 budget was set at $47.4 million, up from $44.6 million a year earlier.

On February 17, the day before their budget figures were released, the senators were caught with their paranoia showing. Senator Al Graham, the government leader in the Senate and the Upper House's representative in cabinet, responded to a question from Tory senator Donald Oliver who asked why Chrétien "remains so silent and takes no initiatives to defend the institution," and about rumours circulating on Parliament Hill that the prime minister may want to "abolish the senate and the monarchy as his legacy to improve the Canadian federation." Graham, whom former senator Finlay MacDonald said "has gone a long way on personality alone," assured his colleagues there was "no secret plot" in the PMO to abolish the Senate. To demonstrate how petty the in-fighting between the two Houses had become, Graham was greeted by enthusiastic applause and wild desk-thumping from the other senators when he challenged an earlier statement by Gallaway that contrary to claims by the senators, MPs on average are better educated.

Graham said, "Senators can do their own research on that. I do not think a university degree is the be-all and end-all, but if a university degree is a criterion, I think the percentage would be higher in the Senate than in the other place." Graham himself has a Bachelor of Arts from St. Francis Xavier University. It's hard to fathom why it would even matter but, alas, the exchange of barbs once again inspired the *Citizen*'s Jack Aubrey to check it out, resulting in this February 25, 1999, front-page headline: "Senate not as erudite as House." A *Citizen* survey of the biographies of 101 senators and 300 MPs found the Commons just squeezes out the Senate. A total of 76.33 per cent of MPs have taken university courses, just slightly ahead of the Senate's 76.23 per cent. There were 69 degrees in the Senate – a rate of 68.316 per cent – compared to 205 in the Commons, or 68.333 per cent.

The antipathy between the two Houses reached such a low point in early March that several Liberals were talking about joining forces with the opposition parties to block the Senate's budget increase. However, a "talking points" memo from Chrétien's office faxed to all Liberal MPs on March 4 ordered the Liberals to approve the budget. The PMO recommended that when asked about the Senate's budget, Liberal MPs should say that the "spending estimates were arrived at in keeping with established Senate procedures, in an open and transparent process. . . . Accordingly, they are part of the government's spending plan," which is political talk for support-the-Senate-budget-or-else.

Responding to questions in the Commons on March 4, Chrétien said he would reform the Senate only once a consensus was reached among the premiers and opposition parties. He denied ever having proposed to abolish the Upper House – even though in 1985, when momentum to abolish the Red Chamber was building, Chrétien said during Question Period that he was "appalled by the attitude" of Brian Mulroney. "He is the prime minister and if he wants to abolish the Senate he has enough members to do it," said Chrétien. "He does not have to play games with anyone in this House and cop out like that." But in March 1999, Chrétien said, "What is important is that the Senate is doing its job and doing it well."

Really?

10

THE BOOZE BROTHERS

JUST MINUTES BEFORE his minority government was about to crash and burn on a 137–123 non-confidence motion on May 9, 1974, Pierre Trudeau told the Commons that he had an announcement to make. He'd appointed two Nova Scotia Liberals to the Senate.

Former prime minister John Diefenbaker protested that given the government's imminent defeat, it could be unconstitutional. It was, at the very least, totally inappropriate. "Following my government's defeat in 1963 I didn't make any appointments to the Senate or the Supreme Court of Canada or any posts like that," thundered Diefenbaker, adding that he was afraid Trudeau would make a series of appointments in the wake of his defeat "because he's trampled on the Constitution so many times."

Procedural nicety is one thing, the selection of senators is another. One of Trudeau's choices was sixty-one-year-old Irvine Augustus Barrow. Governor of Dalhousie University and a past president of the Nova Scotia Liberal Association, Barrow was much better known, and obviously appreciated, as that province's Liberal bagman extraordinaire.

When Barrow walked into the Senate in 1974, one Liberal who was there to greet him was wealthy Montreal businessman Senator Louis de Gonzague "Bobby" Giguere, the first senator Trudeau sent to the upper chamber when he became prime minister in 1968.

Giguere, a native of Hébertville in the Lake St. John region of Quebec, was the ultimate back-room boy in Quebec politics. He played a leading role in establishing the Quebec section of the Liberal Federation of Canada in 1964. He had also been the chief Liberal organizer in Quebec for the previous three federal elections and had arranged for Trudeau to run in the Montreal riding of Mount Royal in 1965. Then when Trudeau, as a relatively new justice minister, sought the party's leadership in 1968, Giguere threw his considerable resources – both political and financial – behind him, acting as chairman of Trudeau's leadership campaign in Quebec. Few men were closer to Trudeau than Giguere.

Giguere and Barrow, in addition to their political fealty for Trudeau and their history as Liberal bagmen, would also come to share another distinction: both would be convicted of influence peddling. Both men subsequently spent several years fighting the convictions and ultimately beat them. But the investigation and legal proceedings drew unwelcome attention to the ties that bind senators and the seedy back-room world of political financing and corporate lobbying.

The problems began for Giguere on November 3, 1975, when Nova Scotia Tory Elmer MacKay tabled a petition in the Commons seeking a judicial inquiry into a possible conflict-of-interest in the renewal of the Sky Shops Export Ltd. lease for its duty-free shop at Dorval Airport in 1972.

MacKay, a wealthy lawyer, had forced a judicial inquiry into Air Canada executive shenanigans a year earlier. In 1983, he stepped aside in Central Nova riding to allow Brian Mulroney, who had just replaced Joe Clark as Conservative leader, to win a by-election and earn a seat in the Commons. MacKay returned victorious in the 1984 national election, and his loyalty was rewarded by a series of cabinet posts in the Mulroney administration. His son Peter now holds the same seat.

Back in the mid-seventies, however, MacKay was the bane of the Liberal benches. His bombshell nine-page legal document tabled in the Commons said that the board of Sky Shops – which included National Hockey League president Clarence Campbell – had voted on June 9, 1972, to sell Giguere five thousand shares of stock, valued at $20 a share, for the bargain-basement price of $1 a share. That came shortly after the federal government had granted the company a five-year extension of its Dorval lease to November 1980. The company, in fact, was awarded a ten-year monopoly on duty-free liquor sales at all Quebec airports. Five months later, when all company stock was sold to P. Lawson Travel (Canada) Ltd., Giguere sold his shares for $100,000, a cool $95,000 profit.

MacKay claimed the conditions of the Sky Shops contract at Dorval were far more favourable than those granted by the Liberal government to duty-free concessions at Toronto's Malton (since changed to Pearson) Airport.

MacKay said the shares were transferred to Giguere by three major shareholders: Campbell; Louis Lapointe, who was Sky Shops chairman; and Gordon Brown, owner of Royark and Co. Brown was also an executive committee member of the company. MacKay said they knew the stock was worth $20 when they sold it for $1. MacKay also demanded an inquiry into Sky Shops' contract for the new Mirabel airport – perhaps Canada's most expensive white elephant – arguing that two competing companies, Cara Operations Ltd. and Host, had offered better terms than the winners did.

The day after MacKay made his charges, Giguere rose in the upper chamber and admitted that he had made a $95,000 profit on the stock deal but denied he had anything to do with the lease negotiation, or that he had intervened with anyone on behalf of Sky Shops. He said, "The story is quite different when you know all the facts." He called for a Senate inquiry.

The senator said his "old friend" Louis Lapointe had discussed the share option about two years before while they were holidaying in Florida. Giguere said the two men met again in June 1972 and he bought the shares, making out a cheque for $5,000. He claimed he "forgot the whole affair" until he was told in November 1972 that Lawson had offered to buy the Sky Shops shares at $20 each. "All the shareholders decided to accept this offer. So did I." Giguere said he had been engaged in "purely private transactions" and he had reported it on his income tax return and paid the required taxes.

Senate opposition leader Jacques Flynn of Quebec said a Senate inquiry would be too limited a forum. "I think a full investigation would be more appropriate." But B.C. senator Ray Perrault, government leader in the Senate, said he would refer the issue to a committee and would convene a Senate inquiry as soon as the opposition requested it.

The Mounties, who had been investigating the deal for nine months, did not wait. Two days after Giguere's speech in the Senate, they raided both the senator's Montreal home and his parliamentary office. An RCMP spokesman said the force "would have preferred not to execute search warrants at this time. . . . However, the searches were carried out as a result of increased media activity due to a series of statements made recently."

On the day of the searches, most Liberal senators and MPs were attending the party's national convention a few blocks from Parliament Hill. Ironically, Senate Speaker Renaude Perrault had just delivered an impassioned speech defending the honour of the Senate during a workshop debate on a resolution, sparked by the Giguere affair, to place senators under the same conflict-of-interest rules that apply to judges and cabinet ministers. The resolution, incidentally, was approved, but like so many others, it was never passed into law.

On November 24, Giguere resigned as director of Campeau Corp. On the same day, Solicitor-General Warren Allmand conceded the RCMP investigation that led to the raids on Giguere and Clarence Campbell's offices was "of a broader nature than one merely involving Sky Shops." The RCMP had confirmed earlier that the warrants authorized them to seize material relating to "the collection of monies for the Liberal party of Canada."

On April 22, 1976, Giguere, Campbell, and three other businessmen were arraigned in provincial court in Ottawa on charges of conspiracy and influence peddling in connection with the Sky Shops affair. They were accused of conspiring to pay Giguere $95,000 through the sale of shares as a consideration for his exercising influence to obtain the lease extension from the federal transport department. Giguere, Campbell, Lapointe, Brown, and former treasurer James Lavery had all surrendered to the RCMP before their court appearance. They were driven to the garage entrance of the courthouse in unmarked police cars, and whisked out of sight of reporters and cameramen up a back stairway to the court room. After their appearance, freed on bail of $100,000 each, they left through a tunnel leading to an adjacent building.

The RCMP had earlier turned the case over to the Quebec attorney-general's department, but decided to proceed in Ontario because of a disagreement with the Quebec prosecutor. Quebec had wanted to hold a pre-enquête, a private preliminary hearing before a judge who then decides whether a case should go ahead, often used in cases involving accusations against prominent people. In spite of the Ontario court action, however, Quebec solicitor-general Fernand Lalonde announced plans to proceed with a pre-enquête anyway, raising the possibility that there would be parallel criminal cases in two provinces. Lalonde announced he had filed a formal complaint of influence peddling against Giguere with a Montreal judge. That hearing opened in Montreal sessions court April 26 – but was adjourned until mid-May. On the same day in the Commons, MacKay charged there had been "great pressure" on Marchand as transport minister in 1973 in awarding the Mirabel bar-restaurant concession. He said the president of Les Enterprises Cara Ltée, which eventually won that contract, had to call deputy transport minister Gerald Stoner to get tenders opened publicly. According to MacKay, Stoner was told he should consider a merger with Kebec Restaurants Ltd., a competitor whose officers included Senator Giguere. Cara corroborated the allegation in a prepared statement but Transport Minister Otto Lang dismissed the merger suggestion as merely "exploratory thoughts."

Judge Maurice Rousseau completed the closed-door pre-enquête hearing in Montreal by concluding that while evidence in the affair was "circumstantial," it was sufficient to support a charge of having illegally accepted benefits of $95,000 to influence the lease extension. Six major private companies were named as having "a special interest" in the charges; to wit: they donated the money that was alleged to have been stolen. The companies were Power Corporation of Canada Ltd., Distillers Corporation Ltd., Steinberg's Ltd., Canadian Pacific Ltd., the Royal Bank of Canada Ltd., and the Bank of Montreal Ltd. Giguere was subsequently ordered to appear in Montreal sessions court on charges of theft of $16,536 and misappropriation of that amount while he was trustee for funds of the Liberal Party of Canada. He made a brief court appearance June 1 and asked for a trial by judge and jury. Three weeks later he joined Campbell, Lapointe, Lavery, and Brown in an Ottawa court and was remanded until October on those charges.

Things got worse for Giguere on October 12 when he was arraigned in Montreal on three new counts of conspiracy to influence the government in connection with advertising contracts. The charges alleged a conspiracy and payment of $87,000 to Giguere between 1965 and 1973. Two Montreal businessmen and two advertising agencies were charged along with him.

On June 29, 1978, however, a seven-woman, five-man jury in Montreal Superior Court deliberated a day and a half and found Giguere not guilty on two counts of conspiracy and influence peddling in the Sky Shops affair. "I feel less tired," said Giguere as his lawyer, Bruno Pateras, led him out of the prisoner's dock. Pateras had argued that Giguere had been given a verbal option on the shares in 1968 or 1969, years before the question of a lease renewal came up.

On July 21, 1979, Giguere was acquitted on breach of trust charges through misappropriation of funds collected for the Liberal Party. Giguere admitted that he had transferred the $16,537 into his own bank account but testified that he never intended to make personal use of it. "I mixed the remaining money from the special fund in with my personal account because I didn't want the source of the money traced by bank employees," he testified. "The companies that had given the money had shareholders, and I had been told their contributions were to be strictly confidential." Montreal Sessions Judge Jean Goulet, in acquitting Giguere, said he did not think the senator was innocent, but he couldn't find him guilty because the Crown was unable to prove the case beyond a reasonable doubt. "The accused has the right of the benefit of the doubt," the judge said. He added, however, that he was not convinced he was told everything that led to the 1970 creation of a special fund to fight the Quebec independence movement. "Not all was revealed – far from that" about what instructions Giguere received from former senator Lazarus Phillips, who had asked the four companies and two banks to send a total of $55,000 to Giguere. Judge Goulet also had harsh things to say about the testimony of some of Canada's most powerful corporate moguls. "Rarely have I had the opportunity to read replies that were so intelligently evasive. I have the impression that these witnesses didn't want to get their feet wet. They couldn't say what they were contributing the money for, the only thing they were sure of was that the money would not be returned."

One of those corporate giants criticized by the judge was Charles Bronfman, chairman of the executive committee of Seagram Co. Ltd. Former senator Lazarus Phillips had been named to the upper chamber by Lester Pearson in 1968. A wealthy Montreal corporate lawyer, Phillips was widely considered the "Seagram senator" during his tenure. He also sat on the Senate Banking and Commerce Committee, while simultaneously holding directorships in several blue-chip companies and acting as vice-president of the Royal Bank of Canada, whose chairman, Earle Mclaughlin, was also criticized by the judge for evasive testimony. Phillips retired from the Senate at age seventy-five in October 1970.

The last charge against Giguere was dropped in October 1979, a few days after the court dismissed similar charges against Clarence Campbell, the former NHL president, and Gordon Brown of the Bahamas because of what the court called "intolerable" delaying tactics by Crown and defence lawyers. In a telephone interview, Giguere told Canadian Press, "We were in and out of court for so long, and each time costs. Over the years, it cost me thousands of dollars."

He wasn't quite out of the woods yet, however. In December, the Ontario Supreme Court in Ottawa acquitted Giguere on three counts of influence peddling concerning the advertising contracts, saying the Crown fell short of proving Giguere received money in return for getting government business for the advertising company. Mr. Justice Jean-Marc Labrosse said that while Giguere "opened doors" for the company, he never did anything more than make appointments and introductions. Giguere had owned a one-quarter share in Canadian Advertising and Publicor Ltd., its parent, but sold it in 1967 for a lump sum of $67,000 and payments of $5,000 a year for five years. The Crown argued the shares were not worth that much. Giguere claimed the four-year-long battle cost him $100,000. Soon after the trial, he left for a Florida holiday.

In January 1980, the Crown lost its appeal of the jury acquittal against Giguere when prosecutors showed up in a Montreal court but said they weren't ready to proceed with the case.

Campbell and Brown weren't quite as fortunate as Giguere. Both men were convicted in February 1980 by a Quebec Superior Court jury of conspiracy to bribe Giguere in the Sky Shops affair. The two men were found guilty on two conspiracy counts, one to give Giguere the benefit, the other to have him accept it. This conflicted directly with the June 1978 jury finding that Giguere was not guilty either of conspiring to accept the bribe or of actually accepting it. Campbell was sentenced to a "symbolic" day in prison and fined $25,000, the same sentence given to Brown. Campbell, seventy-five, was in failing health. He had enjoyed a distinguished record as a Rhodes scholar, soldier, special prosecutor of Nazi war criminals, and NHL president from 1944 to 1976. Mr. Justice Melvin Rothman said in sentencing Campbell, "An agreement to bribe a member of the senate of Canada in return for assistance on a Government contract is an affront to the fundamental values of Canadian society. It must be denounced in strong terms." In the end, the NHL gave Campbell more than $50,000 to help pay his legal bills.

The wheels of justice continued to grind slowly. In June 1981, the Ontario Court of Appeal dismissed an appeal against Giguere's 1979 acquittal in the advertising case. Then in October 1981, the Quebec Court of Appeal upheld Giguere's acquittal on the breach of trust charges involving the $16,536 from the special Liberal fund. In November 1981, the Supreme Court of Canada granted leave for the Crown to appeal Giguere's acquittal on using his influence in return for $87,000 to get government contracts for the advertising agency. Finally, on November 24, 1983, eight years after Elmer MacKay had shocked the Commons with the initial allegations, the Supreme Court of Canada upheld his acquittal in the advertising case by a 4–1 ruling. In her dissent, Madam Justice Bertha Wilson said she would have ordered a new trial. Mr. Justice Brian Dickson said the trial judge had made several errors, but none was sufficient to order a new trial.

"There is uncontradicted evidence that Giguere, after the sale of his shares, arranged meetings between government officials and representatives of Canadian Advertising," said Dickson, "and also that Giguere put in a good word for Canadian Advertising with at least one cabinet minister." Even so, he said, the trial judge apparently had not found enough evidence to warrant a conviction.

Never during these legal proceedings did Giguere offer to resign from the Senate. Neither Trudeau nor Giguere's fellow senators ever asked him to. He retired just before Christmas 1986 and, still fiercely partisan, heaped scorn on former cabinet minister Jean Chrétien for his attempts to undermine embattled Liberal leader John Turner.

"He was liked, but he's finished now," Giguere said of Chrétien. "He left Turner when we were so low in the polls – when the leader needed him."

When Irvine Barrow entered the Senate in the mid-seventies, he was a partner in two chartered accounting firms, Barrow, Nicoll & Co., and Collins, Love, Eddie, Valiquette & Barrow. He was president of Halifax Cablevision Ltd. and a director of Sydney Steel Corp. He had directorships in private businesses as well, but he liked to say those directorships "are my own business."

The public did get a glimpse of Barrow's party business in 1980, however, when federal labour minister Gerald Regan, the former Nova Scotia premier, told a March 19 news conference that he was "morally certain" there was no impropriety in receiving an extra $13,000 a year on top of his $42,000 salary as premier and later as opposition leader in Nova Scotia. Regan said the fund was established ten years before he became party leader and that he had no knowledge of who the donors were. He said he was satisfied that no conflict of interest existed in accepting the money, which he had declared for tax purposes. The fund was administered by lawyer Frank Covert and two Nova Scotia senators – Irvine Barrow and Henry Hicks, a former Nova Scotia premier himself.

Revelations about the fund, the payments to Regan, and the administrators of it, had come to light when documents relating to a two-year RCMP investigation into alleged kickbacks on government contracts were released in a Halifax court. It emerged that Barrow had been engaged in the traditional fund-raising activities on behalf of the Nova Scotia Liberals, dealing with the traditional sources of party funding, the liquor and construction companies, often by designating precisely what each of them was expected to contribute.

In July 1981, Barrow was charged with conspiring to influence the former Liberal government of Regan. Also charged were two other Liberal bagmen, Charles R. MacFadden and James G. Simpson. In February 1982, the three men appeared before Provincial Court Judge William Atton in a Halifax court where they were arraigned on new conspiracy charges that replaced an original one laid against them months earlier.

They were jointly charged with seven counts stemming from activities between October 1970 and September 1978 when Regan was premier. They were alleged either to have or pretend to have influence with the provincial government, or with a minister(s) or government official(s). The Crown said the three men demanded or accepted for their own benefit or that of the Nova Scotia Liberal Association "rewards, advantages, or benefits as consideration for co-operation, assistance or exercise of influence or an act of omission." Barrow and Simpson each faced two other counts as well. All three faced a charge of conspiring to accept benefits as consideration for their exercise of influence on the government.

Five of the counts involved wineries and distilleries: Alberta Distilleries Ltd., Andres Wines, Jordan Wines, McGuinness Distillers Ltd., and Hudson Bay Distilleries Ltd. Two other counts involved Norman Wade and Co. Ltd. and LaHave Equipment Ltd., construction firms. The charges generally involved a practice called "toll-gating," where fund-raisers made liquor companies believe that they had to contribute a portion of their annual sales to the party in power or their brands would not be listed for sale with the Nova Scotia Liquor Commission. In addition, other businesses kicked back a percentage of government contracts to the party in power as the price of securing the work. The case was adjourned until April.

When the three men appeared in court again on April 29, they all pleaded not guilty. Barrow opted for trial by judge and jury on nine counts of influence peddling. MacFadden picked trial by judge alone on his seven counts of influence peddling. Simpson also opted for a judge and jury, but in May he changed his plea to guilty on one count of influence peddling and was fined $75,000. The other charges against him were dropped.

Five days after Simpson was convicted, a preliminary hearing into the charges against Barrow and MacFadden began in Halifax but Provincial Court Judge Charles O'Connell granted a defence motion for a publication ban on evidence. During the hearing, several prominent Liberals were called to testify, including Regan. Also testifying was Gordon L. MacKay, a general manager of the Nova Scotia Liquor Commissioner between 1965 and 1973. In July, Barrow and MacFadden were ordered to stand trial.

When Barrow's trial got under way in April 1983, the Crown produced a seventeen-page list of general supplies needed by the liquor commission and the names of the companies that provided them. This list had been forwarded to Simpson, then the chief Liberal fundraiser who used it, presumably, to identify firms that depended on government business. A. Garnet Brown, Regan's former highways minister, said he had "no idea" how the document reached Simpson, but said, "I could understand how he would want them in the general discharge of his duties on the financial committee." They also produced a letter from Barrow to Simpson asking about the information on the lists. Regan testified that he occasionally took advice from his trusted friend Barrow, but he denied the senator ever tried to influence policy.

Another memo seized from Simpson concerned Barrow and a consulting firm called Acres, which was hired to work at a once-proposed common-user dock in Mulgrave. Simpson's March 9, 1973, memo read: "In accordance with a telephone conversation with A.I.B. (Barrow) he made arrangements with Acres at a figure of approximately $60,000. This figure is based on the gross overall job of $1,500,000, but of course could be adjusted depending on the ultimate size of the job."

On another day at the trial, representatives from three liquor distillery companies testified that paying a percentage of their sales in Nova Scotia to the governing political party was "a way of life." William Thompson, a vice-president of Hudson's Bay Wines and

Spirits Ltd., said his company agreed to pay fifty cents on every case of spirits sold "because it was, and had been, the normal way of doing business in this province." He said he knew of no other province where "toll-gating" was practised. He said they paid the percentage because "we hoped to further our business in the province and presumed if we weren't paying it we wouldn't be in business."

On April 25, a parade of well-known Halifax lawyers and long-time Liberals, including Barrow's fellow senator and former premier Henry Hicks, testified that both Barrow and MacFadden were men "of the highest integrity." Asked if he would expect to see Barrow in a criminal court at the age of seventy, Hicks told Barrow's lawyer, Austin Cooper, "I'm amazed, sir." Evidence earlier in the trial revealed that Barrow, head of the party's finance committee, was a trustee of three funds named after their original trustees and dating back to Angus L. Macdonald's Liberal government in the 1950s. The Crown said Barrow served on several funds described as investment vehicles to which contributions moved from two chief accounts, Cambridge Investments and J.G. Simpson in Trust. Barrow and MacFadden were kept posted on all debits and credits to the two main funds. The three men collected $593,000 for the Liberals under this system, the biggest share attributed to Simpson. Altogether, Barrow raised $3.8 million for the Liberal Association.

On May 12, at the end of their five-week trial, both Barrow and MacFadden were convicted of conspiracy to peddle influence and fined $25,000 each. Mr. Justice Denne Burchell of the Nova Scotia Supreme Court said the wide publicity in the case had been a "devastating" form of punishment and it would be improper to consider rehabilitation or incarceration. By this time, Nova Scotia's Elections Expenditures Act prohibited "toll-gating," which had been practised by both Liberals and Conservatives for decades. None of the three bagmen took any of the money for personal gain. It all went to the party.

In Ottawa following the conviction, Halifax West Conservative MP Howard Crosby said the public would be outraged if Barrow kept his Senate seat. Responding to Crosby in the Commons,

Trudeau said, "It is for the Senate to determine questions relating to the status of its own members." Trudeau cited the British North America Act, which prohibits a person convicted of treason, a felony, or an "infamous crime" from holding a seat. Trudeau said it was not a felony, and it would be up to the Senate to decide whether it was "an infamous crime." He added it would be a "matter of elementary decency" for the Senate to wait to see if Barrow appealed and whether the conviction was upheld.

Barrow had suggested to reporters that an appeal was unlikely. "I'm seventy years old and I'm not sure I want to go through this thing for several more years," he said. He went on to add that he intended to keep his Senate seat until he had to retire at age seventy-five. In June, however, Barrow launched an appeal of his conviction on the grounds that the verdict was unreasonable and unsupported by the evidence and that the presiding judge did not adequately instruct jurors on the use of good character evidence. Barrow's lawyers also argued that under the Criminal Code's definition of influence peddling, the Nova Scotia Liberal Association did not fit the definition of a "person." The Code says bodies corporate, societies, and companies are persons, but evidence heard at the trial with the jury absent was that the Liberal Association did not technically fit into any of these categories. The judge had ruled against the argument, saying such a narrow interpretation would lead to absurd results. Barrow's lawyers also complained that thirty-five prospective jury members were given exemptions by the trial judge while he and his lawyer were not present, thus depriving him of the right to be present during the whole of his trial.

Barrow's conviction apparently did not hurt his standing in the cozy confines of the Senate. In January 1984, the senators elected their convicted colleague chairman of the Senate's most powerful body, the Senate Banking and Commerce Committee.

In September, a three-judge panel of the Appeal Division of the Nova Scotia Supreme Court unanimously upheld Barrow's conviction. The thirty-three-page decision said Barrow "may have honestly thought there was nothing illegal in the collection practices. . . . If

[Barrow] held such mistaken belief his mistake was one of law – not fact – and cannot be called in aid of him as a defence to the charge." As for the argument that the association is not a person, the court dismissed the argument as too "narrow. . . . The object of the legislation is to prevent the payment of rewards of any kind to anyone as consideration for the exercising of influence." It said Barrow's argument would "defeat the clear intent of the legislation."

Ten days later, lawyers for Barrow announced they would seek leave to appeal Barrow's conviction to the Supreme Court of Canada. The appeal was allowed and eventually heard in March 1987, more than four years after the conviction. On December 17, the court ordered a new trial. The 5–2 ruling set aside his conviction on a legal technicality, ruling that the trial judge acted improperly when he questioned eighty-three potential jurors out of earshot of Barrow and his lawyer and excused thirty-six of them. "The public perception of the fairness of the trial process would be damaged if potential jurors were excluded after private conversations with the judge," wrote Chief Justice Brian Dickson in a twenty-nine-page judgement. ". . . It is a breach that casts into doubt the impartiality of the jury, which in turn reflects on the fairness of the entire trial."

Barrow turned seventy-five on February 15, 1988. The Senate paid tribute both to him and his colleague, former Trudeau speech-writer Jean Le Moyne, who retired the same week. Deputy Liberal leader Senator Royce Frith praised Barrow as a model senator who "always did whatever he was asked to do in performing his senatorial duties and he always did it well."

Barrow's retrial finally got under way in January 1989. On February 7 the jury deliberated twelve hours before acquitting him on a charge of conspiring to peddle influence. "I feel elated, I feel vindicated, which I knew I would be," the retired senator said. "It's been a long time, almost nine years and I knew I was innocent from the start and that's why I had to go through with it."

And so, ultimately, both Giguere and Barrow had the means to hang in there and eventually win acquittals from the myriad charges against them. But their high-profile cases, dragged through the courts for years and bringing headlines with them, overshadowed anything positive the Senate may have been doing. Nor did the mindless and enthusiastic support from their fellow senators help inspire public confidence that the Upper House understands the concept of public morality. True, their actions in the end were judged noncriminal by the system. But you don't have to break the Criminal Code to be doing something wrong.

11

To Catch a Thief

H AZEN ARGUE WASN'T the first thief to sit in the Senate. He was, however, the first one caught stealing Senate funds.

To be sure, other senators have been charged with crimes, but they were for offences committed outside the Senate sanctuary. Argue, in 1989, was charged with theft, fraud, and breach of trust for his abuse of Senate resources. The only thing that saved him from being convicted was his timely death.

The eccentric former farmer, raised in grain-farming country around Kayville, Saskatchewan, once rose in the Senate to officially complain that the parliamentary tailor refused to press his rumpled brown suit because of the foul odour.

Argue began his political career in 1945 as an MP for Assiniboia, Saskatchewan, for the CCF (Cooperative Commonwealth Federation), forerunner of the NDP. At age twenty-four, he was the youngest MP ever elected to the Commons at the time. He was re-elected in 1949, 1953, and again in 1957 when he defeated high-profile Liberal Ross Thatcher by just 1,527 votes. Thatcher, a former CCF member for Moose Jaw, had shared an Ottawa office with

Argue before he bolted the party and joined the Liberals in 1956. During the often-bitter 1957 election campaign, Argue, an accomplished orator, constantly attacked Thatcher as a turncoat and a traitor to his political colleagues and supporters. Thatcher subsequently became Saskatchewan Liberal leader and went on to be premier of the province.

In the 1958 election, when the Diefenbaker sweep left a tiny caucus of eight CCF members, Argue was one of them. He was the only CCF member left east of British Columbia and west of the Lakehead. In 1960, at its final national convention, the CCF installed Argue as caretaker leader during the party's transition to the NDP, a party forged from the merger of the CCF and the Canadian Labour Congress. The CCF Establishment hadn't wanted an interim leader because it could complicate the planned coronation of Saskatchewan's popular preacher-premier Tommy Douglas. But Argue thumbed his nose at them and became leader.

Not for long. In August 1961, Douglas and Argue squared off at the NDP's founding convention. In his campaign speech to the delegates, Argue had pledged undying loyalty: "I pledge no matter what my role, I shall speak for you, I shall work for you. I shall never let you down." Douglas easily defeated Argue by a vote of 1,391 to 380.

Things change. Six months after the convention, Argue repudiated Douglas and denounced the NDP at a press conference in Regina. Argue said he left the party because it had become a tool of organized labour and had lost touch with the Saskatchewan people. The feelings he engendered in his former colleagues were summed up years later by veteran Regina NDP MP Les Benjamin, who called Argue's defection "one of the worst, double-crossing betrayals ever pulled on a political party in Canada." Benjamin refused ever again to speak to Argue, even when the two men passed each other in an airplane aisle.

Three days after the press conference, Argue crossed the floor and took a seat on the back benches on the Liberal side in the Commons. He managed to hang onto his Saskatchewan seat by 353 votes in the 1962 election, but he lost in 1963, and was easily defeated in his

1965 comeback bid. A year later, Prime Minister Lester Pearson summoned Argue to the Senate. As a CCFer, Argue had made countless speeches not only attacking the Senate, which he once dismissed as "an old man's home," but calling for its abolition. When his main chance came, however, he didn't waste a second packing up and heading down the road to Ottawa.

From the beginning of his career, Argue was a man who never let principle get in the way of ambition. And so it was that he returned to the nation's capital as a senator and a key spokesman for the Liberal's western farm policies.

After the 1980 election, when Saskatchewan, once a Liberal stronghold, failed to elect a single Grit, Pierre Trudeau desperately needed a Saskatchewan minister. He appointed Argue as minister responsible for the Canadian Wheat Board. Argue knew the wheat business. He had played a leading role in creating the Senate agriculture committee, becoming its chairman, a position he held until his cabinet appointment. And, despite his considerable political baggage, he initially received generally good reviews in his new role as minister. Of course, this may have had less to do with him and more to do with the fact that his Liberal predecessor, Otto Lang, was so widely disliked in the farm community. Conservative critic Alvin Hamilton, a former agriculture minister and long-time Saskatchewan MP, said, "It is nice to have someone who knows something about wheat in the portfolio. . . . [Lang was] such a disaster and by sheer contrast it will be good to have Hazen. . . ."

The honeymoon didn't last, particularly after Argue waded into the critical Crow's Nest Pass Agreements, the deal setting out the terms for transporting western wheat to markets, the closest thing outside of the local church to Holy Grail west of the Lakehead. Typically, Argue ended up on all sides of the issue. Saskatchewan premier Allan Blakeney said in a February 1982 speech in Moose Jaw that Argue's word could not be trusted. "This is the same fellow who, a year ago, said the Crow won't change," Blakeney said.

Argue spent much of his four-year tenure in cabinet jetting around the world, taking in such places as Russia, China, and Hong Kong. At one point, Conservative Don Mazankowski complained that Argue "certainly hasn't been spending much time around here or in the Senate." In November 1982, Argue was criticized for taking his wife, Jean, along on a week-long freebie to Japan. Argue – who never did seem to understand the concept of conflict of interest – said the trip didn't cost Canadians one cent. Why? Because CP Air provided free tickets for both of them.

Argue, who was known to wear two different coloured socks on occasion, seemed pretty clear on the colour of his political allegiance during the 1980s, unabashedly telling reporters in September 1983 that it is "standard procedure" for governments to appoint lawyers who support the political party in power. Argue was responding to criticism of a list of forty-four lawyers appointed to the lucrative task of handling Farm Credit Corporation (FCC) mortgages; he said it had been "a long-term custom for . . . government of all complexions . . . to be somewhat more favorable or fully favorable to the people who have supported them in the past." The lucky forty-four were culled from a list of 1,172 licensed Saskatchewan lawyers, most of them either former Liberal candidates, party business managers, or members of the Liberal Party executive.

Argue was never fully accepted by the Liberals – and continued to be reviled by the NDP – but his own view of his worth never wavered. When Pierre Trudeau stepped down in early 1984 Argue, who was only in cabinet by default, actually toyed with the idea of running for the federal Liberal leadership. He eventually came to his senses and just a few weeks before the leadership convention came out publicly for John Turner. It didn't do him any good. Turner, the short-lived prime minister, booted him out of cabinet and back to relative obscurity in the Senate.

Through the years, Argue's behaviour became even more bizarre. He and his wife got heavily into psychic phenomena. A long-time

friend from Regina recalled an evening when he was drinking scotch
with a few friends in another senator's office. On a trip down the cor-
ridor to the washroom, he noticed a light on in Argue's office.
"'What the hell,' I thought. 'I'll say hello to old Hazen.' I knocked
on the door and stepped into the room and found myself right in the
middle of a seance being run by Jean. Half a dozen middle-aged
women were sitting on the floor in a circle around a light. The only
light. The place was really in darkness. I mumbled to Jean, who did
say hello, and backed out. Neither of us mentioned it later."

In a 1985 trip to the Philippines, the Argues, already strong advocates of alternative medicine, got smitten by the flim-flam of psychic
healers. They claimed they cured Jean's rheumatism and relieved a
painful cyst on Argue's neck – by sticking two fingers up Argue's
nose. Jean took Polaroid shots of these healers performing surgery
without the use of any medical equipment and showed the pictures
to friends back home. Argue enthused, "We watched them operate
behind a glass wall. They use their hands to open the body, blood
flows and they take out the tissue and immediately they are finished.
The wound closes, the blood is wiped off and the patient goes about
his or her business."

The process has been widely discredited as old-fashioned sleight-
of-hand, but the senator was so taken by it that he doubled as a shill
for a Filipino faith healer, helping him round up recruits for
"surgery" in Regina's Sandman Inn in August 1989. Argue was
spotted by a *Regina Leader-Post* reporter greeting people in the hotel
lobby, some of them arriving in wheelchairs, and then escorting them
to the private suites where, for $50, a man registered as A. Orbito
was said by patients to have performed surgical operations with his
bare hands and without the use of anaesthetic. Asked by the reporter
if he was associated with the scam, Argue said, "I have no comment"
and walked out of the lobby.

In 1985, Argue led a group of farmers trying to bust into a
Regina's first ministers' conference. "If you want in, I'll take you in,"
he said. The group was stopped by security guards. Two years earlier,
he and Jean actually picketed outside the U.S. Embassy in Ottawa to

protest Washington's subsidy of U.S. wheat sales to China. And on another occasion he and Jean hooked up an old plywood trailer to their truck and toured rural Saskatchewan. They billed the tour as a fact-finding mission to save rural communities. Argue's affinity for lost causes surfaced again when he also lobbied hard to get the distant Turks and Caicos Islands made part of Canada.

Eccentric behaviour and character quirks are one thing, but misuse of public funds is quite another.

Argue's real problems began in May 1988 when *Ottawa Citizen* reporter Nicole Baer discovered that some residents in Nepean, an Ottawa suburb, were irate about a barrage of letters they'd received from various senators endorsing Jean Argue for the federal Liberal nomination in their riding. Most of the "Dear Resident" letters were sent by Argue himself, but others were sent by Liberal senators Bud Olson, Anne Cools, Jerry Grafstein, and David Croll. Eugene Costello, a retired public servant, complained that they were "making it look like the whole Senate is behind her. It's the perception that to me is less than honest." Argue dismissed the complaints out of hand. "We're all engaged in the political field. . . . There's nothing wrong with that. Everyone does it." Argue and Olson said they and the other senators paid for the mailings themselves.

The Argues had played a similar game in 1984 when Jean tried for the Liberal nomination in Regina East. One close observer said, "Hazen pulled out all the stops for her, all his markers. We were worried for a while, but Jean (and Hazen) were too well known here. She lost convincingly." She lost in Nepean too, to local councillor Beryl Gaffney, but not before the *Citizen* reported on June 18 that Argue had used Senate money to hire seven part-time telephone canvassers for his wife's nomination bid. They worked out of Argue's Senate office and used government telephones and office equipment. Argue had also used more than $1,000 worth of postage through the Senate Post Office and more than $3,000 in taxi chits in connection with Jean's campaign. (Argue once used a Senate taxi chit to send a

Senate worker to his Ottawa home to cut his lawn. The cab was kept waiting, its meter running, while the lawn was cut, after which the worker was taxied back to Parliament Hill.)

The *Citizen* also reported that delegates as young as twelve years old had been given free memberships in the federal Liberal Party after promising to support Jean's candidacy. Party rules say members must pay the $5 membership themselves and must be at least fourteen. Twelve-year-old Peter Worth said he accepted a membership from an Argue organizer because "she said we'd have a party after the meeting at her house with a dance and food and prizes."

In the wake of the *Citizen* stories, the Senate's internal economy committee began an investigation into Argue's spending. The committee found him guilty of misusing $5,607.40 worth of funds, staff and supplies, taxi chits, phones, and mailing privileges. The committee did not put a price tag on Argue's use of Senate messengers during the campaign, used to stuff campaign literature into envelopes, but said their use was "grossly excessive." It also revealed that Argue had allowed a staff member to study French in a $3,570 language course reserved for senators and their immediate families. Argue said he had not "knowingly abused [his] privileges" but said that he had repaid the Senate for the government taxi vouchers. He then rose in the Senate on a question of personal privilege to flatly deny any wrongdoing in his use of public funds. He blamed Senate officials for not alerting him that there might be something wrong. He accused the *Citizen* of establishing a double standard, saying that Joe Clark's wife, Maureen McTeer, won the Conservative nomination (but later lost the election) for the new federal riding of Carleton-Gloucester with the help of strong support from government officials, including members of Clark's external affairs staff. "When looking at the Senate and the Argue campaign, would it be fair to ask why the *Citizen* does not give the same attention to the Clark-McTeer campaign, make an inquiry and apply the same standards of investigation?" Clark staff did work on McTeer's campaign, but strictly on a volunteer basis after hours. No public funds were spent on it.

Several senators demanded a thorough investigation of Argue's use of government supplies and services and said it was time to end the Senate's "honour system" that gave senators enormous latitude in their use of publicly funded privileges. "I cannot help but feel that we are perhaps doing a disservice to the Senate or to Senator Argue by letting the matter drop," said independent Montreal senator Hartland Molson during a debate in the Upper House. Most of his colleagues, however, didn't agree. The committee found that Argue's actions were "not acceptable and . . . cannot be condoned," but recommended no further punishment beyond asking him to pay back the public money he used on Jean's campaign.

Speaker Guy Charbonneau, who also doubled as chairman of the internal economy committee, concluded that there was nothing really wrong with the honour system. "If a senator says something falls within his duties, who is to say otherwise – no one really." He said the only problem is that all senators do not appear to share the same standards. "It's a question of interpretation. As far as Senator Argue is concerned, everything he did was within the guidelines laid out regarding the facilities he's entitled to use to conduct his senatorial duties." (Charbonneau was noted for a certain moral flexibility of his own. Years earlier as chief bagman in the successful leadership run of Brian Mulroney, Charbonneau offered a Senate seat to one eastern Ontario businessman in return for a $75,000 campaign donation.)

Charbonneau actually tried to keep the Senate report secret, but in September 1988 a senior PMO official leaked it to the *Toronto Sun*. The Mulroney government had been upset at what they saw as a series of abuses by the Liberal-dominated Senate in blocking passage of government legislation. But even after the report was released, many of Argue's colleagues were prepared to let the matter drop. Toronto senator Richard Doyle, a committee member and former editor of the *Globe and Mail*, said, "I consider [Argue's use of Senate resources] the most outrageous behavior, but if he broke the law, I'd like to see that law. If anything, he broke a rule of Senate conduct – albeit a rule that is unwritten."

The RCMP didn't see things quite the same way. After the committee's report became public, Cpl. Pierre Belanger, an RCMP spokesman, announced, "We're making inquiries into the allegations contained in that report. . . ." He said that at that stage, it was not an RCMP investigation. "If you're doing an investigation, you suspect certain criminal activities have gone on. This is simply an inquiry to see if a criminal investigation is justified." Months would pass before the investigation bore fruit.

In May 1989, a Senate-financed independent audit of Argue's travel habits dating back to 1980 found that thirty-five of Argue's claims were false, at least thirty-five more could not be substantiated, and another fifty or so were inflated. The audit by accounting firm Peat Marwick included flights taken by Argue and family members on Air Canada and other airlines. It was discussed in a meeting of the Senate's internal economy committee. The *Citizen* and its parent company, Southam News, launched a lawsuit before the Federal Court of Canada after its reporter Charles Rusnell was refused entry to that committee meeting. The Federal Court's trial division ruled that this was a violation of the Charter of Rights and Freedoms. But the Senate appealed, and in August 1990, ten days after Argue was admitted to Regina General Hospital suffering from a heart condition aggravated by a blood clot in his leg, the Federal Court of Appeal overturned the ruling. Chief Justice Frank Iacobucci said the court does not have jurisdiction over the Senate. "Like the House of Commons, the Senate is central to the Constitution. To treat the Senate as though it were a federal board, commission or tribunal not only belittles its role but also goes beyond the ordinary meaning of those terms."

In the meantime, the senators on the committee took drastic steps to ensure secrecy, even kicking out the translators and clerks ten minutes after the meeting started so that no minutes of the meeting were kept. In an unprecedented move, reporters were even barred from their traditional lurking spot in the hallway outside the committee room, making it impossible for them to question senators as they left the meeting.

After the meeting, however, the Senate announced it had asked the RCMP to probe the allegation that Argue had, among other things, claimed travel expenses for trips he didn't take. Argue appeared before the committee and was given a copy of the report but he did not speak. Senator Lowell Murray, government leader in the Senate, who had promised earlier, "I won't allow this thing to be swept under the rug," said after the meeting, "I don't think it would be proper for me to comment."

Under Senate rules, senators were entitled to sixty-four free, first-class, round-trip airline tickets a year. Of those, up to twenty could be used by members of the senator's immediate family or personal staff. Argue wasn't talking about it in public to anybody, but his lawyer, John Nelligan, said that if Argue was reimbursed more than once for the same trip, it was because of poor office procedures. "His office was very poorly equipped to handle these things."

On November 15, 1989, as a result of the earlier investigation, Argue was charged in provincial court in Ottawa with theft, fraud, and breach of trust. He was the first senator in the upper chamber's 122-year history to be accused of criminal offences related to the use of Senate funds. The five charges concerned the use of public funds in his wife Jean's failed nomination bid. On January 24, 1990, Argue, who had repeatedly denied any wrongdoing, was also charged with fraud and uttering forged documents for his use of Senate-financed travel. Argue, suffering from cancer, appeared briefly in court the next day wearing one of his famous blue rumpled suits, said, "I've done no wrong," and pleaded not guilty to all seven charges. He elected trial by judge and jury, and Provincial Court Judge Bernard Ryan set nine days for a preliminary hearing beginning November 25. Argue faced a maximum ten-year sentence for fraud and fourteen years for uttering forged documents.

In the meantime, the Senate had been forced to abandon its "honour system" and introduce proper accounting procedures requiring that expenses be justified and, when necessary, supported by receipts. The Senate even backed off a highly public row with Auditor-General Kenneth Dye, who had demanded the right to complete a comprehensive audit on Senate expenses for the first time in its history. Dye had been regularly denied access, but in light of the publicity surrounding Argue, he stepped up his public campaign to audit the Senate books. Finally committee chairman Roméo LeBlanc gave in but only on condition that Dye leave a series of items, such as attendance records, out of his audit. "How often does the Senate sit? And is it cost effective, etc. That shouldn't be touched," said LeBlanc.

By June 1991, Argue's health had deteriorated badly. He was undergoing chemotherapy treatment for cancer in a Regina hospital. One June 11, Crown attorney Mac Lindsay told an Ottawa court that after reviewing Argue's medical records, he had decided to drop all the criminal charges against the seventy-year-old senator. Lindsay made it clear the decision had nothing to do with the merits of the case. "I'm doing this for sympathetic and humanitarian reasons," said Lindsay. "The gentleman is seriously ill. For humanitarian reasons, I'm moving that the charges be stayed."

On October 2, 1991, Argue died. He was the longest-serving parliamentarian in Canada at the time. He remains the only senator ever charged with the criminal use of Senate funds, a singular accomplishment given the history of rogues, mountebanks, and bagmen who have occupied the place since its beginnings.

12

FRIENDS IN HIGH PLACES

IT WAS 1986, and Michel Cogger was feeling hurt. After all, he was Brian Mulroney's closest personal friend. Or, as Mulroney told his biographer, L. Ian MacDonald, Cogger "will always be number one on my hit parade." Yet while the rest of Mulroney's long-time pals prospered from patronage appointments after Mulroney became prime minister in 1984, the forty-seven-year-old Cogger was stuck practising law in Montreal. Cogger openly admitted after the 1984 election that he was hurt by Mulroney's neglect. He told reporters he felt left out in the cold.

And why not? Cogger was one of the first friends Mulroney made when he arrived at Laval University in 1960. And Cogger, small and roly-poly in stature, was a big man on campus. He was president of the arts student faculty and editor of the college paper. He and Mulroney often wandered over to the Quebec National Assembly together, sometimes joined by Michael Meighen, whose grandfather had been Canada's ninth prime minister, to take in Question Period. Cogger, a Liberal then, had contacts with the government and used them to introduce his ambitious buddy to important people. Years later, Mulroney told MacDonald that "of all the times in my life, Laval was the golden years." And Cogger was a big part of those times.

During their post-graduate carefree bachelor days in Montreal, Cogger, Bernard Roy, Lowell Murray, and some others were charter members of the small Mulroney crowd that gathered at The Swamp, a popular bar on the lower-level shopping concourse of Place Ville Marie. On Sundays they would all meet at Nick's Restaurant to discuss politics – and women – and whatever else turned their fancy. They all lived nearby. At the time, Cogger was practising law in Montreal and it would be his recommendation that got Mulroney a position with the prestigious firm of Howard Cate Ogilvy, et al. In the winter, Mulroney, Cogger, and the gang regularly rented a chalet for ski and party weekends in the Laurentians. In the summer, they often rented a cottage on Nantucket off Cape Cod.

In 1967 Cogger and Mulroney had worked together, along with Murray and an eager young Tory named Joe Clark, on the failed federal leadership bid of Davie Fulton. After that, Mulroney went back to Montreal, but freshly minted Tory leader Bob Stanfield made his first three appointments: Cogger became associate national director of the Conservative Party; Murray became Stanfield's personal assistant; and Clark, a researcher. The three men shared an apartment.

In April 1972, Cogger and Mulroney left together for a planned five-week jet-setting tour of various Mediterranean resorts around the Cote d'Azur. The trip ended prematurely when Mulroney received a telephone call from the Maritime Employers' Association, his first major client, and he had to fly back to Montreal to deal with a nasty longshoremen's strike at the Montreal Harbour.

When Mulroney married Mila Pivnicki on May 26, 1973, Cogger, Murray, and Yves Fortier were the ushers. Bernard Roy was best man. Mulroney was an usher at Cogger's wedding, too, and each is godfather to one of the other's children.

In 1976, when Mulroney sought the Tory leadership – and lost to Joe Clark – Cogger, as national vice-president of the party and

Stanfield's press secretary, ran the leadership campaign. Cogger subsequently hired on as an adviser to Clark and stayed on as part of the transition team in Clark's short-lived 1979 government. But his loyalty was to Mulroney, not Clark, and it wasn't long before he joined a cabal of anti-Clark forces working to undermine Clark's leadership. Cogger was a key Quebec organizer for Mulroney in his successful 1983 leadership bid. He also became Mulroney's personal counsel and worked on the 1984 campaign.

So where, he may have asked, was the beef? After all, Mulroney had once boasted that when he got into office he would appoint Liberals and New Democrats only "when there isn't a living, breathing Tory left without a job in this country."

Unfortunately for Cogger, he had embarrassed his boss through his ties to financier Walter Wolf, a major contributor in the "dump Joe" movement. That wouldn't have been a bad thing had it remained private but, alas, it had become public knowledge that the wealthy Austrian-born entrepreneur had funnelled at least $25,000 – some estimates put the figure at $250,000 – into the dump-Clark movement with the help of Cogger and former Newfoundland premier Frank Moores. In 1985, with Cogger acting as Wolf's lawyer, Ottawa awarded a lucrative contract without tender for undersea work to a Wolf company, Wolf Sub-Ocean Ltd., to help finance a joint project with COSEL Ltd., also of Newfoundland, claiming no other firm could do the work. But Newfoundland premier Brian Peckford said five other Newfoundland firms had applied for funds to develop the undersea vehicle, and opposition critics in Ottawa claimed the $363,000 award was in effect payment of a political debt to Wolf for his help in dumping Clark.

When Cogger went on Mulroney's payroll as his chief counsel in June 1984, he had claimed to have severed all ties with Wolf the year before, yet he was still listed as Wolf's nominee on the board of directors of a Montreal firm, Voyageurs Marine Construction Co. Ltd.

Fortunately for Cogger, however, his days of living in the patronage paddy wagon were about to end.

On March 4, 1966, then Liberal prime minister Lester Pearson, in an orgy of partisan appointments, named ten men to the Senate. Among them were two Liberals who would become nationally known, but for very different reasons: Keith Davey and Hazen Argue. Lost in the publicity around these two appointments, however, was fifty-three-year-old Jean-Paul Deschatelets, a Montreal MP for ten years who had resigned as Pearson's works minister a year earlier and hadn't run in the last election. Deschatelets would go on to become Speaker of the Senate, but by 1986 his health was failing badly and at age seventy-four, just a year before his mandatory retirement, he announced his resignation.

Mulroney knew that naming Cogger to take his place would be controversial. So he left town before anybody knew about it.

On 5:30 P.M. on Friday, May 2, 1986, after most of the Parliamentary Press Gallery members had gone home for the weekend, the PMO issued a news release announcing that Cogger had been chosen to replace the ailing Deschatelets.

About that time, Mulroney was in Vancouver helping to open Expo 86 and preparing to leave for an extended business trip to China, Japan, and Hong Kong.

Sudbury Liberal MP Doug Frith called it "a very cynical appointment. He's looking after his friends." He said the timing of the announcement was also suspect. "It's a typical manipulation of events. [It] was made at the worst possible moment for anyone to comment."

Cape Breton Liberal MP David Dingwall was more direct. "It's a sleazy appointment," he said. Nevertheless, Cogger took his seat in the Senate.

In February 1987, Wolf's business affairs burst into the open again and caused Mulroney's government more headaches. In November 1982, Fred Doucet, another former Mulroney classmate and close friend, and his brother Gerald, a former Nova Scotia education minister, made a public offering of convertible preferred shares for East Coast Energy Ltd. They hoped to raise $8.2 million. Wolf invested $500,000. Mulroney and Michael Meighen also made small investments.

The company, formed by the Doucet brothers, had a small share in the Venture natural gas field off Sable Island and was part of a consortium that wanted to build a pipeline to the mainland. In April 1985, Cogger, then Mulroney's chief counsel, was named co-defendant in a $200,000 suit filed against Wolf arising out of the stock transaction in Doucet's firm. It was filed by McLeod Young Weir Ltd. The action against Cogger was dismissed, but in February 1987 the Supreme Court of Ontario ordered Wolf to repay a $198,000 loan made by McLeod Young Weir on the ill-fated firm. Wolf had also launched legal action against Fred Doucet for misrepresentation. East Coast Energy went bankrupt in 1985 but the Wolf-Doucet lawsuit sparked a political uproar in the Commons early in 1987 amid accusations that Mulroney had personally tried to intimidate Cogger into getting Wolf to drop the lawsuit.

"The prime minister called Mr. Cogger and gave him shit," Wolf said in court records relating to the lawsuit. Cogger said he did have a conversation with Mulroney about the $300,000 lawsuit against Doucet and his brother, but said he made the call, not Mulroney, and "no threats of any kind were made against anyone."

Hamilton Liberal MP Sheila Copps had raised the issue in the Commons, saying that Wolf had raised it with her in a private conversation the year before. Copps said outside the Commons that "when the prime minister uses his influence in whatever way possible to convince someone to drop a lawsuit, then it is an improper use of his position as prime minister and shows very bad judgement." Deputy prime minister Don Mazankowski, in Mulroney's absence, defended his boss by saying, "If there was any such conversation [between Mulroney and Cogger], I would submit it was a private matter." NDP leader Ed Broadbent said it was "quite extraordinary" that Mazankowski would argue that it was a private matter when Mulroney might be involved in discussions of government contracting.

Two days later, Mulroney dismissed the accusations as "speculation, unfounded rumour, unproven allegations." He said that Cogger's statement "disposes of this matter." For his part, Wolf, a globe-trotting, European-based businessman, said through his new lawyer, Michael Eisen, that he "was very upset" about Mulroney's intervention and that his recollection of the incident was "not in accordance" with Cogger's version. Wolf had also complained that he lost $234,000 because of poor investment advice from Cogger, his long-time friend whom he'd hired as his personal lawyer in 1985.

On January 11, 1989, court documents in a civil suit in Quebec Superior Court revealed that Cogger, who was co-chairman of the Tories' 1988 federal election campaign, was paid $110,000 by a computer company to lobby the PMO and senior ministerial aides on its behalf. The fees were paid by GigaMos Corp., a computer semiconductor project based in Vaudreuil and owned by Quebec businessman Guy Montpetit, who was seeking $45 million in joint federal-provincial funds.

Cogger's bill to the company listed discussions he had about the company's funding with Bernard Roy, then Mulroney's principal secretary; Charles McMillan, then Mulroney's adviser on high technology; Tom Creary, chief of staff to Robert de Cotret, minister of regional industrial expansion and minister of state for science and technology; and Paul Brown, then chief of staff for Labour Minister Pierre Cadieux.

Japanese businessman Takayuki Tsuru sued Montpetit for $39 million he had loaned him to start up the business after it became clear to Tsuru that things were not going well with his investment. Montpetit signed the cheques to pay Cogger's bill, which also included fees for trips abroad and meetings and discussions with scientists and others involved in GigaMos. A separate bill showed that Cogger charged GigaMos Research, another Montpetit firm, $4,000 for "services rendered" between January 31 and February 28, 1986. Cogger even billed $95 for roses "sent to the Hon. Barbara McDougall," then minister in charge of privatization.

Creary told the *Montreal Gazette* that he received "at least three or four calls" from Cogger "inquiring" about the status of Montpetit's request for federal funding, but "our evaluation later on was that it [the GigaMos request] did not meet the criteria." He said de Cotret backed his officials' decision that the project not be funded.

The *Gazette* had reported on December 24 that the helicopter firm Les Helicopteres Trans-Quebec Ltée had paid about $37,000 over five years to a man who worked full-time on Cogger's Eastern Townships farm; that a Montreal real estate developer paid $5,000 toward renovations done that year to Cogger's house near Knowlton; and that Montpetit paid $2,416.80 to another man who also worked full-time on Cogger's farm.

In Ottawa, opposition critics in the Commons demanded an RCMP investigation to determine whether Cogger was in a conflict of interest when he accepted money for representing GigaMos in discussions with senior government officials. MP John Rodriguez, NDP critic on parliamentary ethics, said, "It seems to me a senator ought not to be representing companies to the government. They [senators] are paid as part of the Parliament of Canada. The Senate is part of the Parliament of Canada. When they start approaching ministers on behalf of clients, who in turn pay them for services, that is a highly questionable practice. I think it borders on influence peddling."

As the civil action continued, it was learned that Cogger had actually received $229,000 from Montpetit between 1986 and 1988, $150,000 of which came out of Tsuru's $39-million loan to Montpetit. Gabriel Voyer, a senior public servant with the Department of Regional Expansion, testified in June that Cogger had pressured him to recommend that his client receive the government funding. Voyer said Cogger telephoned him in September 1987 and told him to "get moving" on Montpetit's request. He said Cogger told him that provincial officials had already approved the project, but Voyer testified that he spoke to his Quebec counterpart and was told that no decision had been made. On April 18, 1988, Montpetit's request was denied.

Tsuru testified that he believed Cogger when the senator wrote him on July 23, 1987, to say that a building in Vaudreuil had been put on a government "priority list" for renting federal office space.

At the time of Cogger's letter to him, Montpetit had already borrowed $39 million from Tsuru and was asking the Japanese businessman to invest $13.5 million in his computer project to be based in Vaudreuil, in the former Hoffman-La Roche office owned by a Montpetit company. Montpetit wanted to rent out space there to cover a large mortgage. Tsuru, who had since learned there was no such list, testified that at the time, "this was a letter from a senator so I believed it." Cogger had told Tsuru that he had "good news on two fronts – that the Vaudreuil building was on the priority list," and "we can safely assume that we would be going ahead with the governments in the GigaMos project within the next couple of weeks." Montpetit later testified that one of Cogger's jobs was to handle "governmental relations."

In June 1989, *Gazette* reporter Rod Macdonell revealed that several high-ranking Conservative Party officials had been given a free ride a year earlier to Alma, Quebec, aboard Montpetit's private jet – which he had bought for $2.9 million out of Tsuru's $39-million loan – to celebrate Lucien Bouchard's by-election victory in the federal riding of Lac St.-Jean. Bouchard, now Quebec's Parti Québécois premier, was a federal Tory and secretary of state at that time. Jean-Yves Lortie, a senior Tory official, confirmed that he was aboard the flight along with Cogger and Mario Beaulieu, the Tories' Quebec chairman for the November 21 general election. He explained they went to "help organize the press conference" for Bouchard.

The *Gazette* story also revealed for the first time the Saskatchewan connection with Montpetit and Cogger – including news that Senator Eric Berntson, then the province's deputy premier, had also spent time on that jet, as had Saskatchewan's ministers of justice, science and technology, and the ministers responsible for the Saskatchewan Economic Development Corp.

Saskatchewan Tory pollster Ken Waschuk, a former Joe Clark aide, was on that flight too. Waschuk, an adviser to both Mulroney and Saskatchewan premier Grant Devine, had been brought into the mix by his old friend Cogger. Both had been part of Mulroney's inner circle since their Montreal days. Waschuk subsequently was under investigation by the RCMP for possible influence peddling in connection with a $150,000 interest-free loan he had received from Montpetit in 1988. Waschuk helped convince Berntson that Saskatchewan should invest in Montpetit's project. Saskatchewan gave Montpetit $5.25 million and continued to pay $50,000 a month in operating costs for a translation system called GigaText that wasn't working. In a 118-page ruling in October, Mr. Justice André Forget of Quebec Superior Court gave Montpetit thirty days to pay Tsuru $39 million or have his high-tech companies liquidated. That judgement prompted Eldon Lautermilch, then NDP critic for the Saskatchewan Development Corp., to say the province "was suckered by Montpetit" and should cut its losses and run. Montpetit and his partner, Douglas Young, owned seventy-five per cent of GigaText even though they had invested no money in it. The province did, however, force them to give up control and put their shares in escrow after the Quebec court case was launched.

Things grew still bleaker for Cogger. In late October 1989, *Gazette* reporters Rod Macdonell and Robert Winters reported that Cogger had billed the Federal Business Development Bank, a Crown corporation, a total of $74,250 between 1986 and 1988. Under Section 14 of the federal Parliament Act, it is a conflict of interest for a senator to be involved in a contract involving public funds. It expressly forbids both MPs and senators from doing business with the government. Cogger's bill was part of a total of at least $182,000 in invoices sent by Cogger's law firm, Lapointe Rosenstein. Payments for the bills submitted by Cogger and the firm were made out to Lapointe Rosenstein. The FBDB received $35 million in federal money in 1988. Its mandate is to promote small and medium-sized businesses by lending them money and providing management-counselling services.

The Parliament Act provides for fines of $200 for "each day during which the contravention continues," but proceedings to recover the fine have to be launched within one year of the event giving rise to the conflict. A senior partner at the law firm told the *Gazette* that Cogger had left the firm "several months ago."

In a brief statement about the affair in the Senate, Cogger admitted that he had billed the development bank. "I have, in some instances, signed the covering letters accompanying such bills of fees. All payments were made to the firm of Lapointe Rosenstein." Some of them, however, were marked to Cogger's attention.

Mulroney refused to comment, but Industry Minister Harvie Andre, responsible for the bank, didn't seem to be concerned. He said the law firm had done work for the bank for two decades and, anyway, all Cogger did was sign the covering letters. But Liberal justice critic Bob Kaplan said, "I think the law is very clear. The defence the senator has just given in the Senate is no defence at all."

Cogger initially refused to comment on another published story that the development bank loaned the University of Sherbrooke $100,000 in 1987 to produce a home-study course in business management. The university in turn struck a deal with a firm called Pluri-Canaux. Cogger subsequently told the *Gazette* he was not involved with Pluri-Canaux at the time, but in June 1990, an RCMP investigation concluded that Cogger owned between twenty-three and fifty per cent of the company between 1985 and 1988 and earned $259,000 in the deal. Police said the bank loaned the money to the university after Cogger personally lobbied bank president Guy Lavigeur during a private dinner in a Montreal restaurant in early 1987. The RCMP said Cogger received a benefit from Montpetit, who loaned Pluri-Canaux $45,000 at Cogger's request.

And another Quebec company, Hydromega Developments Inc., paid Cogger $2,500 the day after it got the final go-ahead for $340,000 in federal money that Cogger helped obtain. It paid after Cogger sent a bill for "professional services rendered." Maurice Roch, a consultant who handled the grant request for the firm, told the *Gazette* that Cogger was paid because he helped Hydromega obtain money that had already been approved in 1987 by the Department of Energy, Mines and Resources. Despite the approval, however, the department said there was no money in their budget and Cogger "helped in getting this thing [money] through. . . . He [Cogger] was asked for a favour, and he asked for one in return," said Roch. But in a second interview a day later, Roch altered his story and denied Cogger had pulled strings to get the federal money. He said Cogger should not have received any money from the firm and that "Cogger was not Hydromega's lawyer." The reason he had been paid was a "grey area," said Roch.

The company is half-owned by Mayer Lawee and his cousin, Alfred Lawee, Montreal real estate developers. In April 1988, Kesmat Investments, a company owned by the Lawees, paid $5,000 for renovations to Cogger's country home in Quebec's Eastern Townships.

Cogger at the time was also involved with Mayer Lawee in a company called Pluri-Canaux Ltée., which received a $100,000 loan from the business development bank in 1987.

In a terse statement responding to the latest revelations, Cogger admitted he was paid to lobby for the firm but said that "while I have rendered professional services to the said company . . . at no time did I have anything to do with the said company receiving a grant. I have in no way intervened with anyone in the Department of Energy, Mines and Resources and any allegation or representation to the contrary is completely false." Cogger said all he did to help the firm get the grant was set up and attend a luncheon meeting with a co-owner of Hydromega and two Montreal-area Tory MPs.

During the subsequent uproar in the Commons, on November 2, 1989, Kingston Liberal MP Peter Milliken shouted, "He should be in jail!" NDP leader Ed Broadbent accused Solicitor-General Pierre Blais and Justice Minister Doug Lewis of shirking their duties by brushing off demands for an RCMP inquiry and saying it was up to the Senate to settle the matter.

"It is cowardly; it is a complete disregard for the democratic system of justice," fumed Broadbent. "It is to say there is one law for the senators in Canada and another law for everyone else."

While Mulroney's government was trying to downplay the Cogger affair, the RCMP was getting interested. On November 3, during the third straight day of heavy questioning from the opposition in the Commons, Blais admitted that the Mounties were looking into the *Gazette* revelations. Mulroney told the Commons that Cogger had denied the allegations and had asked the Senate to investigate and "I'm informed by the leader of the government in the Senate that will be done."

Cogger had sent a letter the day before to Senate leader Lowell Murray asking for committee hearings so he could respond to the allegations. "Notwithstanding my public denials, some members of the media and of the House of Commons have persisted in these insinuations," he wrote.

Outside the Commons on November 3, Mulroney told reporters that Cogger's request for a Senate hearing was "appropriate and legitimate. An allegation has been made against him and he's denied it, he's invited the Senate to examine his conduct. What could be more forthcoming than that? I think it's the proper way to proceed."

And for the first time, Andre, so dismissive earlier in the week, admitted that day that Cogger had done legal work for the business development bank after he was appointed a senator in May 1986. "He [Cogger] and other members of the firm have been doing work on that file for a long time. . . . The first bill sent in by Michel Cogger was before he was appointed to the Senate, and . . . the other two sent over his signature was after he was in the Senate." Asked specifically whether "in the last two cases, it is clear whether Cogger was directly involved in doing the legal work" Andre replied, "The firm generally is involved but I understand he [Cogger] did some of the work."

The next day, Small Business Minister Tom Hockin said Andre was misinformed and denied that Cogger did legal work for the Crown corporation after his appointment to the Senate. A few days later, however, Mark Rosenstein, a partner in Cogger's law firm, told the *Globe and Mail* that Cogger worked under contract on a part-time basis for the firm and was responsible for handling the firm's dealings with the federal bank, even after he became a senator. He said the contract with Cogger went back to 1983 and "was not altered" after Cogger entered the Senate. "The bank was his client. He was responsible for the bank. That responsibility was an ongoing thing when he became a senator."

On November 7, Cogger resigned from the Tory caucus as the RCMP launched a criminal inquiry into his business dealings. Cogger retracted his call for a Senate inquiry, saying, "I believe that justice would be better served now by suspending my request and waiting for a definitive report from the RCMP." But Cogger's colleagues were having none of that. Despite Cogger's plea, Senate Liberal leader Allan MacEachen demanded an even broader inquiry probing all aspects of Cogger's business dealings since his appointment to the Upper House. Government leader Lowell Murray subsequently asked the Senate to strike a committee immediately to be chaired by Newfoundland Tory senator Gerald Ottenheimer and consisting of B.C. Tory Jacques Flynn, and three Liberal senators – Eymard Corbin, Bud Olson, and Joan Neiman, who was vice-chairman. The committee, with a start-up budget of just $25,000, set out to investigate, as Neiman put it, whether Cogger acted properly "in the context of appropriate standards of conduct for members of the Senate. "We as a committee have to try and determine . . . if there is a standard of conduct that Parliament wants to prohibit that is something less than what is now spelled out in the Criminal Code." They even decided to hold the meetings in public.

In mid-December, RCMP commissioner Norman Inkster stunned the Commons justice committee by testifying that a special economic crime unit of the RCMP was investigating fifteen MPs and senators, saying eight of his officers were working full-time for the unit. Mulroney, who actually had a point, was outraged. He said it was "unacceptable" to leave all politicians under a cloud of suspicion. "It's already tough enough being an MP without having this sort of stuff floating around," he said. "Canadians don't have a high regard for politicians or journalists." Even Liberal leader John Turner, usually a strong defender of the RCMP, said Inkster was wrong to "darken the reputation of everybody by suggesting there may or may not be an investigation. You either lay charges or you don't."

In response to the growing scandal, the Tories re-introduced conflict-of-interest legislation designed to toughen conduct rules for both MPs and senators. It required politicians and their spouses to declare most of their assets and sources of income to a conflicts commissioner.

In January 1990, things grew even murkier when a disaffected RCMP informant, Paul Vidosa, told Southam News that Cogger had been targeted by the RCMP in 1989 in an undercover operation into a suspected international money-laundering ring in Vancouver. "It was just a sting operation," said Vidosa. "It was a trap just to get him. Any reason to get him, any way, just get him. They wanted him and they told me I was the best to get him."

Apparently the RCMP were going after Cogger on other fronts. On January 22 – the same day Cogger made a brief appearance in a Montreal court to set a preliminary hearing for the charges of influence peddling against him – a Montreal businessman said he'd been asked to participate in a sting against Cogger. Pierre Ducros was chairman of DMR Group Inc., a Montreal computer consulting firm that was one of the losing bidders for a $150-million contract awarded by the federal government. He said he was asked by the RCMP to "set a trap" for Cogger after the RCMP were called in to investigate complaints from Ottawa's SHL Systemhouse Inc. and the Canadian Association of Data and Professional Service Organizations that there was political interference in awarding the contract to Fenco-Lavalin, a subsidiary of Quebec engineering giant Lavalin Inc. A subsequent RCMP investigation found the complaints "were totally unfounded."

Perhaps, but the awarding of that contract certainly raised some interesting questions. Cogger had helped to incorporate DMR in 1973, and in 1988 after tendering its second bid for the contract, Ducros asked Cogger to arrange a lunch so they could discuss the contract with Senate Speaker Guy Charbonneau. Ducros would later testify at an inquiry that Charbonneau, nicknamed "The Pope" because of his power within the Quebec Tory party, told him directly that DMR's bid would not be considered because one of his partners in the bid was a French company that had not received NATO security clearance. Charbonneau then asked Ducros if he would be interested in making a deal with Fenco-Lavalin. Systemhouse president Rod Bryden, now owner of the Ottawa Senators hockey team, was offered a similar deal by another Tory official. These offers were made five months before the government officially awarded the contract to Fenco-Lavalin.

RCMP commissioner Norman Inkster had responded to these allegations in November by ordering an internal inquiry. At the same time, Ducros had complained to the RCMP's special federal inquiries unit that he had not been interviewed by police about the bidding process. Unit chief Rod Stamler and RCMP inspector André Beauchemin heard his story and initiated another investigation. But this time they concluded the process had been badly flawed, although it was uncertain whether any criminal act had occurred.

In her book, *On the Take: Crime, Corruption and Greed in the Mulroney Years*, author Stevie Cameron writes that as a result of meetings with Ducros and others, the two police officers prepared a memo for what they called Operation Sack, saying that "intelligence has been received by this Section to the effect that senators have been involved illegally in the process of awarding Federal Government contracts to private industry, more specifically Senators Cogger and Charbonneau have been mentioned in several investigations as having been involved in suspicious circumstances in relation to various large Federal Government contracts. . . . From our inquiries, it appears to be generally understood in the business community, that the only way to obtain government contracts is to cultivate political connections and to contribute a portion of the profits to these government connections." They said traditional investigative techniques wouldn't work and suggested a pro-active method using a police agent to "attempt to confirm or dispel that Senators Cogger and Charbonneau accepted by corruption, money or non-monetary benefits for intervention or influence. . . ."

On February 13, a teary-eyed Cogger rose on a point of privilege in the Senate to paint himself as a victim and to accuse the RCMP of "bias and prejudice" against him, suggesting that police investigators "may be guilty of criminal conspiracy." He said his fundamental rights as a Canadian citizen were being threatened because of "malicious prosecution, entrapment, undue suspicion [and] police harassment." Speaking in the Senate, where parliamentary privilege gave him immunity from libel or other legal recourse, Cogger said the RCMP was unfit to conduct an internal investigation. "Why should one believe that the RCMP will now clean up its act, will now voluntarily expose its own wrongdoing?" he said.

In March, after a six-week internal review, Superintendent John L'Abbe found there was no criminal wrongdoing by the police although he did find "errors in the handling of human police sources" and concluded there was a need "to review the force's policies relating to the management and control of human sources."

Inkster's next move was to ask the independent RCMP External Review Committee consisting of one person, former Ontario County Court Judge René Marin, to conduct its own investigation. He said the extra review was needed in order to avoid the appearance of a "whitewash. . . . I think it's important that justice not only be done, but be seen to be done."

That one-man review committee of inquiry began its closed-door hearings in mid-April, but the process was delayed again when Southam News launched court action to have the hearings made public. In November, Inkster moved to end a constitutional challenge by Southam by announcing that the inquiry would be open except for evidence dealing with active RCMP investigations, national defence or security, police techniques and the identity of targets, sources, or informants. Marin was told he could no longer determine whether there was any wrongdoing by the Mounties involved, only assess their "ethical conduct." The change was made because under the RCMP Act, disciplinary action cannot be taken against an officer more than a year after an allegation is made. The process got bogged down even more because of a dispute over access to RCMP documents and other legal issues and at one point Marin said he would quit his inquiry unless lawyers for the current and former Mounties involved were allowed to study the secret documents.

While all this was going on, Cogger's lawyer pleaded with the Senate to suspend its inquiry until after the public review was completed. The Senate agreed. And Cogger asked Marin to order the RCMP to pay for his legal fees claiming "my financial situation is difficult."

Months earlier, Revenue Canada had shown considerable interest in Cogger's financial situation when it slapped a $68,588 lien on his eighty-hectare Eastern Townships estate for non-payment of his 1987 and 1988 taxes. It was Revenue Canada's fourth lien against the farm, which was already burdened with $350,000 worth of mortgages and liens. The previous summer, the estate – two houses, stables, and swimming pool – was offered for sale for $950,000 but Cogger, his wife, Erica, and three children decided not to sell when reporters, posing as potential buyers, started snooping around.

On May 24, 1990, about two dozen RCMP officers raided Cogger's home and his offices on Parliament Hill and in Montreal. Cogger told the *Globe and Mail* May 29 that the RCMP were out to get him because of his close friendship with Mulroney. "The police operation conducted last Thursday was not part of a genuine investigation . . ." he said, "but rather a massive display of police power designed to harass and intimidate me. . . . I don't believe I'm being paranoid." He added he believed the RCMP was tapping his phone and that the force was so powerful Canada had become a police state.

In a 144-page affidavit filed by the RCMP in Quebec Court on June 18, 1990, police said they believed Cogger received more than $200,000, including $5,000 in home renovations, and committed fraud against the federal government five times in 1985. They also alleged that Cogger billed the Federal Business Development Bank for $74,250 for work he never did. They said he used half the money to help pay his overdue Quebec income tax.

On June 10, 1991, Marin concluded that the Mounties had done nothing illegal in their probe of Cogger, but he questioned the judgement of some officers and the ethical standards of their investigations. Making no judgement on Cogger, Marin offered several recommendations to tighten up RCMP investigations, including establishment of an RCMP informant review and approval unit, better training for use and handling of informants, setting ethical standards and education seminars for rookie MPs and senators on political influence laws. Later that month, the government said it would pay more than $27,000 for Cogger's legal bills from the inquiry.

By this time, Cogger's legal business had almost completely dried up and the Quebec Revenue Department was garnisheeing some of his Senate salary for nonpayment of $107,000 in Quebec income tax. A big chunk of Cogger's $74,5000 Senate salary was already being withheld to pay off $83,000 in unpaid federal income taxes, and the Toronto-Dominion Bank foreclosed on his farm near Knowlton for $304,000 in delinquent mortgage payments. An affidavit from the Senate's director of finance showed that because of the garnishees, Cogger's take-home pay was only $17,112.96.

Cogger said in August that he had worked out a deal to sell his estate and would be able to pay off both Ottawa and Quebec. After the bank had foreclosed, Senator John Lynch-Staunton told writer Mordecai Richler that he and David Angus passed the hat among the old Tory gang in Montreal. (Angus, the long-time PC Canada Fund head who later was named to the Senate by Mulroney, denies playing a role in saving Cogger's farm.) On December 5, 1991, Cogger sold the property to a numbered company, 2732611 Canada Inc., whose only officer was listed as Jean-Yves Lortie, a charter member of

Mulroney's circle. Also registered with the deed was an undertaking by the numbered company to be a guarantor for Cogger's debts to Revenue Canada.

In August, Cogger had publicly complained through *Toronto Sun* political columnist Michel Gratton that his livelihood had been destroyed by the RCMP investigations. "This thing has got to end," he said, adding that "no charges have been laid against me yet. . . ."

That changed on September 12, 1991, when Cogger was formally charged with influence peddling for allegedly receiving $212,000 from industrialist Guy Montpetit in return for his help in seeking a large federal government grant. The charge, laid by the RCMP under Section 121 (1) of the Criminal Code, was sworn before Louise Bourdeau, a justice of the peace at the Montreal courthouse. The next day, Cogger said he was innocent of the charge and would not resign his seat in the upper chamber. A few days after that, Montpetit was charged with giving the money to Cogger as payment for the senator's influence in seeking government contracts.

On May 22, 1992, Cogger was ordered to stand trial on the charge that he peddled his influence with governments to Montpetit between 1986 and 1988. After a preliminary hearing in Montreal, Judge Joel Guberman also ordered Montpetit to stand trial for buying Cogger's influence. In June 1993, Quebec Court Judge Jean Falardeau acquitted Cogger of influence peddling. Cogger did not contest the facts presented by the Crown, but argued in court that the billings to Montpetit were for ordinary legal work done by a lawyer on a client's behalf.

Falardeau ruled, "In effect, the circumstances are that I cannot convince myself beyond a reasonable doubt that the accused posed the alleged actions with the guilty mind or blameworthiness required for a conviction under the charge."

In February 1996, a three-judge panel on the Quebec Court of Appeal upheld Cogger's acquittal, concluding that "the concepts of a 'guilty mind' and a 'blameworthy state of mind' . . . have been used for a very long time in Canadian jurisprudence."

In the Crown's appeal, prosecutor Pierre Levesque had argued that the evidence showed Cogger clearly broke the law by continuing to work at influencing government officials on Montpetit's behalf after his appointment to the Senate. He said he shouldn't have to prove that Cogger had a guilty conscience as well.

Later that month the Crown requested permission to appeal the Cogger case to the Supreme Court of Canada. Maurice Galarneu, head of the team of Crown lawyers who prosecute economic crimes, said, "Our position is that a person who is a senator, who receives sums of money either for his lobbying or to obtain a contract for his client, we think that he has voluntarily put himself in that position, and has committed an act of corruption."

In April, prosecutor Pierre Levesque, in an argument filed with the Supreme Court, said if the precedent of Cogger's acquittal is allowed to stand, public officials will be able to hawk their influence like "door-to-door salesmen." He said the Cogger ruling would create a new burden on the prosecution not only to prove the crime was committed, but that the accused had a "feeling of acting wrongfully or that he was conscious of breaking the law."

On October 3, 1996, the Supreme Court granted the Crown leave to appeal the case. In July 1997, the Supreme Court quashed Cogger's acquittal and ordered a new trial on the charges against him. Justice Claire L'Heureux-Dubé, writing the opinion for the Supreme Court, called Quebec Court Judge Jean Falardeau's reasoning in the original trial "curious." She said Cogger's "situation regarding the Criminal Code changed from the moment he became a government official. The fact that he did not know the law, or his status regarding the law, is simply not a factor relevant to his innocence or guilt. . . . Ignorance of the law is not an excuse."

Cogger, a practising lawyer since 1964, also testified at Montpetit's corruption trial in March 1998 telling Quebec Court Judge Suzanne Coupal that he had consulted with a "beige or green book" of parliamentary law to determine whether he would be in a conflict of interest if he continued to work for the businessman after his Senate appointment, but could find nothing in the book that described a situation comparable to the one he was in. He said he also consulted with lawyer Charles Lussier, the Senate clerk, but he didn't realize he was considered a public servant under Section 121 of the Criminal Code until "the accusations were brought against [him]." During the trial, evidence came out that in 1989, Montpetit told an RCMP officer that Cogger's role was to "cut through this shit. Apply pressure to make sure civil servants do their job. That he not be bypassed for other paper in the basket."

Montpetit was found guilty May 1, 1998, of trying to buy Cogger's influence. Once a jet-setting businessman, the slight, grey-haired Montpetit was then living on welfare. Judge Coupal said, "All elements of the crime have been proved. . . . Michel Cogger took several steps, which were without success, at various levels, often the highest, of the federal and provincial government with the ultimate goal that his client obtain a financial benefit."

Cogger's retrial on the influence-peddling charges began again in Montreal on May 4 – the fourth time they had come before the courts – with the Crown once again laying out all the facts that had been known for several years. On the opening day of the trial, former Tory industry minister Michel Côté testified that Cogger had approached him several times at Tory caucus meetings and pressed him on the Montpetit project. On the second day of the trial, Louis Doyle, a project officer with the industry department, testified he attended a 1986 meeting with Montpetit and Cogger that was unprecedented in his eight-year government career. He said the two men met with Côté and Labour Minister Pierre Cadieux at Côté's cabinet office, and they complained about the bureaucratic stonewalling that was holding up Montpetit's project. Doyle said it was the first time for him that two ministers attended a meeting with a grant applicant like Montpetit. "Normally, such representations are made with the project officer and not at the minister's office."

Public interest in the trial, already high, exploded on the fourth day when Quebec premier Lucien Bouchard was called to testify. Cogger, Bouchard, and Mulroney were good friends from their student days at Laval's law school. Before testifying, Bouchard told the *Gazette* that the Cogger case was "not [his] favorite subject." He said Cogger "has always been my friend. We have been friends since our early years. We were very, very close." Bouchard had testified at Cogger's 1992 preliminary hearing that Cogger had tried to pitch Montpetit or his product to him twice, once during lunch in Ottawa and again on the night that Bouchard was elected to the Commons in Lac St. Jean, when Montpetit, Cogger, and others used Montpetit's Cessna to fly from Montreal to Alma to celebrate the by-election victory.

Security was tight on May 9 when Bouchard arrived to testify that when he became a federal cabinet minister in 1988, Cogger complained to him over lunch that Montpetit's translation technology was not getting a fair shake from Bouchard's bureaucrats. Bouchard told Quebec Court Judge Robert Sansfacon that his friendship with Cogger dated back to the early 1960s at Laval. He said that he was new to town and that Cogger, a Quebec City native who sat next to him in class, befriended him. He said that for a "fleeting" few minutes during an Ottawa lunch, Cogger raised the topic that secretary of state bureaucrats were giving short shrift to Montpetit's translation technology. As secretary of state, Bouchard was responsible for government translation. He said it was a pressing issue in his department at the time because Ottawa was preparing to give Saskatchewan $20 million so the province could abide by a Supreme Court ruling to translate its laws into French. Montpetit wanted the translation contract.

After the luncheon, Bouchard instructed his deputy minister to set up a committee to scientifically evaluate Montpetit's technology. "I wanted to make sure a bad decision had not been made [by bureaucrats]," Bouchard said. The committee's evaluation was "negative" so Bouchard warned cabinet ministers from western Canada that the Montpetit system did not work. Saskatchewan went ahead and poured money into it anyway, thanks partly to the support of Senator Eric Berntson, then the province's deputy premier.

On June 2, 1998, ten years after pocketing the last payment of $212,000 from Montpetit, Cogger was convicted of influence peddling. Judge Sansfacon ruled that "all elements constituting the offence were proven beyond a reasonable doubt." He said even though Montpetit didn't get the government grant, Cogger made "numerous efforts" on his behalf.

Sansfacon said that shortly before Cogger's appointment, the Supreme Court had made a ruling on influence peddling by senators – in the case involving former Nova Scotia senator Irvine Barrow – "and it was thus a well-established and unambiguous rule of law." He said he found it "unreasonable" that an experienced lawyer such as Cogger, "aware of the prosecution of a senator for influence peddling [Barrow], did not find it appropriate to obtain a legal opinion from a competent authority" before deciding to continue to represent Montpetit.

At a pre-sentence hearing ten days later, Cogger's wife, Erica, took the stand to seek clemency for her husband. She described how their lives had become a "nightmare" since the RCMP began investigating him nine years before. She said Cogger had lost all his clients and the family had been financially devastated. She said she went to work as a sales clerk for several years to help out, but had to quit when she suffered a nervous breakdown. He and his wife had been together since 1972, when he worked for Robert Stanfield and she worked for Stanfield's wife.

Sansfacon appeared moved by her testimony, but told her in what a journalist described as an "apologetic tone" that "the cloud will have to remain over your heads a while longer." Needing "time to reflect," he ordered Cogger to appear July 7 for sentencing. At the sentencing, Judge Sansfacon ordered Cogger to pay a $3,000 fine and do 120 hours of community work. He also put Cogger on probation for a year.

Cogger had requested an unconditional discharge – a sentence that would wipe his conviction from the books and improve his chances of hanging on to his Senate seat.

Sansfacon said, "This is the hardest sentence I have ever had to render in my career." He said he had "great empathy for the family drama" caused by the "hellish" affair, but said it was "not in the public interest" that Cogger be given total clemency. He said as a senator, Cogger held one of the highest posts in government, and it was in that very capacity he had committed his crime. "It is for reasons of deterrence that a condemnation [of Cogger's actions] is imperative."

The sentence renewed opposition demands that he resign his Senate seat – or be booted out – but Senate leaders say they can't discuss the matter until after Cogger has exhausted all his appeals.

During a staged media event in Ottawa on July 14, Reform MP Deborah Grey, the party's deputy leader, mailed Cogger his "pink slip," a giant slip emblazoned with the words "Notice of Termination." "I think people are pretty tired of paying this guy," she said. "He is a convicted criminal and I think it's just high time he was out of office."

In late August 1998, the Quebec Court of Appeal gave Cogger the right to appeal both his influence-peddling conviction and his sentence.

In a *Gazette* editorial published after his conviction, the newspaper likely reflected the view of most Canadians when it argued that the conviction "does more than disgrace the man. It also risks shaming the Senate itself, adding to its already low standing in public esteem." It pointed out that legally, the question is not simple. The Constitution says senators should leave office if convicted of a "felony or infamous crime," but the word "felony" has been deleted from the Criminal Code and "any semantically inclined lawyer could question whether influence-peddling qualifies as outright infamy." The *Gazette* said Cogger should resign, but failing that "the Senate should suspend Mr. Cogger, and without pay. If an appeal process should vindicate him, fine. The Senate should then reimburse him for every last nickel it denied him. So long as [the] guilty verdict stands, Mr. Cogger has no business in the Senate chamber."

For nearly a year after the verdict, in fact, Cogger was not seen in the Senate. He did, however, return on March 17, just in the nick of time to sign in and thus meet the onerous demands of the Senate in order to continue being paid.

Cogger was joined in the Red Chamber that day by Saskatchewan senator Eric Berntson, who had been convicted of fraud just the day before in Regina. Neither man had anything to say to reporters and neither spoke during the ninety-minute Senate session. Berntson, however, was approached by several senators who offered hand-shakes and pats on the back. Liberal senator Raymond Perrault complained that he and his colleagues were getting "damned annoyed" at all the negative publicity surrounding the Senate. "I have been in many chambers. I was nine years in the B.C. legislature, leader of the Liberal Party out there. I was elected to the House of Commons . . . and this [Senate] chamber here, its ethics are as high as any chamber I have ever served in in my life."

If that is true, it's hardly comforting. Perhaps if Perrault and his cronies would take some action to clean up the place, their image would be enhanced. As things stand, however, both convicted criminals have vowed to stay as long as their appeals are outstanding. And their Senate colleagues have agreed.

Given the record so far, that could be forever.

13

THE PHANTOM OF THE CHAMBER

THERE ARE TWO things to remember about the Andy Thompson saga: First, he embarrassed the Senate – not an easy thing to do – but he did not break the attendance rules. And second, on February 19, 1998, when Thompson's chronic absenteeism made him the first senator in the upper chamber's 130-year history to be suspended, barely half the Senate showed up for the vote.

Just 54 of the 104 senators bothered to cast a ballot. They voted 52–1, with one abstention, to suspend him for the two years remaining in that session, in effect to throw him out of the Senate because his seventy-fifth birthday, which means mandatory retirement, was just two years away. Manitoba Tory senator Terrance Stratton voted against the suspension, saying the penalty was too lenient. He wanted Thompson kicked out, period. So did Alberta Tory Ron Ghitter, who walked out of the chamber rather than vote.

Thompson, who had attended just 2.5 per cent of the sittings since 1990, was living in Mexico. He claimed he was receiving special treatment there for cancer that is not available in Canada. Over the years, he had also listed a heart condition, high blood pressure, and immune problems as reasons why he was unable to warm his seat in the Red Chamber. Still, all a senator has to do to keep his or her seat is show up during one of the first twenty sittings of a new Parliament.

Thanks primarily to the splendid and relentless work of *Ottawa Citizen* reporter Jack Aubrey, Thompson's chronic no-shows – along with those of many of his colleagues – had become front-page news in the weeks leading up to the 1997 Christmas break.

Prime Minister Jean Chrétien, who had ignored Thompson's chronic absenteeism for years, suddenly became deeply concerned and booted Thompson out of the Liberal caucus on November 19. He wrote in a letter to Thompson that "absence from the sittings of the Senate and the record of non-participation in the work of the caucus over many years are totally unacceptable." Not that it mattered much, since, as Chrétien acknowledged in his tardy note, Thompson never showed up in caucus anyway. What's more, neither expulsion affected his pay and perks. After several days of hemming and hawing, the senators unanimously approved two unprecedented motions on December 16, 1997, stripping the truant senator of his office budget and secretary (worth about $90,000 a year), and demanding that he show up on Parliament Hill after the Christmas break or face being held in contempt of the Senate. He didn't, and they exacted the threatened penalty.

One night in 1940, Joseph Thompson and a friend were riding their horses on patrol for the home guard when the roar of Nazi bombs blitzing nearby Bristol prompted his companion to say he was going to send his children to Canada.

"I could do so much more if I knew they were safe," he said.

"Not me," said Joseph. "I'll keep mine here."

When they returned to Bristol in the morning, the man discovered that his children were dead. It was then that Joseph Thompson decided to send Andy, fifteen, the youngest of his four children, to the far-away safety of Canada.

Andrew E. Thompson arrived in Toronto's Forest Hill and spent the next three years working on an Ontario farm and then a western ranch before spending a year at the University of Toronto. At eighteen, he was an able seaman. At nineteen, he was commissioned, but the index finger of his left hand was crushed while loading depth charges aboard a corvette in Halifax. All that remains of that finger is a stump.

After the war, Thompson studied politics and history at Queen's University in Kingston, then took his master's degree in sociology at the University of British Columbia. In 1949, a year after he took out Canadian citizenship, Thompson got a job with the parole and probation service. It was there, he once told a journalist, where he produced the first stirrings of what he called "a social conscience of the kind which made me suspect I might be a political animal at heart."

In 1950 he began working for the new department of citizenship, initially encouraging ethnic groups in the prairie provinces to work with established Canadian communities, then as an ethnic liaison officer in Ontario. He spent 1957–58 working as a national program organizer for CBC radio and then, "out of the blue," he was offered a job as researcher, speech writer, and aide to newly elected Liberal prime minister Lester B. Pearson. "I was a Liberal," he said, "but not then a party member. I'd studied all three major parties, found the CCF too doctrinaire and inflexible and the Tories too reactionary. Liberal governments, historically, were the only ones which had initiated social reforms. So I took the job with Mr. Pearson."

The Liberals lost that election, and Thompson, looking for practical experience in campaigning, was asked by Pearson if he would contest Toronto's Dovercourt seat in 1959. Dovercourt, traditionally a Tory riding, had not voted Liberal since Confederation.

He ran in Dovercourt "for the experience" and won, even though he campaigned for just three weeks. It was after this unexpected victory that many senior Liberals, Pearson and Walter Gordon in particular, began to express high hopes for Thompson's future with the party.

Thompson had met his Estonian-born wife, Amy Riisna, at the 1958 Couchiching Conference, where they were both delegates. She too had been brought to Canada by her family at age fifteen after living in Sweden for several years. She proved to be a valuable political asset for her husband in a riding that was about sixty per cent ethnically diverse.

After his own electoral success, Thompson helped the party campaign in by-elections in Russell, a Liberal riding, and Leeds, a Tory stronghold, and the Liberals won them both. Still a close Pearson adviser, Thompson helped construct the two major planks in the party's successful 1963 federal election: the national medicare plan and the contributory old age pension scheme. He also campaigned for Walter Gordon and was beginning to enjoy a growing reputation within the party as a comer – a winner. With his rugged good looks, his shock of blond hair, some people compared the six-foot politician to Robert Kennedy.

Thompson won again in 1964 but still, the mighty Tories, who had ruled Ontario since 1943 – and would stay in power until 1985 – rolled up a huge majority under the leadership of Premier John Robarts. Liberal leader John Wintermeyer had attempted to run what was called a scandal-a-day campaign against the Tories. But Ontarians weren't buying it. Not only did the Liberals get crushed, but Wintermeyer lost his own seat, leaving the party suddenly without a leader.

Thompson seemed the natural choice. In stark contrast to his later non-performance in the Senate, Thompson had risen to speak in the legislature 1,100 times during his first term at Queen's Park. He was clearly the party's star. And in September 1964, he defeated six other candidates for leader, winning on the sixth ballot. He and Amy were redecorating a west-end Toronto house with a mixture of modern and antique furniture. They had bought a farm near Bowmanville, forty miles east of Toronto, and had plans to build a house there. Life was good then for Andrew and Amy Thompson.

But it didn't last. By 1966, Thompson was being publicly attacked from both inside and outside his caucus for his low-key political style. He believed the attacking opposition of Wintermeyer or federal Tory chieftain John Diefenbaker had gone out of style. His new tack, he argued, was to present the Liberals as a responsible alternative government. "I'm a stubborn person," Thompson said, "and I'm not going to be pushed by any criticism into becoming some demagogue – and I won't be raving every day in the House just to capture headlines. Headlines can be destructive to you as well as helpful."

Thompson could not have known then just how prescient that comment would be. On October 6, 1965, Thompson and another Toronto Liberal, Bracondale MPP George Ben were driving through Peterborough on their way back to Toronto from Millbrook. Thompson, who was driving, suddenly pulled out into the other lane and smashed into a car carrying four women from Harwood, Ontario. All four women were treated in hospital – one of them, Ida O'Connell, was listed in serious condition with head injuries. Police charged Thompson with dangerous driving, impaired driving, careless driving, and failure to yield one-half of the road. Ben posted the $100 bail so Thompson could get out of jail.

Thompson appeared in a Peterborough court the day after the accident and was remanded until later that month. On December 1, he was convicted of dangerous driving and fined $250 plus $67.10 in court costs. Magistrate W.A. Phil said the conviction carried a mandatory six-month driving licence suspension when injuries were involved. Charges of impaired driving were dismissed. In an interview later, Thompson said he didn't feel the conviction would affect his political career. "I feel I should be judged on my political performance rather than a car accident."

Less than a year later, suffering from a combination of influenza, high blood pressure, and exhaustion, Thompson went into several weeks of seclusion at his Durham County farm. On November 17, less than a month before his forty-third birthday, Thompson sent a film clip taken in his Toronto home to be shown at a Queen's Park news conference to announce he was stepping down as Ontario Liberal leader.

On April 4, 1967, Thompson was given a standing ovation by 150 delegates at the nomination meeting in his riding of Dovercourt after he announced he was leaving elective politics because of a worsening heart condition. Speculation was rampant that his old pal Lester Pearson would reward him with a Senate seat. Walter Gordon, then federal minister without portfolio, told reporters at the meeting he hoped Thompson would have a chance to devote his talents not only to the people of Ontario, but to all of Canada. "We simply can't let a man of these kinds of attributes return to the sidelines once the immediate health problem is corrected," said Gordon.

Two days later, Thompson was one of four Liberals elevated to patronage heaven. And so a bit of Senate history began.

In September 1997 the *Ottawa Citizen*'s intrepid reporter Jack Aubrey published the results of his survey of Senate attendance. It showed that about one-fifth of the 104 senators had missed more than half the sittings during the previous two years. Only eight of those missing-in-action senators received the prescribed financial penalties for their truancy. (The Senate began keeping attendance records only in 1990.)

Aubrey's survey put Thompson right at the head of the class – a significant accomplishment considering the competition – for having attended just 12 of the 459 sittings over the two Parliaments.

Toronto business entrepreneur Trevor Eyton wasn't much better. A lawyer and Brascan Ltd. chairman, Eyton showed up for just seven of the ninety-six sittings between February 1996 and April 1997. During that period, Eyton collected about $170,000 in salary and allowances yet paid only $720 in fines. He used a loophole in the rules to avoid fines, claiming sixty-one of the missed sittings fell under the nebulous category of "non-paying public business." He cited his chairmanship of Toronto's SkyDome, activities as chancellor of King's College in Halifax, and attendance at meetings of the International Chamber of Commerce in Paris. Eyton said he told Mulroney from the outset that he would not attend regularly, but Mulroney wanted him anyway, to act as a liaison between the senior business community and the Senate. That prompted Senator Marjory LeBreton, a Mulroney loyalist, to deny Eyton's claim. Since it was LeBreton who made at least the initial calls for Mulroney – and who arranged for the necessary clearances by the RCMP, the tax department, and security officials – she is the one who would have made the first call to Eyton. "People like to blame Brian Mulroney for a lot of things," she said, "but I very much doubt you can blame him for someone else's attendance records."

Mulroney dismissed Eyton's claim out of hand. When I asked Mulroney if LeBreton's version is accurate, he said, "You can be certain of that . . . as an article of faith, had Trevor Eyton or anybody else said, 'I'll accept the job but I won't be able to attend very often,' I'd say 'Thank you very much.' I wouldn't call back, you can sure of that."

Senators are allowed to miss twenty-one sittings during each session without penalty. After that, they're docked $120 for each absence. However, it doesn't count as a "miss" if the senator is ill, on parliamentary delegation work, at out-of-town Senate committee meetings, or on "public business."

The *Citizen* survey showed that B.C. Tory senator Pat Carney attended just thirty-one of the eighty-seven sittings, the same number as another B.C. senator, Ed Lawson. Both avoided fines, however, by booking large numbers of public business days. In July 1992, when he had received considerable flak for his poor attendance record and hefty travel expenses, Lawson said, "Why does everybody pick on senators? What have we ever done?" That, of course, is the point.

The survey found that Lawson, the former Canadian Teamsters' Union boss, had missed 1,111 of 1,379 Senate sittings since his appointment twenty-two years before. Between February 1996 and

September 1997, he did better, but still attended only thirty-seven per cent of the sittings.

The same thing is true of Toronto lawyer Michael Meighen, grandson of the former prime minister, who missed fifty-two sittings but claimed thirty-three public business engagements. Meighen explained that his work on the Senate's bank, trade, and commerce committee led to meetings in Toronto with the heads of banks and insurance companies. He also claimed his work as president of the Stratford Festival as public business, including attending opening week activities. "I think my record isn't bad considering I don't live in Ottawa and [considering] my work on the banking committee," he said.

The rules also say that in addition to showing up from time to time, senators are supposed to own property in the province or, in the case of Quebec, the district they represent. Trudeau appointee Paul Lucier of the Yukon failed on both counts. Lucier, a former mayor of Whitehorse and one-time deckhand on a Yukon stern-wheeler, was the first senator from northern Canada, appointed in 1975 shortly after the Commons increased the Senate by two seats to 104 – one each for the Yukon and Northwest Territories. Lucier showed up for only twenty-one per cent of the sittings in 1997. But more to the point, Lucier lived in British Columbia, not the Yukon, from the early 1990s, a clear violation of the Constitution, which states emphatically that a senator must "be resident in the Province (or Territory) for which he is appointed." Lucier said it was okay for him to break the rules because the Senate staff said he could as long as he owned property in the Yukon. "This is perfectly accept-able," he once explained. "I'm in constant touch with the Yukon and I probably visit there a half dozen times a year." Nice place to visit, but . . .

Ironically, Lucier explained his chronic absenteeism the same way Thompson explained his – he said he had to live in Vancouver for his bone cancer treatments and, like Thompson, he avoided financial penalties for his absences by claiming sick days. The difference between them was that, even though Lucier ran roughshod over the rules, he never became a public embarrassment to his colleagues. Senator Lucier died in July 1999.

In sharp contrast to the senate slackers, Senator Michael Pitfield, one of Trudeau's most controversial appointments, paid $3,480 in fines after missing fifty-six of eighty-seven sittings, even though he suffers from Parkinson's disease. Pitfield refuses to submit a doctor's certificate to avoid the fines. "I feel, quite frankly, a little bit like boarding school. . . . If one needs a doctor's letter, that sort of leaves the impression that one is inventing." He added that "I have not called government business anything but government business. Perhaps it doesn't stand me in good stead when it comes to attendance, but at least it keeps me feeling honest."

Pitfield was closely followed by Senator Leo Kolber, who paid $3,360 in fines, and Senator Walter Twinn, an Alberta Indian chief, who paid $2,880.

Day after day, Aubrey hammered away at the senators. On September 22 he wrote about the use of the "public business" category to excuse chronic absences. The next day he reported that female senators had much better attendance records than their male colleagues, attending about ten more sittings on average and sitting in on seventeen more committee meetings. Senator Anne Cools, for example, had a perfect attendance record. This prompted Senator Jacques Hébert, the Liberal whip who is ever-ready to show he's a man of the nineties, to claim that "women are more conscientious, they are more dedicated, and they are more passionate about the work around here." Of course, their record might also have something to do with the fact that the female senators don't sit on as many corporate boards as their male colleagues. Indeed, women listed only about half the "public business days" claimed by the men.

On September 25, Senator Colin Kenny, chairman of the committee on internal economy, budgets, and administration, told Aubrey that the committee would re-examine the use of public business days and sick leave by the senators. "The majority of senators are hard-working and the attendance stats don't show half the work that we do around here," said Kenny. "But it seems some things need to be clarified."

A secret memo was circulated to senators in the midst of the kerfuffle advising senators to blame a handful of truants for their image problems. But the Senate sits only three days a week at the best of times. It held just fifty-six sittings in all of 1997. Senators counter that they spend considerable time outside the Red Chamber working on committees. Most of them do. Some of them don't. There's certainly nothing in the rules to force senators into extensive committee work.

As for Thompson, who seems to have been ill most of his political life, he did manage to be conveniently healthy enough over the previous decade to show up about once every two years, which is all that is required to meet the rigorous standards of Senate membership. Thompson did disappear for thirty-nine months between October 1990 and January 1994, but here again, his illness claims kept him from being penalized. All he needed was a letter from a doctor. And since the place operated on the "honour" system, nobody verified any of the claims.

With his annual salary of $64,400 plus a $10,100 tax-free allowance, Thompson had collected more than half a million dollars in the previous seven years alone. Between 1990 and 1997, Thompson collected $519,550 in salary for attending fourteen days in the Senate. That works out to $37,110 per day, putting him right up there with superstar baseball pitcher Roger Clemens in his rate of pay per outing.

To make matters worse, Thompson was living in Mexico for four months each winter. He claimed he needed to be there because of his own ill health and that of his ailing wife. Even so, he says he was spending much of his time doing good works for the locals, such as coordinating the provision of seventy-five hospital beds and two hundred crutches to poor hospitals and providing "Newcastle, Ont." T-shirts to poor Mexican children to wear while playing soccer. He said he had thought about resigning his seat, but decided to continue to protect the "legacy" of his office, which goes back to his first election as an MPP in 1959.

He appeared in the Senate in late September and early October of 1997 for the Throne Speech. In December, the Senate privileges committee recommended that he be ordered to appear in Ottawa in February, after the Christmas recess, to explain his absences and to determine whether he was in contempt of the Senate. "If the committee determines that he is in contempt, they will so report," said chairman Senator Colin Kenny. "If this House agrees with such a report, then he could be expelled for the remainder of the session and if that were the case, he could lose his indemnity and his allowance."

On December 16, 1997, the senators unanimously agreed to strip Thompson of his office and secretary. The next day, Ontario Tory senator William Kelly, a member of the rules committee, said stiffer sanctions aren't the solution and attendance should not be the main basis on which to judge performance. "At the end of the day, we have to accept the fact people will behave as people will behave," Kelly said. "You can't legislate morality. It is just not possible. If people are dishonourable, no matter what the rules you have, they will find a way around them." Kelly earned his reputation as chief bagman for the vaunted Ontario Tory Big Blue Machine. He gained some notoriety for his system of imposing specific donation quotas on corporations rather than simply leaving it up to the companies to decide how much they wanted to donate.

Kelly said, "The cynicism that surrounds our political process is quite scary. People have become convinced right down to the municipal level that these people just don't do anything – they draw their salaries and they just laze away."

The Day of Reckoning arrived clear and cold on February 10, 1998, with a welcoming party of Reform MPs wearing giant Mexican-style sombreros, singing Mexican folk songs, dancing to a hired three-piece mariachi band, and serving burritos to themselves and a crowd of curious journalists in the foyer outside the Red Chamber. They were waiting for Andrew Thompson. He didn't show.

But this being the Senate, it took three hours of debate to determine that, well, the senators had goofed. They'd ordered Thompson to appear, but they hadn't said exactly when. So they had no choice but to give him another week to show up. Instead of immediate expulsion, they sent him another order to appear before the Senate's rules committee at 7 P.M. February 17.

Senate committee clerk Gary O'Brien said that Thompson had provided valid medical certificates over the years indicating that he was ill, including one dated November 27, 1997. "I have lost patience with Senator Thompson too and I'm one of his oldest friends," said Liberal senator Richard Stanbury. "On the other hand . . . legally, he's done everything that we're supposed to do."

Reform, in addition to their Mexican musical interlude, had also prepared an easy-to-use map of Parliament Hill to remind Thompson exactly where the Senate is located.

Senate Speaker Gildas Molgat, a veteran Manitoba Liberal, was not amused. He called the Reform demonstration "a circus." Reform's Deborah Grey shot back that Thompson's failure to show up was "a slap in the face of all Canadians." She said the problem is deeper than just Thompson – "something is sick here in the Senate."

Certainly Thompson continued to be sick. He faxed the Senate rules committee to say that he respected the institution but his health prevented him from travelling to Ottawa to testify.

So with Thompson supposedly ill in bed in Le Paz, Mexico, his colleagues, to spare themselves the ongoing embarrassment, overlooked their own rules – all of which Thompson had complied with – and found him in contempt. They voted to suspend him without pay for the rest of the parliamentary session, likely to end in the fall of 1999, just months before he reached the mandatory retirement age of seventy-five. It was the first time in Senate history that a senator had been suspended.

Tory senator Lowell Murray acknowledged that he and his colleagues hadn't exactly been diligent in demonstrating concerns about Thompson's attendance over the years. "I am in my nineteenth year here and it was open to me at any time to stand up and draw attention to what we all knew to be the . . . flagrant absenteeism of our colleague," said Murray. "Others have been here longer than me, still others have been here three, five, eight, and ten years. None of us ever raised this matter in public because it is not done. What we are guilty of is treating this place like a club instead of doing our duty by one of the houses of Parliament."

Finally, on March 23, 1998, Thompson sent a fax to Governor-General Roméo LeBlanc announcing his retirement. In a telephone interview with the *Ottawa Citizen*, Thompson said he would collect almost as much money from his pension as he was receiving from his salary. "I had only a year and a half to go. Frankly some [of the $75,000 salary] was taken in taxes. I think there is not that great a difference between the [$45,000] pension and salary."

The fall-out from the Thompson fiasco led to a committee report in June raising fines for missing a sitting to $250 from $120, but maintaining the lenient twenty-one-sitting grace period. In addition, senators now need a doctor's certificate if they miss more than six days for medical reasons and the certificate must be renewed every three months. Senators who claim to be away on business will have to declare the nature of their business, including the date and location where it took place. The good senators decided, however, to allow time spent on Senate junkets to be counted as a valid reason for missing sittings, along with out-of-town committee meetings on public business.

As a result of all the publicity, Senate attendance improved – from sixty-three per cent to seventy-eight per cent. Senator Sharon Carstairs, the government's deputy leader, acknowledged that media coverage had been instrumental. "Sure, there is no question about it.

I think it was the attention and also a wake-up call. And senators accepted that."

In September 1998, however, the *Citizen*'s Aubrey was at it again, catching the senators at their silly little games. Aubrey reported that the senators were restricting access to their attendance records by placing them in the upper chamber's communications office – which is open for public consultation only during weekday office hours – and by refusing to make copies available to the public. Before then, the documents were regularly reproduced by the Senate clerk's office and provided on request. Brad Bos, a Senate policy adviser who works for rules committee chair Senator Shirley Maheu, told Aubrey that the restriction on access was "under investigation" and a cost-recovery program to recoup the expense of copying the attendance sheets was being studied. He said the clerk's office had been swamped with requests for attendance records. Other government departments simply allow interested parties to use on-site, coin-operated photocopy machines. Britain's House of Lords has its own Web page, which lists each member's attendance.

The next day, in a damage control exercise, Carstairs said the Senate would make every effort to be more open about its attendance and would even supply a photocopy machine. "The intent of the change was to increase – not diminish – access to the documents," she said. "If you want to go in and make photocopies, that is fine. I will make sure that it is in place."

As for Andrew Thompson, when last heard from he was still living in his Mexican villa, making ends meet thanks to a lifetime of public pay and a generous taxpayer-provided pension. He once told a reporter that his favourite Andrew Thompson joke was the one about "the only way the Senate could guarantee my presence up there would be to build a statue of me."

Well, he won't get his statue. But he won't soon be forgotten either.

THE WEST WANTS IN

S TAN WATERS WAS never one to mince words.

On October 17, 1989, the day after he easily defeated five other candidates to win Alberta's first Senate "election," he made a few things clear.

He wanted to scrap official bilingualism, along with universal social programs and the then proposed GST. He found the distinct society clause in the Meech Lake Accord "offensive," and he demanded extensive federal spending cuts and a balanced budget within two years.

Waters, then sixty-nine, was a former lieutenant-general whose troops called him "Muddy." He was commander of the Canadian Army from 1973 until he retired in 1975. A Second World War veteran, Waters also served as assistant deputy minister of defence and after retiring from the service became a corporate executive.

Asked by reporters if he spoke French – hardly a prerequisite for appointment to the Senate, one would think – Waters characteristically replied, "No, I don't speak French, and no, I don't plan to learn." He said he had once been bilingual, "but I haven't used the language in fifteen years and at my age I have other priorities."

He had another message for Prime Minister Brian Mulroney that day: start working on severance plans for the existing senators as step one toward a fully elected Senate. And Mulroney had a message for Waters: don't hold your breath waiting for a Senate appointment.

And so had begun another modest step along Alberta's self-chosen path to become the Oregon of Canada in its effort to shame the other provinces and the federal government into at the very least giving the public the chance to choose their own senators.

Waters would have to wait eight months, until June 11, 1990, before Mulroney would cave into public pressure and appoint him. Fifteen months later, on September 25, 1991, Waters died of cancer, but the idea of Senate reform, particularly of a Triple-E Senate – elected, equal, and effective – did not die with him. Even though Canada is unlikely to see a Triple-E Senate in our lifetimes, the pressure to move in that direction continues to exercise a profound impact upon constitutional politics in this country.

In April 1984, a farmer, a small-town lawyer, and an oil tycoon, three men who would not appear to have much in common, met in a farmhouse near Kathyrn, not far from Calgary.

Bert Brown, the farmer who once carved the message "Triple-E Senate" in his wheat field, was host. Alex Rose, a small-town lawyer from Lacombe was there too, and he had persuaded the third man – high-powered Calgary oil baron Jim Gray, co-founder of Canadian Hunter Exploration Ltd. – to come along. It was the beginning of the Canadian Committee for a Triple-E Senate.

For Gray, the impetus for Senate reform was clear: the hated National Energy Program. "Where was this sanctimonious body of sober second thought when the west was being raped by the NEP?" asked Gray.

Gray raised another issue then that remains equally valid today: how is it fair that Quebec, with its twenty-four senatorial seats, can overrule any regional objections that the six senators from each of the four western provinces might raise? And is it fair that British Columbia has six senators while New Brunswick has ten? The answer, of course, is that no, it isn't fair, and it's just this inequity, and central Canada's historical nonchalance toward it, that still fuels western resentment against central Canada.

Gray's anger over the NEP – which became a symbol to westerners of all that's wrong with our current political system – was just one manifestation of a deeply held historical sense of grievance in the west against the power of central Canada. This anger has expressed itself in the formation of many of this country's most prominent populist, grass-roots reform movements.

For much of the first quarter of this century, the western-based Progressive Party played a major role in both federal and provincial affairs. At its peak in 1921, the party had sixty-five seats in Parliament, mostly from the west, and was entrenched in nine provinces, even winning forty-three seats in the Ontario legislature. Then there was the United Farmers Party of Alberta, which ruled that province until the upstart Social Credit Party swept into power in the Depression-ridden province in 1935 to the rousing music of William "Bible Bill" Aberhart's campaign theme song, "Onward Christian Soldiers." One of Aberhart's cabinet ministers was twenty-six-year-old Ernest Charles Manning, a farmboy and radio preacher who at the time was the youngest cabinet minister in the Commonwealth. At thirty-four, Manning, the father of current Reform Party leader Preston Manning, became the youngest premier in Canada. He ruled Alberta for twenty-five years, retired in 1968, accepted a host of company directorships, then joined the Senate two years later. At one point, the Social Credit movement became a power in Ottawa and for decades held sway in both Alberta and British Columbia.

While all this was going on, the left-leaning Co-operative Commonwealth Federation also came roaring out of the west, eventually merging with the Canadian Labour Congress to form the New Democratic Party. It had a major impact at various times

in Ottawa – where it held the balance of power during Pierre
Trudeau's second mandate – and boasting a history of winning
provincial elections in British Columbia, Saskatchewan, Manitoba,
and Ontario, with a realistic chance of adding Nova Scotia to that
list in a future provincial contest there.

And on November 1, 1987, forty-five-year-old Preston Manning
easily defeated leadership rival Stan Roberts at the founding convention of the Reform Party of Canada. Manning asked people in
Ontario and Quebec to view western political action as "a necessary
part of nation-building" and promised "to make phrases like 'Triple-
E Senate' and 'economic justice for the resource-producing regions'
the subject of serious discussion in Montreal, Ottawa, and Toronto,
just like 'sovereignty-association' and 'What does Quebec want?'
became subjects of serious discussions in the 1970s."

By the time Reform came on the scene, the gospel of Senate
reform made converts of more than forty MPs, seventeen senators,
several premiers, and provincial legislators in almost every province.
The Triple-E plank was also endorsed by two other short-lived
western parties, the Western Concept Party and the Representative
Party of Alberta. It was arguably an idea whose time had come.

Pierre Trudeau did not help matters. Shortly after the July 8, 1974,
election, when the Liberals were shut out of Alberta and didn't fare
much better in the other western provinces, Trudeau met the
defeated Liberal candidates at a fog-shrouded golf club on the outskirts of Calgary. He was accompanied by Senator Earl Hastings,
Alberta's Liberal campaign chairman, who had been appointed as
the official link between Albertans and the Liberal government.

Trudeau proceeded to scold Albertans for their lack of wisdom.
"No matter how good our policies are, they are not generally well
explained because we have no elected Liberals to explain them," he
said. "The people of Alberta have to decide for themselves to participate in the national government and not sit around and wait for it
to come to them. To take power means to get with the party which

forms the government and which has formed the government for a large part of our history."

In 1980, Manitoba Liberal MPs Robert Bockstael and Lloyd Axworthy, the only western Liberals to survive the February 18 election, told Trudeau that he should make use of western senators by naming them ministers to compensate for the lack of elected western Liberals. The short-lived Tory government of Joe Clark had done the same thing the previous year to make up for their lack of MPs in Quebec. Clark named two Quebec senators and a defeated Ottawa candidate to the cabinet, a move bitterly criticized by the Liberals.

Trudeau appointed Alberta senator Bud Olson, a former CCFer, as minister of state for economic and regional development and as a member of the powerful economic development committee of cabinet. Senator Jack Austin of British Columbia, a former Trudeau aide, became junior minister of state for northern affairs. Another British Columbian, former provincial leader Senator Raymond Perrault, later became minister for fitness and amateur sport, while Saskatchewan senator Hazen Argue was named minister for the Canadian Wheat Board.

A poll released by the Canada West Foundation on November 24, 1980, showed while support for outright separation was weak, some eighty-five per cent of the 1,370 westerners polled felt that the west was being ignored in national decision-making.

Two days later, a Senate subcommittee report said the Senate should grow from 104 seats to 126 with 20 of those extra seats going to the west. It also recommended that the prime minister should share senatorial appointments 50–50 with the provinces to appoint senators to ten-year terms.

In 1981, Trudeau tried to counter the anger provoked by the National Energy Program by resorting to the age-old Liberal tactic of buying electoral support with taxpayers' money. Trudeau appointed Alberta-born bureaucrat Bruce Rawson as the federal government's first senior adviser on western Canadian affairs. Based in Edmonton, Rawson reported directly to Privy Council boss Michael Pitfield to coordinate federal funding projects in the west.

In June 1983, Justice Minister Mark MacGuigan told the parliamentary committee on Senate reform that the quickest and least controversial first step toward improving the Senate would be to double the number of senators from western Canada. MacGuigan, who was co-chairman of the parliamentary committee that recommended the same thing in 1972, said it would help the Senate do a better job in representing regional interests. The four Atlantic provinces hold thirty Senate seats, compared to twenty-four for the four western provinces, yet the combined population of Nova Scotia, New Brunswick, Newfoundland, and Prince Edward Island is less than one-third that of the west. The committee was set up after a federal Senate reform bill had been rejected by the Supreme Court of Canada in 1979 on the grounds that Ottawa couldn't tinker unilaterally with the upper chamber. But like so many committees before and since, nothing came of it.

In a speech to the committee in Edmonton in October 1983, then Alberta Liberal leader Nick Taylor – later appointed a senator himself – said his party supported an elected Senate. He said the existing distribution of senate seats was "perfectly acceptable" but that voters in each province "would have as many votes as there are senators to be elected [in that province]. It would certainly give voters the eminently proper right to choose their representatives."

Another poll commissioned by the Canada West Foundation in 1984 just a few weeks after the Liberals were routed by Brian Mulroney's Tories found that little had changed. Roger Gibbons, a University of Alberta professor and a co-author of the study, said, "My own expectation was that there would be a more substantial shift away from Senate reform since the major rationale for it relates to exclusion from government." The Canada-wide poll conducted by CROP, a Montreal-based polling firm, found fifty-eight per cent of those polled thought the Senate should be either reformed or abolished. A separate question found that eighty per cent of westerners and seventy-six per cent of all Canadians favoured an elected Senate. In the west, thirty-seven per cent favoured reform while twenty-one per cent wanted abolition. Some twenty-four per cent of Canadians favoured the status quo.

In 1985, an Alberta legislative committee called for a Triple-E Senate and the Canadian Chamber of Commerce endorsed the idea at its annual convention.

In April 1988, Preston Manning and his year-old Reform Party announced a radical Senate reform plan that would be "held under the nose of every western candidate for Parliament" in the next election. Manning called for wide-ranging constitutional amendment allowing each province to elect ten senators each, giving those senators power to appoint members of some federal commissions and a veto over spending legislation. "We want a Senate with the power to stop things like the National Energy Program or to hold up CF-18 maintenance contracts," said Manning. He was referring in part to a controversial 1986 decision to award a $1-billion maintenance contract for the CF-18 to Canadair of Montreal instead of Bristol Aerospace of Winnipeg, even though Bristol's bid was $3.5 million cheaper and a panel of experts gave Bristol a far higher rating. Even the Manitoba Conservative Party condemned Mulroney for "abandoning the tender process" in favour of Quebec political favouritism.

The year before, Alberta premier Don Getty had convinced Mulroney and his fellow premiers to agree that Senate reform would be the first priority once the Meech Lake constitutional accord was ratified by all the provinces and by Parliament. Manning said that deal was unacceptable: "I don't feel the west should go along with any future constitutional amendments to make Quebec feel at home until we get this." He said Meech Lake "was an old case of Ontario and Quebec and the feds outsmarting the west. . . ." He said western provinces should withhold their support for a year to compel Ontario and Quebec to approve a "western Meech Lake accord. . . . By dividing into two rounds there will be no meaningful second round," he said. He had no way of knowing, of course, that two years later the accord would crash and burn when both Manitoba and Newfoundland failed to endorse it.

In May 1988 in Parksville, British Columbia, a small resort town on the east coast of Vancouver Island, Canada's four western premiers emerged from two days of working sessions to unanimously call for an elected Senate. In a communiqué entitled the Parksville Accord, the premiers said they agreed that a Triple-E Senate "would provide the basis for a more representative national Parliament." Alberta's Don Getty said, a bit precipitously as it turned out, "I think it's very important to the Senate reform process. I think we're going to be able to carry the momentum to the rest of Canada." Getty said he had convinced Ontario premier David Peterson and Quebec premier Robert Bourassa that an efficient and elected Senate is required, but he was still working on the third E – equality of the provinces in the Upper House.

Clearly the premiers were responding to the mood of the times. An August Gallup poll sponsored by the National Citizens' Coalition, a conservative lobby group, found fifty-five per cent of Canadians polled favoured a Triple-E Senate, with just sixteen per cent opposed. Twenty-nine per cent were undecided. Not surprisingly, support was strongest in the west but even in Ontario, the idea was supported by fifty-five per cent compared to sixteen per cent who said no. While support was highest in British Columbia, at seventy-one per cent, in Quebec it plummeted to forty-one per cent, with twenty-two per cent against and thirty-seven per cent undecided.

In September, Alberta's intergovernmental affairs minister, Jim Horsman, rejected the idea of an election to fill a vacant Senate seat formerly held by Donald Cameron. Both Edmonton Strathcona MP David Kilgour and provincial Liberal leader Nick Taylor said Alberta should produce its nominee by holding an election. But Horsman said, "We're not as interested in tinkering with that current body as we are in seeing the long-term prospects, which are to see a proper Upper House elected in Canada. I'm not about to be diverted by the red herring of the current Senate vacancy," he said.

Four months later, however, in January 1989, Alberta's deputy premier Dave Russell said the cabinet was studying a plan to hold an election to fill the seat vacated by Cameron in 1987. He said the province would pass a law setting up the vote and the winner's name would be proposed to Mulroney. Under the terms of the Meech Lake Accord, which were being recognized by Mulroney pending formal agreement of the pact, each province got to submit a list of names from which the prime minister would pick a senator, but Getty was refusing to because of his push for a Triple-E Senate. Senator Lowell Murray, Mulroney's minister of federal-provincial relations and a key architect of Meech, was cool to the idea, saying, "Any reading of the accord would suggest that there has to be more than one name."

On February 1, Mulroney went much further, calling the idea "unacceptable" because the accord clearly called for a list of five names. (Not true. It called for "names" to be submitted.) And Alberta Liberal senator Earl Hastings dismissed Getty's plan as "strictly a pre-election ploy," a sentiment shared by Senator Bud Olson, another Liberal, who accused Getty of "desperately looking for a good political issue." B.C. premier Bill Vander Zalm didn't see it that way, however. He announced plans to follow Alberta's lead and introduce a Senate election process in that province.

In March 1989, former school teacher Deborah Grey won a by-election in the Alberta riding of Beaver River, easily outdistancing the runner-up Tory and becoming the Reform Party's first elected MP. Her election guaranteed that the notion of a Triple-E Senate would soon be heard regularly on the Commons floor.

In the meantime, campaigning continued for the March 20 Alberta provincial election, which Getty had called more than a year before the normal term of a majority government expired. Getty said he needed a mandate to continue his battle with Ottawa over Senate reform, high interest rates, and a proposed national sales tax. After easily winning re-election (although, embarrassingly, Getty lost his own seat), Getty introduced the Senatorial Selection Act on June 26 to allow the province to choose a senator-in-waiting by a public vote held in conjunction with the October 16 municipal elections.

In July, the Alberta NDP rejected Getty's plan to elect a senator on the grounds that the party favoured abolishing the Senate. Alberta Liberal leader Laurence Decore said the Liberals were considering fielding a senatorial candidate. He said the Liberals objected to a clause that forbade sitting MLAs to run. It was dubbed "the Nick Taylor clause" because it would prevent the popular Liberal MLA from running. As for Taylor, he threatened to launch a legal challenge over the clause, which he said contravened federal legislation and civil rights laws, but he didn't follow through.

Alberta Liberals, of course, weren't the only Grits embroiled in a political battle at the time. The federal party was gearing up for its June 1990 campaign to replace outgoing leader John Turner. In September, Hamilton Liberal Sheila Copps, campaigning in Alberta, called Getty's senate election "a reasonable approach." Copps said the Triple-E "is a dream that will likely never be achieved because successive governments are too into their power basis." She said Mulroney, for example, "cried Senate reform before he got in there [and] basically forgot it." As for Turner, he said the Albertan elected to fill a Senate vacancy would be more legitimate than current senators. Turner, who wrote his university thesis in 1949 on Senate reform – and still believes it should either be turned into an elected body or scrapped altogether – said, "Anyone who is elected has more legitimacy than anybody who's appointed, period."

The moment Waters won the election, Mulroney began feeling the heat. On the one hand, his Quebec caucus, outraged that Waters was opposed to Meech Lake, official bilingualism, and Quebec's sense of its place within Canada, were apoplectic at the prospect. On the other hand, the Alberta Conservative federal caucus called on Mulroney to appoint Waters, understanding that his refusal to do so would mean the destruction of Fortress Alberta, a province that had voted overwhelmingly Tory since the days of John Diefenbaker thirty-five years before.

Reformer Deborah Grey said, "If the prime minister and his party ignore this election, they will make Mr. Waters a symbol and it will be my party that benefits."

Getty wasted no time in calling for Mulroney to appoint Waters to the Senate. He also sent a confidential letter to the prime minister

giving him the list he demanded: it was headed by Waters and contained the names of the five other candidates who ran against him
and lost. Waters quickly flew to Ottawa, arriving at the front door
escorted by both Grey and Manning for a symbolic stroll to the Red
Chamber. "I'm prepared to be quite patient," Waters said. "Until the
end of the month. After that I will become very impatient."

An Angus Reid poll in November 1989 found that sixty-seven per
cent of the 2,006 Canadians polled the week before wanted
Mulroney to appoint Waters to the upper chamber. Only twenty-
three per cent said Mulroney should appoint whomever he wants.
Support for Waters was at eighty-five per cent in Alberta and eighty-
three per cent on the Prairies as a whole. It was seventy-eight per cent
in British Columbia, sixty-eight in Ontario, ninety-seven in Atlantic
Canada and, not surprisingly, lowest in Quebec at fifty-two per cent.

During a lively exchange in the October 30 Question Period,
Mulroney's comments remained ambiguous. "I will be happy to
respond as soon as I can," he said, adding that it was his "preroga-
tive. . . . There is nothing automatic." Grey said Mulroney had a
simple option: "You give us one seat in the Senate . . . or we'll take
twenty" seats in the next federal election. Grey, although she
couldn't have known it at the time, underestimated her own party's
appeal in Alberta.

In December, Senator Lowell Murray, the intergovernmental
affairs minister, floated the first trial balloon, saying Alberta's election was not valid because the provinces have no power to pass laws
involving the Senate. In January, Mulroney, who by this time must
have been wishing the premiers had accepted his 1987 challenge to
abolish the Senate, hinted his government might mount a legal challenge. Alberta's deputy premier Jim Horsman replied that the
province would fight Ottawa if it insisted on a constitutional challenge, but a court battle would be a waste of taxpayers' dollars and
only delay real Senate reform.

In the midst of all this, Liberal leadership contender Jean
Chrétien told 640 Albertans at a Chamber of Commerce luncheon

in Edmonton on February 1, 1990, that if he was prime minister, Canada would have a Triple-E Senate. "You want the Triple-E Senate and I want one too," Chrétien said. But later, when he actually was prime minister, Chrétien flatly refused to appoint the winners of another Senate election to the cabinet. He continued to load it up with loyal Liberals or left-leaning Tories instead.

During an April 5 swing through Calgary, Mulroney said, "The idea of appointing someone simply because he has been elected may have a great deal of attractiveness, but it carries with it the seeds of destruction of legitimate and complete Senate reform." With the June 23 deadline for ratification of the Meech Lake Accord swiftly approaching, Mulroney tied the two issues together. "If Meech Lake dies there will be no Senate reform."

Finally, on June 11, just days after Getty finally signed Meech and the first ministers agreed on a process for Senate reform, Mulroney appointed Waters. He said that it was on the condition all provinces wait five years before holding future Senate elections, a condition flatly rejected by both Alberta's Getty and B.C.'s Vander Zalm.

The first thing Waters did after his formal swearing-in on June 19 was to attack Meech Lake as a "seriously flawed document" and call on other provinces to hold Senate elections and promise to push for reform of the Upper House. "This is a historic occasion," he said. "If the prime minister has a sincere commitment" about reform, he "should welcome this first step."

When Meech collapsed, Getty said, "Senate reform is dead, and that's a real sense of loss." Waters didn't agree. "Senate reform can and should be a stand-alone reform measure. There's nothing to prevent Canada from carrying out constitutional change of that nature."

In July 1991 Reform Party officials announced that Waters was undergoing cancer treatment at a Calgary Hospital. He died there on September 25, 1991. He was seventy-one. And while his death ended the short senatorial career of Canada's only elected senator, the movement he represented certainly wasn't buried along with him.

On May 6, 1996, veteran Liberal senator Earl Hastings died of heart disease. He was seventy-two. A past president of the Alberta Liberal Association, the twice-defeated Sun Oil Co. executive was rewarded for his faithful service by Prime Minister Lester Pearson in March 1966. Two days after his death, Alberta's Tory premier Ralph Klein, a former Liberal himself, said Chrétien could prove his commitment to national unity by giving Albertans a chance to vote on Hastings's replacement. Calling for a second Senate election in Alberta, Klein said, "To me, it represents what democracy is all about." It did to Chrétien too just six years earlier when he promised to bring in a Triple-E Senate if he got to be prime minister.

Three Albertans had been appointed to the Senate since Waters's election, two by Mulroney. First it was Conservative Walter Twinn in September 1990, part of the disreputable GST Gang. Then, in March 1993, shortly before Mulroney slunk out of town, leaving his once-mighty party in shambles, he appointed former Tory MLA Ron Ghitter, a human rights activist and darling of the small "l" liberal set.

Three years later, in March 1996, Chrétien named Nick Taylor to the Senate to replace the retiring Bud Olson. Taylor, a former provincial Liberal leader, had been a champion of Senate elections. He was named to the Senate just an hour after resigning his seat in the legislature, leaving Klein no time to seek a province-wide Senate election.

Klein then said he'd write to Chrétien asking him to honour the choice of Albertans if another Senate election was called. "We still have a commitment to elect a senator as long as we get a commitment from the prime minister that the person elected will be appointed," said Klein. Chrétien responded by telling Klein he would not let Albertans elect their next senator. He said he intended to pick a suitable Liberal for the patronage post to do his bidding and make sure the Liberals keep control of the upper chamber. "I will use my privilege and exercise my duty to name a senator who will respect the will of the House of Commons," he said.

Just ten days after Hastings died, on the very day Klein was writing his letter to the prime minister, Chrétien appointed sixty-nine-year-old Jean Forest, a former University of Alberta chancellor who was named to the first Alberta Human Rights Commission in 1974 and subsequently joined Ghitter's private human rights organization, The Dignity Foundation. She claimed she favoured direct elections. Not enough, it seemed, to actually get involved in one.

Nick Taylor insisted he still liked the idea of elections, but he supported Chrétien's move, saying, "Unless the public demands an election, it's not something you're going to see soon." Ron Ghitter also endorsed Chrétien's appointment. He said he was undecided about an elected Senate and added that "being unelected brings a certain amount of freedom." It certainly does.

Throughout the 1990s, Alberta kept pushing for the idea of Senate elections and Chrétien kept dismissing the idea. In November 1997, both Klein and Alberta Liberal leader Grant Mitchell joined Reform MPs in calling for an election because of the death of Conservative senator Walter Twinn. Chrétien added a new wrinkle when he rebuffed the request, saying that because Twinn's appointment was a special measure and Alberta already had its six regular senators, there wasn't really a vacancy to fill.

During this period, Chrétien consistently resorted to two cheap shots to counter Reform leader Preston Manning's insistent calls for reform. First, he'd remind Manning that Reform helped defeat the 1992 Charlottetown Accord, which proposed an elected Senate. It wasn't the Senate provision that upset Reform, it was myriad others, as Chrétien knew. What's more, Reform wasn't alone in rejecting Charlottetown: a solid majority of Canadians did the same thing, including voters in Chrétien's home province of Quebec. Second, Chrétien stooped to attacking Manning because his father, Ernest, had served as an appointed senator. "I will name the next senator the same way as the father of the Leader of the Opposition was named," Chrétien said.

Chrétien's other favourite response, equally stupid, is that since the Constitution requires him to appoint senators, Alberta's elected route is unconstitutional. Justice Minister Anne McLellan embraced this argument too, saying elections would be "violating the terms of the Constitution." Nonsense. Under Alberta's system, Chrétien would still make the actual appointment, as Mulroney did with Stan Waters. There's nothing in the Constitution to rule out such elections. The fact is, given the political realities in this country, this slow, turtle-like approach to reform, allowing the election of senators as vacancies arise, could be the only way an elected senate will ever happen. Eventually, as the numbers of elected senators grew, the political appetite to revamp the system could grow along with it.

Mulroney, the only prime minister ever to appoint an elected senator-in-waiting, called Chrétien's argument "absolute nonsense. You can do whatever you want in this regard. All the Constitution says, although this isn't the exact wording, is that appointments must be made by the prime minister. There is nothing to stop him from appointing somebody who has been elected by provincial voters. Now, if you say that he can be re-elected and you change the whole system from an appointive to an elective system, well, that's a different thing."

On March 5, 1998, twelve of Alberta's Reform MPs held an Edmonton news conference to announce they would be asking Albertans to help them convince Klein to hold Senate elections in the fall. Brandishing an Environics Research poll of a thousand Albertans that found ninety-one per cent supported Senate elections, Reform argued that the Senate election winners would provide two senators-in-waiting, ready to be appointed the moment another vacancy occurred. Most days, politics moves slowly. But not this day. At about 12:40 P.M., while the news conference was still on, sympathetic Tory MLAs calling from Government House began dialling the cell phones of Reform staffers sitting in the back of the room where the news conference was being held to say that the provincial Tory caucus had just approved elections in principle.

Calgary Conservative senator Ron Ghitter said the idea was "well-intentioned but futile" and would cost Albertans $1 million.

Ghitter said he'd resign if Chrétien promised to accept the winner. "Until he does that, I'm not going to resign for someone in waiting because all Chrétien will do is appoint another Liberal in my spot. What does that solve? There would be six Liberals from Alberta instead of five." One of those Liberals, Senator Thelma Chalifoux, said it was all a waste of money. She supports an appointed Senate. It certainly worked well in her case.

Senator Nick Taylor, the man often credited with originating the Alberta Senate election idea, was dismissive. Firmly ensconced in his own bit of patronage heaven, Taylor predicted that Klein didn't have the guts to call the election. He was wrong. Klein did decide to hold elections for two nominees that October. Taylor then accused Klein of "kowtowing" to Manning and predicted it will only be contested by mental patients on leave from psychiatric wards and a couple of Reform "spear carriers. . . . There's going to be a loud round of applause from a crowd of one-handed people. It will be a little like the Castro elections," he said. Taylor also argued that if Klein was going to do it, the only way to attract good candidates would be to pay the winners the equivalent of a senator's annual $64,000 salary, plus a $10,000 tax-free allowance. "Klein is a master at appearing to make strides forward while in effect he's tippy-toeing backwards."

On April 20, 1998, Manning used a debate to amend the Constitution to establish the new territory of Nunavut to launch a scathing seventy-five-minute attack on "the [Senate] sheep" who were discrediting Parliament. In one of the toughest speeches ever delivered in the Commons, Manning said the cost of the Senate far outweighs the benefits received by Canadians. He said the Senate does not represent regional interests, is hopelessly tainted by patronage, refuses to deal with the ethical misconduct of some of its members, and is marred by the unconscionable spending habits of many senators. He painted a picture of a Senate full of greedy, lazy, unethical patronage appointees who not only abuse their travel and office budgets, but who often don't even bother to show up for work.

In August, Chrétien released a letter he'd sent to Klein in January saying "it would not be fruitful" to broaden the national unity agenda to include Senate reform, "a complex issue on which agreement is far from evident." He said Mulroney's 1990 appointment of Stan Waters does not set a precedent for filling Senate vacancies and that "partial modification" of the current appointment practice would be "neither appropriate nor desirable." Chrétien said his government viewed talk of changing the Senate appointment system as a "distraction" from the broader unity agenda, federal political code for saying that if Quebec doesn't want it, then it shouldn't be on the agenda.

In addition, the *Ottawa Citizen* obtained two memos on the subject under the Access to Information Act. A November 1997 memo from Chrétien's Privy Council Office claimed that appointing elected senators would require a constitutional amendment needing the approval of seven provinces with at least fifty per cent of the country's population. In addition, it said each of the five regions would have a right of veto over any change to the appointment system. A less political view of the legal requirements of the Constitution, however, was provided by Queen's University constitutional scholar C.E.S. Franks in May 1997. He told the Privy Council that no constitutional amendment was needed to routinely appoint senators chosen by voters in elections.

The political war between Ottawa and Alberta exploded just before Labour Day 1998 when Alberta Liberal senator Jean Forest announced she was retiring three years early to look after her ailing husband. With the Senate election campaign already in progress, Klein faxed Chrétien a letter urging him not to name a replacement for Forest until "Albertans have the opportunity to voice their democratic choice" in the October 19 election. "As the Stan Waters precedent suggests, you can accommodate Albertans' desires without constitutional change." He said if Chrétien chose to deny Albertans "the opportunity to democratically select their representatives, Albertans will take your actions as a provocation." Provincial Liberal leader Nancy MacBeth said Forest's resignation meant that her caucus would review its earlier decision not to run Liberal candidates in a contest where no openings existed. In the end, the Liberals stayed out of it, no doubt realizing that their party label wasn't exactly a bonus.

In Ottawa, Reform rushed into federal court to seek an injunction to suspend any Alberta Senate appointment until after the election. Mr. Justice John Richard ordered both parties back in court three days later. On September 1, Justice Donna McGillis dismissed Reform's application, saying that Chrétien would "proceed at his own political peril" if he ignored Alberta's vote, but he has "unfettered discretion" under the Constitution to name any qualified person to the Senate. She said changing the Senate is a political matter and it's not up to the courts to decide. Reform was back in court the next day appealing the ruling.

Alberta treasurer Stockwell Day, a Reform supporter being touted as a potential leader of the proposed United Alternative movement, said he welcomed the Reform appeal but he still did not "believe in my heart that the prime minister would be as harsh and as undemocratic as to slam dunk the process we're involved in by going ahead with a patronage appointment."

Wrong! On September 17, Chrétien, who'd attacked the election plan as a "ludicrous charade" and a "joke," deliberately thumbed his nose at the province by appointing one-time Tory MP Douglas Roche, sixty-nine, an international arms control activist, to fill the seat vacated by Forest. Roche, who was Canada's disarmament ambassador in the 1980s, announced he would sit as an independent. Klein called the appointment "a slap in the face to Albertans. . . . To me, the issue is simple. Who should decide who represents Alberta in Parliament? The people of Alberta, or the prime minister? . . . Clearly, it is the people who should decide. . . . Albertans will remember," Klein told a business luncheon, drawing a sustained ovation. As for Roche, he too holds the convenient view of so many of his Senate colleagues: he believes in the concept, but elections should be only part of a comprehensive reform. Reform MP Deborah Grey, her party's deputy leader, called Roche a "good fellow" but said she'd "respect him a lot more if he ran in the election." Given Roche's left-wing politics, it's doubtful he could win an election in Alberta, a fact that demonstrates once again how unrepresentative Alberta's senators are of the prevailing political views in the province.

On September 24, during a rowdy exchange in the Commons between Reform and the Liberals, deputy prime minister Herb Gray, who usually has better control of his senses, charged that Albertans voting in the Senate election will be engaged in "undemocratic conduct." Gray, booed by Reform MPs, argued that it is undemocratic because the people selected would be elected for life and unaccountable forever to the voters who put them there. "That is not democratic," he huffed.

An incredulous Manning replied, "They're certainly more accountable than the current senators. They're not accountable to anybody except the prime minister and some of those prime ministers are dead." (Actually, there was just one senator at the time who owed his seat to a dead prime minister, Prince Edward Island's Orville Phillips, who was appointed by John Diefenbaker in 1963 and who retired in 1999.)

On October 18, long-time Triple-E champion Bert Brown, running as a Reformer, collected some 327,000 votes to lead the four-man field. University of Calgary political scientist Ted Morton finished second with 257,000, followed by independents Guy Desrosiers, 145,000, and Vance Gough, 130,000. There were 858,108 ballots cast, but each voter was allowed to pick two candidates.

A week after the election, the two winners, Brown and Morton, met with Klein for several hours in his office to plot strategy. In early December, Reform paid their way to Ottawa to visit the Red Chamber. They invited Alberta's six senators for a meeting at the Chateau Laurier, but none accepted. They asked again for meetings but only two of the six obliged. Their request to be introduced while sitting in the Senate gallery was also turned down. "We're not going to let ourselves be discouraged," Brown said. "We're putting the appointed senators on notice that at least one of us is going to be here every month, monitoring this system of legalized bribery, and detailing what elected senators would be doing differently."

In the meantime, the senators-in-waiting are, well, waiting. The next scheduled Alberta vacancy comes in 2002 when Nick Taylor must retire. Both Doug Roche and Thelma Chalifoux retire in 2004. Ron Ghitter must give up his patronage plum in 2010, while both Joyce Fairbairn and Dan Hays can hang around until 2014.

On the campaign trail during the Senate elections, Morton regularly told the joke that his wife, Bambi, had dreamed up the perfect epitaph to put on his tombstone. It reads:

"He couldn't wait any longer."

He may have to.

15

FOREIGN HOUSES

WHEN THE FIFTY-FIVE delegates to the U.S. Constitutional Convention met in Philadelphia during the spring and summer of 1787, one thing they quickly disposed of was a motion that senators be elected. Reflecting the same elitist attitude that would guide our own Fathers of Confederation some eighty years later, delegate Roger Sherman said: "The people immediately should have as little to do as may be about the government. They lack information and are constantly liable to be misled." Democracy, you see, was far too important to be left to the people.

The U.S. delegates also rejected the British notion of lifetime appointments – which the Canadians later accepted – and nixed another scheme to have senators elected by the House of Representatives, based on nominations from the respective state legislatures, a proposal that has often reappeared during interminable Senate reform debates in this country.

Unlike the 1864 Quebec Conference, where the existence and make-up of the Senate was the make-or-break issue, the Philadelphia delegates spent little time on the issue, deciding after a brief debate that the selection of senators was best left to the state legislatures. This, they reasoned, would insulate the senators from public pressures and what were referred to as "the passions of the moment" that plague elected bodies. Anyway, it was exactly how the delegates themselves were chosen, so it hardly came as surprise that they decided it was a good system. Nor was it surprising that since they all represented a state, they would decide that the Senate should do the same, providing the only direct tie between the national and state governments. The Quebec delegates adopted the same principle, slightly amended so that instead of equal numbers of senators from each state, Canada had equal numbers from each of the three regions: Ontario, Quebec, and the Maritimes, a decision that has been at the root of much of the regional unrest in western Canada over the past three decades.

And so, Article 1, section 3 of the U.S. Constitution read, in part, that the Senate "shall be composed of two Senators from each state, chosen by the legislature thereof, for six years." Section 4 said "the times, places and manner of holding elections for Senators and Representatives shall be prescribed in each State by the Legislature thereof; but the Congress may at any time by law make or alter such regulations, except as to the places of choosing Senators." The system was approved during the state ratifying conventions in 1787 and 1788. Up until the mid-1800s it worked well.

The first big problem cropped up in Indiana where the two state houses – the House and the Senate – were controlled by competing parties. In 1857, one of Indiana's federal Senate seats was still vacant because the Republicans from the state's northern counties and Democrats from the southern counties were deadlocked. Hostilities reached the point in February 1857 where armed Republicans charged onto the floor of the state Senate, surrounded the Democratic lieutenant governor, and foiled his attempts to call the roll.

Realizing they couldn't restore order in their own chamber, the Democratic senators charged down the hall to the House where, in joint session, they used their majority to elect two Democrats as their men in Washington. A year later, when the Republicans took control of both houses of the Indiana legislature, they decided that the two Democratic senators had been illegally elected, so they elected two new national senators, both Republicans, of course. But when the new Indiana senators arrived in the nation's capital to present their credentials, the Democratic majority in the federal house refused to recognize them and sent them packing back to Indiana.

Years earlier a vote to choose a federal senator almost resulted in bloodshed in the Colorado legislature. Their partisan dispute became so hostile that Democrats in the legislature called the Denver police to help maintain order, while the Colorado Republicans turned to the governor to have the state troopers sent in to restore order.

Throughout the post-Civil War days, when the passions of that bloody war were still fresh in the minds of the politicians, the problem became even more acute. And despite a series of reforms, there were forty-five House-Senate deadlocks in twenty different states between 1891 and 1905. As a result Senate seats often remained vacant for entire congressional sessions. Worse, state legislatures became increasingly open to bribery in their Senate selections: nine major cases of bribery were exposed between 1866 and 1906.

In Delaware in 1895, the legislature in joint session took 217 ballots over a period of 114 days and still failed to elect a senator. Nearly two years passed before they did. In 1899, they took 113 votes over sixty-four days without picking a senator, and their Senate seat remained vacant for four years. In 1901 and again in 1905 they had periods of up to two years without representation in the U.S. Senate.

For those who think the wild debates in the Canadian Senate during the 1990 GST battle were unprecedented, writer George Haynes provides us with an account of the Senate deliberations in the Missouri legislature in 1905:

"Lest the hour of adjournment should come before an election was secured, an attempt was made to stop the clock upon the wall of the assembly chamber. Democrats tried to prevent its being tampered with; and when certain Republicans brought forward a ladder, it was seized and thrown out of the window. A fist-fight followed, in which many were involved. Desks were torn from the floor and a fusillade of books began. The glass of the clock-front was broken, but the pendulum still persisted in swinging until, in the midst of a yelling mob, one member began throwing ink bottles at the clock, and finally succeeded in breaking the pendulum. On a motion to adjourn arose the wildest disorder. The presiding officers of both houses mounted the speaker's desk, and, by shouting and waving their arms, tried to quiet the mob. Finally, they succeeded in securing some semblance of order."

Clearly this couldn't continue. During the 1870s citizens began petitioning the House of Representatives for a system of direct popular elections. Between 1893 and 1902, the House passed several joint resolutions by overwhelming margins favouring popular elections. With little support in the Senate, however, the resolutions were quietly allowed to die in the Senate Committee on Privileges and Elections.

In 1899, powerful newspaper publisher William Randolph Hearst launched an editorial campaign in his newspapers for direct elections. After he was elected as a Democratic congressman from New York in 1902, he introduced a direct election constitutional amendment and continued to speak out regularly on the subject, helping to mobilize public opinion. The Democratic Party even included a plank on direct election in its 1900 national party platform.

Oregon, which Alberta hopes to emulate in this country, was the first state to attempt to democratize the process when it enacted a law in 1900 allowing voters to express their choice for senator. The results of the election would then have to be put before the legislators when they met to choose their Senate representative. The first attempt didn't work. The candidate who had won a plurality of the popular votes was supported by a small minority. Others split their votes among the fourteen candidates, and it took the legislature five weeks and forty-two joint ballots to elect John H. Mitchell, who had not received a single vote in the popular election.

They tried again, however, and in June 1904 established a "direct primary nominating elections law." Now anyone wanting to become a Senate candidate had to submit a duly signed petition and a one-hundred-word statement on their position on major issues. They could also prepare a twelve-word statement to be printed along with their name on the nominating ballot. In addition, candidates running for the Oregon state legislature had to declare their support for either "Statement Number 1" or "Statement Number 2." The first statement was a pledge to vote for the candidate for U.S. senator in Congress "who has received the highest number of the people's votes for that position at the general election next preceding the election of a senator in Congress, without regard to my individual preference." Statement Number 2 said that the legislative candidate "would consider the vote of the people for United States senator . . . as nothing more than a recommendation, which I shall be at liberty to wholly disregard if the reason for so doing seems to me to be sufficient."

The system was first tested in 1907 and it worked. In 1909, Oregon's overwhelmingly Republican legislature was faced with a Democratic winner in the popular election for U.S. Senate and the Republicans, despite the bitter partisanship of the day, set aside their own wishes and cast their ballots for the Democrat.

Other states were watching. Nebraska introduced a statement on the ballot for candidates to the legislature indicating that the candidate either "promises to vote for the people's choice for United States senator" or "will not promise to vote for the people's choice for United States senator."

In 1905, Hearst bought *Cosmopolitan*, a mass-circulation family magazine soon to be turned into what former U.S. senator Robert C. Byrd described as "one of the nation's more sensationalized muckraking journals and a vehicle for Hearst's views on the direct election."

One of Hearst's editors, Charles Edward Russell, lobbied Hearst for a series of articles focusing "on the fact that strictly speaking we had no Senate; only a chamber of butlers for industrialists and financiers." Hearst hired popular novelist David Graham Phillips to produce a series of nine articles called "The Treason of the Senate," portraying senators in a way that reverberated north of the border as well – and still does to a degree – as corrupt front men for big business. *Cosmopolitan*'s circulation doubled and the series was widely reprinted in newspapers across the country.

As the Hearst campaign continued and a growing number of senators owed their seats to popular referenda on the Oregon model, it became rather difficult for them to oppose the notion of direct elections. The concept was, finally, gaining a foothold on the Senate floor.

The first senator to stand in the chamber and call for Senate elections was Robert Marion La Follette of Wisconsin in April 1906. Over time, he was joined by others, particularly Idaho's William Borah and Kansas senator Joseph Bristow, who proposed the resolution that laid the foundation for the Seventeenth Amendment in 1913. By 1909, thirty-five states had declared support for direct Senate elections, but a resolution proposed by Bristow fell just five votes short of the necessary two-thirds majority needed for a constitutional change.

In April 1911 the House of Representatives overwhelmingly approved a motion for direct elections identical to the one the Senate had killed. When voting on an amendment ended in a tie, Vice-President James Schoolcraft Sherman cast the deciding vote in favour and the Senate then voted 64–24 for a constitutional change to allow elections. But Georgia senator Augustus Bacon later challenged the vice-president's authority, but he lost that fight and this challenge still stands as the precedent, giving the vice-president authority to break a tie vote in the Senate on constitutional amendments.

But the battle wasn't over yet. The Senate's amended resolution was defeated in the House. The Senate then voted to insist on its amendment and both sides appointed conferees, ending up delaying the reform again. The conferees met sixteen times but in April 1912 reported to the Senate that they could not agree.

Fortunately for the advocates of direct elections, the Democratic

National Convention was about to begin and House Speaker Champ Clark, a leading figure for his party's presidential nomination, with one eye on the growing popularity of the idea among the general public, decided it would be best to accept what they could rather than scuttle the entire direct election movement. So on May 13, 1912, with 110 members not voting, the House voted 238–39 to send the direct election amendment to the state legislatures for ratification. Less than a year later, on April 8, 1913, Connecticut's legislature ratified the amendment, giving it the required three-quarters of the states in agreement.

On May 31, 1913, Secretary of State William Jennings Bryan signed the Seventeenth Amendment. It reads:

"The Senate of the United States shall be composed of two Senators from each State, elected by the people thereof, for six years; and each Senator shall have one vote. The electors in each State shall have the qualifications requisite for electors of the most numerous branch of the State legislatures.

"When vacancies happen in the representation of any State in the Senate, the executive authority of such State shall issue writs of election to fill such vacancies; Provided, That the legislature of any State may empower the executive thereof to make temporary appointments until the people fill the vacancies by election as the legislature may direct.

"This amendment shall not be so construed as to affect the election or term of any Senator chosen before it becomes valid as part of the Constitution."

The results of changing the U.S. Senate to an elective body were evident immediately. Not only did the average age and length of service of the senators decline rapidly, but public support for the institution grew to the point where it soon bypassed the House of Representatives in credibility and power. Now, when people think of the major political players in the United States, it's the senators who come to mind – next to the president, of course – not the representative from the thirteenth district of New York City.

This undoubtedly is why prime ministers in Canada, despite their rhetoric to the contrary, are reluctant to legitimize the Senate in this way. Elected senators would not be directly beholden to the prime minister, nor could the prime minister stack the Red Chamber with supporters.

One of the truly undemocratic results of our current patronage system can be demonstrated by the fact that while the Senate is supposed to represent the interests of the regions, there is not a single Reform Party senator, even though that party currently enjoys overwhelming public support in the western provinces. Albertans, for example, have been asked twice in provincial referenda to show their preference for senators to represent them, and both times they opted first for a Reformer. Yet Alberta's "representatives" in the chamber are four Liberals, one Tory, and an independent, Doug Roche.

Alberta, of course, is not the only example, but as Reform leader Preston Manning has pointed out, our system of prime ministerial patronage appointments "virtually guaranteed . . . [the] Senate would decline in influence, respectability, and effectiveness in relation to the Lower House . . . [and] rather than representing local and regional interests they ended up representing the partisan interests of the Prime Minister who appointed them."

Amen, to that!

In his 1996 book, *Comparing Federal Systems in the 1990s*, prominent political scientist Ronald L. Watts points out that with the move by British prime minister Tony Blair to democratize the House of Lords, Canada's Senate would become the last remaining wholly appointed upper chamber among the world's democracies.

Watts, the principal emeritus and professor emeritus of political studies at Queen's University, is a long-time adviser to federal and provincial governments on constitutional affairs and was a commissioner on the 1979 Task Force on Canadian Unity, the Pepin-Robarts Commission. He was also assistant secretary to the (federal) cabinet for federal-provincial relations (constitutional affairs) during the 1991–92 constitutional talks. Having studied bicameral systems around the world, Watts concludes, "Where Senators are appointed by the federal government, as in Canada, they have the least credibility as spokespersons for regional interests, even when they are residents of the regions they represent."

One of the few comparable nations is Malaysia, hardly a model of democratic freedom. But even there, just 42 of the 110 senators are appointed by the federal government to represent the country's minorities. India also allows some appointments to represent particular minorities, but just 12 of the 250 members in its Rajya Sabha – or Council of States – get their seats this way. As in Malaysia, the remainder are elected.

Watts told *Toronto Star* national affairs columnist Rosemary Speirs, "Maybe there is an obscure country somewhere that also has a wholly appointed Senate, but I don't know of it. Canada would be the last. . . . It tells you something, doesn't it?"

In February 1998, Peter St. John of Winnipeg, a terrorism expert at the University of Manitoba, was getting ready to retire when news came that a second cousin in England had died, and he was now the Earl of Orkney and Lord of Dechmont. The hereditary titles, alas, did not come attached with a castle, or property, or even money, making him a member of what one wag called the "landless gentry." The only perk it did include, besides the right to use the titles, was status of a voting peer in the British House of Lords, a seven-hundred-year-old tradition of inherited privilege that St. John will not likely get to enjoy for long because Britain's Labour prime minister Tony Blair is in the process of ending it.

Canada's Senate, like the rest of our parliamentary system, is a hybrid of the British and American systems. St. John became one of Britain's 759 hereditary peers: dukes, marquesses, earls, countesses, viscounts, barons, baronesses, lords and ladies, most of them Conservatives, some ninety-eight per cent of them men, all of whom inherited their titles from their ancestors. Eighteen of them are Canadian, the best known being Lord Thompson of Fleet. They get to enter the gold and crimson chamber of the Upper House and share the red leather benches with 485 "life" peers, patronage recipients appointed by the prime minister in the same way our senators are picked, except that they don't have to retire until they're carried out. Fortunately, only about three hundred of them show up on any given day to cry "Content" or "Not content" as various pieces of legislation flow from the Commons for their perusal. An additional twenty-eight Law Lords and twenty-six archbishops and bishops fill out the roster of 1,289 who have a right to sit in the chamber.

Blair, of course, has established a royal commission to study the alternatives for a reformed House of Lords, including the possibility of elections, and report back by 2002. The current battle over the Lords burst into the open last November when Blair tried to enact a bill introducing proportional representation in European parliamentary elections. The Lords balked at the bill, not once, but five times, and the government withdrew it. Blair was furious that the Lords used their majority to "overturn the will of the democratically elected House of Commons," and he promised to strip the hereditary peers of their right to sit in the Upper House.

And so, in the November 24, 1998, Queen's Speech, Queen Elizabeth II, introducing the Labour government's second legislative program said: "A bill will be introduced to remove the right of hereditary peers to sit and vote in the House of Lords. It will be the first stage in the process of reform to make the House of Lords more democratic and representative. My Government will publish a White Paper setting out arrangements for a new system of appointments of life peers and establish a Royal Commission to review further changes and speedily to bring forward proposals for reform."

That single paragraph dominated the day and the political fall-out afterwards. Conservative leader William Hague, setting the stage for what the *Daily Telegraph* predicted would be "a fierce and prolonged fight," accused Blair of "constitutional vandalism" while Blair replied that the Conservatives were ready to "die in the ditch" to preserve the "feudal domination" of the Upper House. Hague said abolishing the rights of hereditary peers without setting out what would be put in their place was an attempt to "neuter" the Lords. He said Blair will not await the outcome of a promised royal commission because he wants to create a "House of Cronies" beholden to him.

The Conservatives do have a point. Lord Jeffrey Archer, a prominent novelist and Conservative life peer, wrote in *Time* magazine, "There is no denying the unfairness of a system that gives legislative power to men . . . just because they were born into the right family." He said reform "would be welcome if there were a coherent plan. . . . Surely we shouldn't destroy a great institution before we have thought of something better to replace it?

"After all," Archer continued, "if we remove the hereditary peers, we will be left only with those who have received their peerages through political party patronage. . . . And over the next few years, the Labour government will be tempted to pack the upper house with more and more of its own supporters – 'Tony's cronies' as some would have it. It could become a place of unelected hacks and dogsbodies, unlikely to provide independent and considered advice. There is at least some legitimacy in ancient tradition; there will be none in the short-term political convenience of the executive."

Champions of Senate reform often point to Australia. In many ways, the Australian experience parallels our own. Although it's a relatively homogeneous society – overwhelmingly descended from British and European settlers – it is a vast nation geographically with a relatively small population, sixty per cent of it concentrated in two of its six states. While it inherited our British style of parliamentary government, it has evolved, much like we have, into a combination of the parliamentary and the American congressional style of government. In June 1982, the Special Joint Committee on a Renewed Canada chose Australia as a good framework by which to restructure Canada's Senate.

While Australians rejected the Canadian model of a centralized distribution of powers, they did incorporate a powerful, directly elected Senate (by proportional representation) while adopting the American notion of equal representation of the provinces. While the theory was that the Senate would be a "regional house," with each senator/legislative councillor reflecting a "geographical expression," the reality is that it has become what Watts described as a "party house."

The Australian Constitution gives the Senate virtually the same legislative power as the House of Representatives, except that it cannot introduce money bills. There is no time limit on debate on bills. Senators are elected for six-year terms, half of them rotating every three years – members of the House of Representatives have to go to the polls every three years. Senate vacancies between elections are filled by the state premiers, the same way that U.S. governors can fill Senate vacancies in that country. Under Section 15 of the Constitution, Australian premiers are encouraged to fill vacancies with a representative from the former incumbent's political party. Most honour this tradition, although one former Tory premier from Queensland once filled a vacant socialist seat with a Tory who, as it turned out, provided the key vote that defeated socialist prime minister Gough Whitlam's bill to nationalize offshore oil. In the ensuing election, fought mainly over that issue, Whitlam lost.

Senators are elected by state to statewide constituencies. Each state elects twelve senators, each territory, two, and unlike our system, Senate representation tends to reflect the political leanings of each state. The Constitution also says the number of members in the Lower House must be double the number of senators, or as close as practicable, the so-called "nexus provision" designed to prevent the Lower House from becoming disproportionately large in relation to the Senate.

Before 1919, senators were elected on a Canadian-style, first-past-the-post system. Until 1948, a system of preferential voting was used. The elections were held at the same time as those for the House of Representatives, so there tended to be a similar partisan make-up in both houses. The current system of proportional representation has been in effect since 1949. While it better reflects the overall votes cast, its downside is that it results in a plethora of minor parties.

Since that system was introduced, however, the Senate is no longer dismissed as a bad joke. It has in some ways overtaken the House of Representatives in importance, becoming the main forum for groups seeking publicity for their policies.

Alberta Liberal senator Dan Hays, in releasing the 1982 select committee report, said the Australian reforms mean that its Senate "provides an effective check on the executive branch of government because it is no longer directly aligned with the House of Representatives. Having elections at a different time, it tends to scrutinize the activities of government more rigorously, making government more accountable."

Voting is compulsory in Australia. The system used is called a single transferable vote. Voters are asked to rank candidates in order of preference. In order to make the system work, voters must rank a minimum number of candidates. For example, if there were five vacant seats, the voter has to rank at least six candidates in order of preference, the number of vacancies, plus one. In order to win a seat, candidates must obtain a certain quota of the votes based on a mathematical formula.

The imperial parliament of Germany was constituted in April 1871 and consisted of two houses, the Bundesrat or federal council, and the Reichstag or Diet of the Realm. The Bundesrat, or Upper House, was set up to represent the German states. It had fifty-eight members, appointed by twenty-five states. Each state according to its size appointed a fixed number. Unlike other Senates, members were not appointed for a fixed term, but could be recalled at any time by their state rulers. Both houses were given equal powers with regard to legislation – which must be approved by both houses to become law – but the budget was strictly the business of the popularly elected Reichstag. In addition, each German state had both an upper and lower house operating on the same principles. Things changed slightly, although the basic structure remained the same in 1949 when West Germany became the Federal Republic of Germany composed of eleven Lander. The 1990 German re-unification added five new Lander to the country of eighty million people.

The German Landers are more directly involved in the federal decision-making process through the Bundesrat, or Senate, because of the presence there of first ministers and senior cabinet ministers from the Landers. The Bundesrat also enjoys considerable power, holding a veto on all federal legislation affecting the Lander – this covers about sixty per cent of all federal legislation – making it a significant player in federal-state relationships. Each Lander is allowed to send either three, four, or six representatives to the Bundesrat, depending upon population. This system is quite common in upper houses. Switzerland, for example, sends two representatives from each of twenty cantons to its Council of States, with six "half-cantons" represented by one each. Their representatives are directly elected by proportional representation chosen by cantons. In Austria's Bundesrat, the number of representatives from each of the nine Lander varies from twelve for the largest to just three for the smallest. India's Rajya Sabha varies from a high of eighty-six representatives to a low of twelve. Canada, in fact, is the only federation in the world that bases its Senate representation on regional groups of provinces, with the four basic regions given twenty-four seats each, plus an additional six for Newfoundland and three for territories.

Unlike Canada, where the senators are usually beholden to the prime minister who appointed them, members of the German Bundesrat, loosely based on the Austrian model, are under express orders to vote the way the Land governments tell them to vote.

Several countries have a mix of directly elected and/or federally or locally appointed members of their upper houses. In the Belgian Senate, for example, forty of the seventy-one senators win their seats by direct election. The Spanish Senate has 208 directly elected senators and 49 appointed regional representatives. In Malaysia's Dewan Negara, the appointment system closest to our own, sixty per cent of the seats are filled by indirect election by the state legislatures and forty per cent appointed by the national government.

In his study of the various systems, Watts concludes that the primary role of most of the federal second chambers is to review federal legislation "with a view to bringing it to bear upon regional and minority interests and concerns. . . .

"What is clear," he writes, "is that of all the federal second chambers, the Canadian Senate has the least public legitimacy. But while most Canadians agree that it should be reformed, disagreement about the appropriate reform has left it unreformed."

SENATE SURGERY

WHAT TO DO?
The late senator Eugene Forsey, perhaps Canada's greatest constitutional scholar, put it best in 1985 when he said, "There are two types of Senate reform proposals: the practicable and the impracticable." Canadians, he told the Canadian Bar Association, spend most of their time pursuing the impracticable – those that would require constitutional amendments to bring them into effect – rather than seeking more modest change that can be done without falling into Canada's hopeless constitutional muddle.

And then, of course, there's the other option many people want for the Senate: nuke it. But as Forsey points out, that too would take a constitutional change.

The ink was barely dry on the Confederation documents in 1867 before people began agitating for Senate reform. Every prime minister in our history has promised reform – but apart from Lester Pearson's imposition of the mandatory retirement age – nothing much has happened. As Mark Twain said about the weather, every-body talks about it, but nobody does anything about it. There are nearly as many plans for Senate reform as there are Canadians.

In his 1949 political science thesis as a graduating student at the University of British Columbia, John Turner argued that at the very least the Senate should be an elected body, and if that can't be done, abolish it. He hasn't changed his mind. In another paper in the mid-1950s, Turner argued that the Senate has completely failed to meet its original purposes – a chamber of sober second thought and a champion of the regions. Turner said Sir John A. Macdonald's "sober second thought" argument "is now merely a hollow echo from an optimistic past." Much of the time senators sit around waiting for bills to be passed on from the Commons. Often, when they do come, these bills arrive at the last minute before a prorogation or some other break deprives senators of the time needed to exercise sound judgement or suggest useful modifications. And because senators are all appointed by the prime minister, they're only there to represent their parties, not their regions. "The plain truth of the matter seems to be that the Senate today has very little to do with the provinces. Political theory and principles are often not reflected in practice. . . . In practical terms, it is doubtful whether today any provincial gov-ernment would look towards the Senate as its spokesman or cham-pion. The role intended for the Upper House by the statesmen of Confederation was never achieved."

Constitutional Senate reform essentially breaks down into argu-ments about changing the method of appointments, imposing a fixed term of office, limiting the Senate's veto power, making senators elected, or outright abolition.

On the final option, Liberal MP Roger Gallaway and NDP MP Lorne Nystrom are currently waging a country-wide campaign to garner public support for abolition. Gallaway and Nystrom both see the institution as redundant and self-serving. Nystrom says it's not worth the $50-million-plus that it costs, and anyway, the provincial governments provide the checks and balances the Senate once did.

Public opinion polls have consistently shown a relatively even split between Canadians who want to abolish the Senate and those who want to reform it. Very few want to leave it as it is.

Reform leader Preston Manning, who is pushing the Triple-E Senate – an absurd concept that in the name of "equality" would give Prince Edward Island the same number of senators as Ontario – opposes abolition because that would mean "a One-House Parliament in which the heavily populated areas of southern Ontario and southern Quebec would have a majority of the seats. And in such a Parliament," he asks, "how would the regional interests of Atlantic Canada, the West, the North, and northern and rural Ontario and Quebec, ever be properly addressed?"

If our democracy was operating the way it should, the argument for Senate abolition would be stronger. But because of the unhealthy growth of cabinet-style government, even the vast majority of our elected representatives in Ottawa have become political eunuchs, not much more able than senators to represent the needs of their constituents. The prime minister, a few senior ministers, and a coterie of elected aides run the government. The Commons, like the Red Chamber, is more often than not a charade, a sorry parody of what is was designed to do. A legitimate Senate – first and foremost elected and not beholden to the prime minister – could return some democracy to the process. Certainly more than there is now.

Many have argued that the power to appoint senators be taken from the prime minister and handed to the provincial premiers, but why replace unseemly federal patronage with tawdry provincial patronage?

In his 1985 speech to the Canadian Bar Association, Forsey recommended that Canadians start with the 1982 report from a sub-committee of the Senate's Standing Committee on Legal and Constitutional Affairs that contained fourteen proposals, only three of which were impracticable because of the 1982 Constitution Act, but several of which could be put into effect by ordinary acts of Parliament. These practical proposals included giving senators a fixed term of ten years, with the possibility of renewable terms of five years; allowing any senator who reaches age sixty-five with fifteen years' service (or seventy, with ten) to retire on full pension; firing any senator who failed for two consecutive years to attend at least one-third of the sittings in each year; legislation to abolish the property qualification; abolition of the twenty-four separate senatorial divisions in Quebec, set up in 1867 to protect the English-speaking minority.

Forsey said the Senate itself could establish regional all-party caucuses to fight for their regional interests. He also advocated the appointment of every second senator from a list submitted by the provincial government concerned. "This would mean more effective voices for provincial interests in matters under Dominion jurisdiction; a more varied membership, politically, economically, and socially; and less danger of huge, long-lasting one-party majorities," he said. Finally, Forsey said no Senate seat should be left vacant for more than six months. "There have been cases in the past when seats have been left vacant for years (in one case, eight years). This is outrageous and intolerable. . . ."

A 1984 committee co-chaired by Liberal senator Gil Molgat and Liberal MP Paul Cosgrove envisioned an elected Senate with 144 members, regionally tilted toward the west and the Maritimes, with elections at a fixed date every third year for one-third of the senators. Their Senate could not hinder "supply" (i.e., monies) or stop or kill legislation from the Commons, although it would be able to delay it for 120 sitting days. The Senate would also be able to approve government appointments to any agency with a regional reach, such as the Supreme Court and the CRTC, and legislation involving francophone and/or bilingual affairs would require a "double minority" – which means a majority of the entire Senate plus a majority of the senators who have declared themselves as francophones. This proposal has popped up many times since as a transparent sop to Quebec, but would have the unsavoury effect of turning non-francophone senators into second-class legislators.

During the seemingly endless constitutional talks of the 1980s, Senate reform was constantly on the agenda, although its importance depended to a large extent on where you lived. If you resided west of Ontario, it was the major issue. If you were a Quebecker it was something to be dealt with after the "important" issues were resolved.

Quebec's definition of the "important" issues – which led directly to the 1987 Meech Lake meetings – were the five demands announced by Quebec premier Robert Bourassa in 1986 in return for his province resuming its role in the constitutional talks. Bourassa demanded recognition of Quebec as a "distinct society" – a code word for special, privileged status – along with the right to opt out of national programs and be compensated for them anyway, more power over immigration to Quebec, a role in Supreme Court appointments, and a veto on all future constitutional amendments.

Ever eager to please, Mulroney and the premiers met in private at Meech Lake, and as Reform leader Preston Manning put it, "without consulting their legislatures or electors, drafted an agreement to meet Quebec's five demands and provide for a second round of discussions on further constitutional changes, including senate reform."

In return for giving Quebec a veto, Mulroney had to hand vetoes out holus-bolus. This resulted in a deal so rigid that, according to Manning, "the chances of securing a constitutional amendment to reform the Senate . . . would be drastically reduced." Westerners also objected to the "token references to Senate reform and the lack of substantive assurances that real progress would be made in this area in any second round of constitutional negotiations."

In any event, Meech Lake didn't make it past Manitoba or Newfoundland, so it died, only to rise again in a different form in the 1992 Charlottetown Accord.

Charlottetown did call for an elected Senate – either by the people directly or members of the legislative assemblies – with sixty-two senators, six from each province and one from each territory. It also guaranteed extra aboriginal seats and permitted some senators to be chosen solely on the basis of gender, i.e., female. It listed four categories of legislation for the Senate: revenue and expenditure bills; legislation materially affecting French language and French culture;

bills involving fundamental tax policy changes directly related to natural resources; and ordinary legislation.

Revenue and expenditure bills would be subject to a thirty-calendar-day suspensive veto, those affecting the French language or culture would require a double majority, senators would have to dispose of bills approved by the Commons within thirty sitting days, and bills involving tax policy changes on natural resources could be defeated by a majority vote in the Senate. In addition, senators would not be eligible to serve in cabinet, and the Senate would have the power to ratify or reject federal appointments to regulatory boards and agencies. But Charlottetown, of course, went down to defeat in the national referendum.

The Senate as it is currently constituted is certainly not representative of anything except a narrow class of political bagmen, organizers, and assorted hangers-on. When Canadians demonstrated their absolute revulsion for the Tories in 1993, for example, reducing them from a majority in the Commons to just two seats, the unelected Tory troopers still held a majority of the seats in the Senate. Even today, the Tories are in fifth place in the Commons, but in second in the Senate. The three parties ahead of the Tories in elective preference – Reform, Bloc Québécois, and NDP, in that order – have no representation at all in the Senate. None.

Does anyone believe that the four Alberta Liberals, one Tory, and one radical left-wing "independent" Alberta senator really represent the political culture of that province?

Does anyone really believe that unelected legislators should be legislating anything?

Does it make sense to anybody that New Brunswick and Nova Scotia each have ten seats, while British Columbia and Alberta only have six each?

Bill Fox, Mulroney's former director of communications, has one suggestion that might make the Senate a little more relevant. He agrees that the Senate's overall image is "among the lowest of the low," but says it might help some if the entire management of government communications were assigned to a senator. "Increasingly," says Fox, "political communications are at the heart of government. It should be directed by somebody who is part of cabinet, but the problem of giving it to an MP is because he has to be elected you create a vulnerability. . . . You have to answer questions about why this group got an $8,000 grant and that group didn't, that sort of thing. A senator wouldn't have the same problem. I just don't think communications can be an afterthought for government any more. . . . That's why you have the rise of the apparatchik. A generation ago, if you summoned the leadership of the party, it tended to be community leaders, the head of a service club, that sort of thing. For a long time, the party was less relevant and communication was through the mainstream media, either through earned messages or bought messages.

"But today, who represents the leadership of the party? Well, they tend to be advertising experts, public relations or media relations. . . . I think that's what Trudeau figured out when he brought in [Michael] Kirby and [Jerry] Grafstein. He didn't give a shit about journalists. He openly despised them. . . . There is a lot of expertise in the Senate and it could be put to good use in this way."

It certainly would take a communications expert to make the public think the upper chamber is doing good work. In fact, it would take a drastic overhaul, almost an impossible thing to do given the rigidity of our Constitution and the number of players who get a say. The west, quite legitimately, wants more power in the Senate, but Quebec will never agree to anything that diminishes its authority. And so it goes. About the only reform that draws wide public support is that if we must have senators, they should be elected, a change a prime minister might be able to find agreement on with the provinces. Beyond that, however, it's a mess.

To Mulroney the real problem is the 1982 constitutional deal negotiated by Pierre Trudeau, with Chrétien one of the major players. In order to change the Senate, all the provinces and the federal government must agree. "The most crucial thing concerning

Senate reform is the amending formula," he says. "Before that the Constitution wasn't a serious impediment to change. Now it is. Big time. It's a big straitjacket for reform." Not only must everybody agree, says Mulroney, but the Constitution allows provinces to revoke their agreement if governments change.

In any event, says Mulroney, "Jean Chrétien doesn't want to reform the Senate. He doesn't want to reform anything. He's the most successful practitioner of patronage of any prime minister in Canada, and he gets no blame for it. . . . If you don't at least try to get something done in a country as resistant to change as Canada is, then nothing will happen. . . . Now if you try, as we did, and bring it to fruition when all the signatures are there, that must be deemed a success by any objective measure. But once one premier withdraws that consent then it is deemed a failure. That's the reality of it. Why would any prime minister even consider getting into that scenario? The 1982 Chrétien-Trudeau amending formula is a killer."

One thing most Canadians do agree upon is that the Senate, as it stands, is desperately sick. But because of the amending formula, conflicting interests, and a general lack of political will, there is no politically practical cure in sight.

My own preference for a renewed Senate would be a dramatically reduced elected Senate of sixty-seven members: twelve each from Ontario and Quebec, seven each from British Columbia and Alberta, five each from Manitoba, Saskatchewan, New Brunswick, and Nova Scotia, four from Newfoundland, two from Prince Edward Island, and one each from the three territories, with provisions to alter the numbers as population shifts, but with a strong bias in favour of Atlantic Canada and the western provinces. That would give the west twenty-four senators, matching the combined total of Ontario and Quebec, surely better than the current situation where Ontario and Quebec each have as many senators as the four western provinces combined. Atlantic Canada, under my plan, would have sixteen seats, also a significantly higher number than their population warrants, and strong enough to give them real clout in the legislative process.

Senators, elected in senatorial districts, would sit for six years and be restricted to two terms – the way U.S. presidents are – with half of the senators elected on a fixed date every three years. They would not belong to their party's Commons caucus and could not sit in cabinet. They would have the power to review – and reject if they wish – all senior government appointments, including those to the Supreme Court. In addition, given the wide spectrum of specific expertise in the Senate in any number of fields, Senate inquiries would replace expensive royal commissions to study matters of national concern. They would elect their own Speaker and enjoy the same legislative powers they do now. The defeat of a government bill in the Senate would not constitute a question of confidence against the government. Finally, senators would be allowed – actually encouraged – to have free votes on everything except, of course, the government's budget, since the inability of the government to approve its budget would clearly spell curtains for the administration.

Indeed, if more free votes were allowed in the Commons – without being considered matters of confidence or cause for partisan reprimands – much of the current dictatorial control vested in the prime minister and his cadre of chief advisers would disappear and we'd get a lot closer to practising real democracy in this country.

But that's another book.

BIBLIOGRAPHY

Berton, Pierre. *The Last Spike: The Great Railway 1881–1885*. Toronto: McClelland & Stewart Limited, 1972.

Cameron, Stevie. *On the Take: Crime, Corruption and Greed in the Mulroney Years*. Toronto: Macfarlane Walter & Ross, 1995.

Canada. *Senate Reform*. Ottawa: The Library of Parliament, 1986.

Canada. *Senate Reform: Proposals in Comparative Perspective*. Ottawa: The Library of Parliament, 1992.

Clarkson, Stephen, and Christine McCall. *Trudeau and Our Times, Vol. 1: The Magnificent Obsession*. Toronto: McClelland & Stewart Inc., 1990.

Cleverdon, Catherine L. *The Woman Suffrage Movement in Canada*. Second edition. Toronto: University of Toronto Press, 1974.

Crosbie, John C., with Geoffrey Stevens. *No Holds Barred: My Life in Politics*. Toronto: McClelland & Stewart Inc., 1997.

Fife, Robert, and John Warren. *A Capital Scandal: Politics, Patronage and Payoffs: Why Parliament Must Be Reformed*. Toronto: Key Porter Books Ltd., 1991.

Frith, Royce. *Hoods on the Hill: How Mulroney and His Gang Rammed the GST Past Parliament and Down Our Throats.* Toronto: Coach House Press, 1991.

Government of Alberta. *Strengthening Canada: Reform of the Canadian Senate.* Report of the Alberta Select Special Committee on Upper House Reform. Edmonton: Plains Publishing Inc., 1983.

Government of Canada. *Reform of the Senate: A Discussion Paper.* Ottawa: Queen's Printer of Canada, 1983.

Granatstein, Jack. *Who Killed Canadian History?* Toronto: HarperCollins Publishers Ltd., 1998.

Granatstein, Jack, et al. *Nation.* Third edition. Toronto: McGraw-Hill Ryerson Limited, 1993.

Hoy, Claire. *Friends in High Places: Politics and Patronage in the Mulroney Government.* Toronto: Key Porter Books Limited, 1987.

Kluckner, Michael. *Toronto: The Way It Was.* Toronto: Whitecap Books Ltd., 1988.

Mallory, J.R. *The Structure of Canadian Government.* Revised edition. Toronto: Gage Publishing Limited, 1984.

Manning, Preston. *The New Canada.* Toronto: Macmillan Canada, 1992.

McRoberts, Kenneth, and Patrick Monahan (Eds.). *The Charlottetown Accord, the Referendum, and the Future of Canada.* Toronto: University of Toronto Press, 1993.

Morton, Desmond, and Morton Weinfield. *Who Speaks for Canada? Words That Shape a Country.* Toronto: McClelland & Stewart Inc., 1998.

Reedy, George. *The United States Senate: Paralysis or a Search for Consensus.* New York: Crown Publishers Inc., 1986.

Walker, Frank N. *Sketches of Old Toronto.* Toronto: Longmans Canada Limited, 1965.

Watts, Ronald L. *Comparing Federal Systems in the 1990s.* Kingston: Institute of Intergovernmental Relations, Queen's University, 1996.

Watts, Ronald L. *The Reform of the Federal Institutions*. Kingston: Institute of Intergovernmental Relations, Queen's University, 1993.

Zolf, Larry. *Survival of the Fattest: An Irreverent View of the Senate*. Toronto: Key Porter Books, 1984.